# BUILDING A GREEN WALL

Irish America's Resurgence
Post-Brexit

Kimberly Cowell-Meyers and
Carolyn Gallaher

First published in Great Britain in 2025 by

Bristol University Press
University of Bristol
1–9 Old Park Hill
Bristol
BS2 8BB
UK
t: +44 (0)117 374 6645
e: bup-info@bristol.ac.uk

Details of international sales and distribution partners are available at
bristoluniversitypress.co.uk

© Bristol University Press 2025

British Library Cataloguing in Publication Data
A catalogue record for this book is available from the British Library

ISBN 978-1-5292-3799-3 hardcover
ISBN 978-1-5292-3800-6 paperback
ISBN 978-1-5292-3801-3 ePub
ISBN 978-1-5292-3802-0 ePdf

The right of Kimberly Cowell-Meyers and Carolyn Gallaher to be identified as authors of this work has been asserted by them in accordance with the Copyright, Designs and Patents Act 1988.

All rights reserved: no part of this publication may be reproduced, stored in a retrieval system, or transmitted in any form or by any means, electronic, mechanical, photocopying, recording, or otherwise without the prior permission of Bristol University Press.

Every reasonable effort has been made to obtain permission to reproduce copyrighted material. If, however, anyone knows of an oversight, please contact the publisher.

The statements and opinions contained within this publication are solely those of the authors and not of the University of Bristol or Bristol University Press. The University of Bristol and Bristol University Press disclaim responsibility for any injury to persons or property resulting from any material published in this publication.

Bristol University Press works to counter discrimination on grounds of gender, race, disability, age and sexuality.

Cover design: blu inc
Front cover image: Getty/Alexi Rosenfeld

# Contents

| | | |
|---|---|---|
| List of Abbreviations | | iv |
| About the Authors | | vi |
| Acknowledgements | | vii |
| 1 | Phoenix Rising | 1 |
| 2 | A Short History of Irish America | 19 |
| 3 | Irish America as an Ethnic Lobby | 47 |
| 4 | Brexit and the Problem of Northern Ireland | 70 |
| 5 | Irish America Remobilizes | 92 |
| 6 | Facing Down the Internal Market Bill | 119 |
| 7 | Irish America, Joe Biden, and the Path to the Windsor Framework | 132 |
| 8 | Legacy and the Limits of Irish American Influence | 169 |
| 9 | The Elephant in the Room: Irish Unity after Brexit | 193 |
| 10 | Irish America: A Force to Be Reckoned with on Brexit | 218 |
| Appendix: Interviews | | 236 |
| References | | 240 |
| Index | | 276 |

# List of Abbreviations

| | |
|---|---|
| ABC | American Brexit Committee |
| ACCIA | Ad Hoc Committee on Irish Affairs |
| AIPAC | American Israel Public Affairs Committee |
| AISLC | American Irish State Legislators Caucus |
| AOH | Ancient Order of Hibernians |
| AUKUS | Australia/UK/US Trilateral Security Strategy |
| CANF | Cuban American National Foundation |
| CCE | Comhaltas Ceoltóirí Eireann |
| CFPB | Consumer Financial Protection Bureau |
| CODEL | Congressional Delegation |
| CTA | Common Travel Area |
| DOJ | Department of Justice |
| DUP | Democratic Unionist Party |
| ECHR | European Convention on Human Rights |
| ECtHR | European Court of Human Rights |
| ECJ | European Court of Justice |
| ECSC | European Coal and Steel Community |
| EEC | European Economic Community |
| ERG | European Research Group |
| EU | European Union |
| FEC | Federal Elections Commission |
| GAA | Gaelic Athletic Association |
| HET | Historical Enquiries Team |
| HIU | Historical Investigations Unit |
| ICIR | Independent Commission on Information Retrieval |
| ICLVR | Independent Commission for the Location of Victims' Remains |
| INC | Irish National Caucus |
| IFI | International Fund for Ireland |

# LIST OF ABBREVIATIONS

| | |
|---|---|
| IRC | Independent Reporting Commission |
| IRA | Irish Republican Army |
| MLA | Member of the Legislative Assembly |
| NATO | North Atlantic Treaty Organization |
| NHS | National Health Service |
| NI | Northern Ireland |
| NIB | Northern Ireland Bureau |
| NICS | Northern Ireland Civil Service |
| NIO | Northern Ireland Office |
| NSA | National Security Administration |
| NSC | National Security Council |
| NORAID | Irish Northern Aid Committee |
| PAC | Political Action Committee |
| PONI | Police Ombudsman of Northern Ireland |
| PSNI | Police Service of Northern Ireland |
| RUC | Royal Ulster Constabulary |
| SDLP | Social Democratic Labour Party |
| SHA | Stormont House Agreement |
| SOSNI | Secretary of State for Northern Ireland |
| UDA | Ulster Defence Association |
| UK | United Kingdom |
| UKIP | United Kingdom Independence Party |
| US | United States |
| USTR | United States Trade Representative |
| UUP | Ulster Unionist Party |
| UVF | Ulster Volunteer Force |
| VAT | Value Added Tax |
| WIP | Washington Ireland Program |

# About the Authors

**Kimberly Cowell-Meyers** is Associate Professor in the School of Public Affairs at American University. She specializes in the politics of identity broadly, and focuses on Northern Ireland and women's political representation and social movements. She has published in journals including *British Politics, Political Studies, Politics and Gender, Perspectives on Politics, Politics, Groups and Identities, Irish Political Studies*, and *Scandinavian Political Studies*. She has also written a book on Catholic mobilization in the 19th century (*Religion and Politics in the Nineteenth Century: The Party Faithful in Ireland and Germany*).

**Carolyn Gallaher** is Professor at the School of International Service at American University. She is an expert on non-state armed groups. She has written a book on Loyalist paramilitaries in Northern Ireland (*After the Peace: Loyalist Paramilitaries in Post-Accord Northern Ireland*) and a book on militias in the US (*On the Fault Line: Race, Class and the American Patriot Movement*). She has published in journals including *Antipode, ACME, Space and Polity*, and *Gender Place and Culture*. She also writes for Political Research Associates, a social justice research and strategy center devoted to protecting democracy.

# Acknowledgements

Although our book has two authors, it is really the product of an ongoing dialogue between ourselves and the people we interviewed, many of whom worked to protect the Belfast/Good Friday Agreement in the wake of the 2016 Brexit referendum. We wrote the words, but they were shaped by what our interview subjects shared with us in formal interviews, at events during St. Patrick's week in Washington, DC, and over lunches, coffees, and the occasional dram throughout the year.

All of this is to say that this book could not have happened without the generosity of every person we interviewed. They gave us time, allowed us to ask nosy questions, and engaged in fruitful exchanges as we tried to clarify things in our heads. We left every interview feeling energized for the next one. That a portion of these interviews takes place during the pandemic was a blessing in disguise. It was often a lonely and terrifying period. The chance to engage with people in a normal way felt like a gift.

We would especially like to thank Kevin Sullivan for inviting us to attend numerous meetings of the Ad Hoc Committee to Protect the Good Friday Agreement. These meetings follow Chatham House rules, so we did not include any of these conversations in our book. But attending these meetings gave us a sense of the stakes of the issue for Irish Americans, and an inside view of how Irish America re-energized itself to meet the moment. We'd also like to thank Andrew Elliot, who was the Director of the Northern Ireland Bureau for the vast majority of the time we were doing our research. Though he could not (and did not) speak to us about the debates surrounding the border, legacy, and the potential for reunification, he recognized our deep interest in Northern Ireland and offered financial and in-kind support for events that we hosted on Northern Ireland, beginning with several online webinars during the pandemic, a respective on the 25th anniversary, and a conversation with the First Minister and the Deputy First Minister in 2024.

We would also like to thank our families. We both admit a talent for weaving Northern Ireland into the most unlikely of conversations, from soccer and music to domestic US politics. Both our spouses know more about Northern Ireland than they bargained for. A willingness to talk about Northern Ireland was in neither's marriage vows, so we are thankful for their cheerful endurance. Our parents and children also deserve our gratitude for their patience, especially Kimberly's dad, whose own work sparked her initial interest in Northern Ireland and who read multiple drafts.

We are also grateful for all the conversations we've had with students on the topic of Northern Ireland. Kimberly would like to thank the students who have taken her Politics of Peace in Northern Ireland class, and Carolyn would like to thank the students in her Complex Problems class. As researchers, we've found conversations with students are often generative of good research. Over the years, our students have asked questions about Northern Ireland that seasoned hands never think to ask and, in so doing, have pushed us to rethink our assumptions and explore new lines of argument.

We are also especially grateful to Bristol University Press and our publisher and editor Stephen Wenham for giving this book initial consideration and working with us to improve our proposal, then our rough draft, and finally the camera-ready version. He chose excellent reviewers who pointed out the weaknesses in our argument and offered useful advice for strengthening it. And as we made our revisions, Stephen gave us great advice on how to proceed. His advice was both incisive and gently delivered. We also missed a deadline or two and offer our sincere apologies and gratitude for his patience. Zoe Forbes' team also gave us excellent cover options and helped us think through multiple titles. We always felt like we had Stephen and Zoe's unyielding support. Though we may not have deserved it, we are so happy to have had it.

Finally, a book about protecting the Belfast/Good Friday Agreement could not have happened without all of the people in Northern Ireland who have worked mightily to keep the peace. Peacebuilding is ultimately the compilation of thousands of people doing their part to maintain and nurture concord amid division. Maintaining peace isn't easy or glamorous, so it is a true testament to this collective labor that the 1998 agreement still stands.

# 1

# Phoenix Rising

> Building a green wall to protect the Good Friday Agreement is something we know how to do.
> Jim Walsh, former Congressman, cited in Manley, 2020

> The Irish have few cards to play but Irish America is one of them.
> Irish Senator Peadar Tóibín, 2022, comments at an event at the Irish Embassy in Washington, DC

By most accounts, Irish America was tremendously influential in the Irish peace process in the 1990s (see, inter alia, O'Clery, 1996; Arthur, 2001; Lynch, 2004; MacLeod, 2016; Cooper, 2017; Fitzpatrick, 2019; Sanders, 2019). During the 1992 presidential campaign, Irish Americans united across traditional divides to persuade Bill Clinton to agree to appoint a special envoy to Northern Ireland if elected. The promise was important because it signaled Irish America's intention to make Northern Ireland a US foreign policy priority, despite the longstanding tradition (in the US and the UK) that matters in Northern Ireland were considered British domestic affairs. As President, Clinton made good on his promise, selecting former Senator George Mitchell for the role in 1995. Mitchell laid the groundwork for peace talks and would go on chair the talks that produced the Belfast/Good Friday Agreement in 1998.

Irish Americans also incentivized the Irish Republican Army (IRA) and its political party, Sinn Féin, to abandon their violent campaign and in so doing helped normalize their participation in politics. They pressured President Clinton to grant travel visas to the US for Sinn Féin leader Gerry Adams and other IRA leaders, prevailing over the opposition of the US Departments of State, Justice, and the Treasury as well as vociferous back-door protests from the British government, who were reportedly "apoplectic" that Clinton had ignored their concerns (see Duffy, 2021). Clinton would remain engaged until the agreement was signed, even nudging the various parties late into the night right before the deal was signed. Today, the Belfast/Good Friday Agreement is considered a seminal achievement of US foreign policy and it continues to enjoy broad, bipartisan support among US politicians and diplomats.

However, after the Belfast/Good Friday Agreement was signed, Irish America retreated from political engagement. With its animating issue resolved, the dominant narrative was that Irish America was ageing, graying and its influence waning. Though some 30 million Americans trace their heritage to Ireland, and Irish America has a long history of social and cultural organization, contemporary Irish Americans are more divided by class, religion, and political party than they have been at any point in their history. On the eve of the 2016 Brexit vote, there was no unified Irish American vote to mobilize or to cater to.

This decline was also evident in organizations devoted to Irish American causes. In 1979 during the Troubles, for example, the Ancient Order of Hibernians (AOH) had 171,000 members (Schmidt, 1980). Today, its membership is just over 46,000 (AOH, 2025a). Irish American organization in Congress has also declined. There used to be two Irish caucuses in the US House of Representatives, but only one remains—the Congressional Friends of Ireland Caucus. In its heyday, the group had 90 members. Today it has 30, just three more than the number in the new Congressional UK Caucus.

What little lobbying Irish America did in the decades after 1998 was focused on immigration policy, and even then was limited in terms of its scope. Irish American organizations did not vet candidates, organize grassroots campaigns, fundraise, make political action committee (PAC) contributions, or provide other forms of material support to politicians. In fact, there are no organizations with "Ireland," "Irish," "Hibernian," and so on in their name in Federal Election Commission (FEC) data of PAC contributions in the last decade, except the Irish American Democrats, a small group that only raised $72,000 in 2020 when Joe Biden, a proud Irish American, was on the ballot.

In his 2000 book on ethnic lobbies, Tony Smith predicted that "there are no conceivable foreign issues that might trigger an ethnic awakening for Irish America" (2000: 117). Paul and Paul found a similar trend in their book (2009). Their interviews with policy makers underscored the conundrum the Irish American lobby faced after the Troubles: it was large and historically influential, but could not get co-ethnics or the US government to focus on Northern Ireland. Before Brexit, few would have disagreed with Smith's prediction that that the normalization of politics in Northern Ireland after 1998 peace accord meant that "Irish American activism with respect to foreign policy will become a subject for the history books" (2000: 117).

And yet, Irish America re-emerged like a phoenix in the aftermath of the Brexit referendum in the UK. Indeed, Brexit threatened the Irish American lobby's signature achievement— fostering peace in Northern Ireland—and would ultimately lead to its re-activation. This book examines that remobilization, following Irish American activists as they flexed dormant political muscles to defend the Belfast/Good Friday Agreement from the threats posed to it by Brexit. Our central argument is that they did so by shaping America's foreign policy approach to the UK's withdrawal agreement with the EU as it pertained to Northern Ireland. Their efforts were bolstered by the Irish government and the EU, who vigorously defended the agreement and the dividends it has produced over 25 years. These combined efforts constrained what the UK government could do as it negotiated its withdrawal from the EU.

## Brexit and the peace process

The Belfast/Good Friday Agreement transformed the conflict in Northern Ireland. Known locally as "the Troubles," the conflict began in the late 1960 and would drag on for nearly 30 years. At the heart of the conflict was a constitutional question—should Northern Ireland remain in the UK or unify with the Republic of Ireland?

The contemporary importance of this question is rooted in Ireland's colonial history (Sulzberger, 1971). Although English forces first invaded the island in the 12th century, the British crown managed to achieve only partial control for centuries. To secure its colony and bring the Irish under more direct control, one strategy the English crown used was to offer Irish land to loyal British subjects, starting in the 16th century. Most settlers arrived in the 17th century and were Scottish Presbyterians. They settled primarily in the northeastern part of Ireland in the region of Ulster. Their arrival and subsequent dominance supplanted the Irish, Catholic population.

In December 1922, the UK government partitioned the island of Ireland into two entities: the Irish Free State[1] and Northern Ireland. Partition occurred in the context of the Irish War of Independence, which was rooted in a long history of Irish mobilization for greater autonomy from the British. The War of Independence began in 1919 as a guerilla war between the original IRA and British military forces. The two sides called a ceasefire in July 1921 and negotiated a peace agreement known as the Anglo-Irish Treaty five months later. The treaty resulted in a portion of Ireland becoming a free state with dominion status in the British Empire, while Northern Ireland, then dominated by Protestants, would remain part of the UK.

After partition, Protestants dominated government and business in Northern Ireland and kept Catholics in a subordinate position in society. Catholics faced discrimination in housing and employment, and had difficulty using the political system for redress because gerrymandering and the franchise favored Protestants. This context meant that Northern Ireland politics diverged from the rest of the UK, where parties were organized along class lines (for example, Labour and Conservatives). In Northern Ireland, politics was defined by religion and constitutional concerns. Nationalist parties were largely composed of Catholics who wanted to reunite with the rest of Ireland, while Unionist parties were primarily Protestant and wanted to remain part of the UK.

---

[1] The Irish Free State became the Republic of Ireland in 1948.

In the mid-1960s, inspired by the US civil rights movements, Catholics began marching for equal rights. They met with stiff resistance from the Royal Ulster Constabulary (RUC) and so-called Paisleyites, who followed the firebrand Free Presbyterian minister Ian Paisley. By the late 1960s, armed groups[2] had joined the fray. The fighting that emerged would pit the Provisional IRA against the RUC and British military forces. Loyalist paramilitaries would also join the fight, sometimes colluding with security forces. At its end, more than 3,500 people had died—a majority of them civilian—and thousands more were injured or otherwise traumatized.

The Belfast/Good Friday Agreement did not settle the constitutional question, but provided a mechanism for answering it peacefully. Specifically, the Agreement committed all sides to a constitutional arrangement that reflects majority consent. If a majority of the population indicates in a referendum that it no longer wants to be governed by the UK, the UK government pledged to allow Irish reunification. The agreement also established a devolved Assembly and Executive in which the political parties of the two communities shared power. The Assembly also contained rules to mitigate the core sources of conflict between them. These rules were meant to channel disagreements by guaranteeing fair play, requiring cross-community consent for Assembly decisions, ensuring each side's representation in proportion to its share of the vote, and giving expression to the multiplicity of identities in Northern Ireland. Two and a half decades after the Belfast/Good Friday Agreement was signed, the violence has largely ceased, but the peace is a cold one.

Brexit, which has been unfolding since the UK referendum in 2016, threatened to undermine this functional status quo in Northern

---

[2] Nationalism and Unionism do not as a general rule support violence to meet their respective goals. However, both positions include elements willing to use force (Republicans on the Nationalist side, and Loyalists on the Unionist side). These internal relationships were often fraught during the Troubles, though Nationalists tended to be more accepting of Republicans than Unionists were of Loyalists. This is due in large part to the fact that Unionists controlled local law enforcement and could not publicly embrace Loyalists paramilitaries while at the same time disparaging Republican ones for using violence (Gallaher, 2007).

Ireland. The UK and the Republic of Ireland had both been members of the EU's single market for nearly 30 years (1993–2021). During that time, goods, capital, and services could move freely between them because EU regulations were the same in both places. The only exception was the border between Northern Ireland and the Republic of Ireland. Even though there were no customs checks to pass through after 1993, the border was fortified for security reasons during the Troubles, and trade was relatively slow. Within a few years of the signing of the Belfast/Good Friday Agreement, the UK government had dismantled its checkpoints and military installations, and the border between the two parts of Ireland began to look like those between other sovereign nations in EU territory—virtually invisible. Goods and people flowed seamlessly across it, and manufacturers developed supply chains as if the island was fully integrated. In 2016, the year in which the Brexit referendum was held, there was $7 billion in cross-border trade between the two parts of Ireland (Haverty and Reaney, 2018).

The common membership in the EU also softened the distinctions between Northern Ireland's two main national identities—Irish and British. Indeed, the two countries' joint EU membership allowed the agreement to include what Brendan O'Leary has called "imaginative elements of co-sovereignty" (1999: 68). In particular, shared EU membership meant that the agreement could allow citizens of Northern Ireland to claim British, Irish, or dual citizenship, and, as a result, to hold British, Irish, or both passports.

Brexit disrupted this arrangement because it re-ignited questions about the border. Because the UK voted to leave the EU, there would have to be a border where goods crossing into or out of the EU could be checked and customs could be paid.[3] There were two options going forward—re-instate a land border and build the infrastructure necessary to carry out checks and tariff collection, which would disrupt the all-island economy, or move the border to the Irish Sea and put customs infrastructure at ports in Northern Ireland, which

---

[3] Brexit did not affect freedom of movement between Ireland and the UK because both countries have a Common Travel Area (CTA) agreement, which is separate from the EU. The CTA allows Irish and British citizens to live, travel, work, and study in the CTA.

would disrupt trade within the UK.[4] Both options risked reviving conflict between the two communities. For Nationalists, a land border looked like a form of retrenchment and to some a potential site for violence by dissident Republicans. For Unionists, a sea border was a new barrier between Northern Ireland and the rest of the UK, creating a de facto form of Irish unification.

The Irish government was adamantly opposed to a land border, and the EU backed that position in its negotiations with the UK government. In 2022, nearly six years after the initial referendum, the UK finally approved the Withdrawal Agreement with the EU. This agreement included a provision known as the Northern Ireland Protocol, which put the customs checks at ports in Northern Ireland. Most of the Unionist political establishment was dead set against it. And in protest, the Democratic Unionist Party (DUP) withdrew from the Northern Ireland Executive, effectively shutting down the Assembly. The party did not go back into government until two substantial rounds of revision had occurred—the Windsor Framework in 2023 and the Securing the Union deal in 2024.

Adding to the tension surrounding the border was the fact that Northern Ireland's two communities viewed Brexit differently. Although a majority of total residents in Northern Ireland voted to remain (56 percent) in the Brexit referendum, support for the remain position varied substantially across the two communities. While 88 percent of Nationalists voted to remain, only 34 percent of Unionists did (Garry, 2016: 2). This means that in Northern Ireland, Brexit is largely interpreted through existing conflict divides. The post-Brexit deterioration in the relationship between the UK and the Republic of Ireland, which was crucial to the success of the Belfast/Good Friday Agreement, also pulled the communities in Northern Ireland further apart.

The state of the British-Irish relationship also alarmed advocates of the peace deal on both sides of the Atlantic. The behavior of the UK government as it attempted to withdraw from the EU was especially alarming for Irish Americans. In fact, during the governments of

---

[4] Although some goods coming into Northern Ireland stay there, the integration of the two economies since 1998 means that most products are designed for sale on both sides of the border.

Boris Johnson and Liz Truss, the UK government appeared ready on several occasions to leave the EU without a withdrawal treaty or to renege on the agreement it had signed, an approach that would have led to a hard border and potentially dire consequences for the still-unfolding peace process in Northern Ireland.

## The US and the peace process

This project considers how Irish America responded to the threat Brexit posed to the ongoing peace process in Northern Ireland. Contrary to expectations, Brexit triggered a dramatic re-escalation of efforts by Irish American groups to shape US policy and protect the gains of the Belfast/Good Friday Agreement. Existing organizations expanded their efforts. The AOH, for example, hired its first full-time lobbyist in 2022. New organizations also formed, including the Ad Hoc Committee to Protect the Good Friday Agreement (hereafter the Ad Hoc Committee), the American Brexit Committee (ABC), and the American Irish State Legislators Caucus (AISLC). These groups engaged in vigorous efforts to lobby Congress, the State Department, and the White House to pressure the UK government into protecting the Belfast/Good Friday Agreement as it negotiated its withdrawal from the EU. Their efforts were complemented by Irish Americans in Congress, especially members of the Congressional Friends of Ireland Caucus, as well as various Executive Branch members in both the Trump and Biden Administrations. The lobby reached an apex in Biden himself, a self-declared Irish American who would go on to appoint top advisors with extensive knowledge about the Northern Ireland peace process.

### *Changing strategic considerations and the role of Irish America*

In the history of US foreign policy, Irish American activism has always intersected uncomfortably with the so-called "special relationship" between the US and the UK (Arthur, 2001; MacLeod, 2016; Cooper, 2017). The shared strategic interests and decades of close diplomatic relationships between the US and the UK largely kept the US from formally challenging British policy toward Northern Ireland during most of the Troubles, *despite* considerable pressure from Irish America. American policy only began to shift in the 1990s, first, with the extension of travel visas to prominent Irish Republican figures and, second, with the creation of a special envoy to Northern Ireland. As mentioned earlier, both moves happened over and against UK government objections. Over time, however, British policy makers and diplomats came to view the American role as useful.[5] Indeed, the US supported British and Irish efforts to implement the peace agreement and facilitated solutions on outstanding issues after it was signed.

The examination of the Irish American response to Brexit is also interesting because Brexit altered US strategic considerations and as such changed the opportunity structures for Irish American mobilization. It did so in three ways. First, Brexit pitted some of the US's closest allies against each other, thus complicating US foreign policy. Brexit not only forced the US to navigate the new and, at times, acrimonious division between the UK and the EU, it also strained the relationship between the Belfast/Good Friday Agreement's two formal co-guarantors, the Republic of Ireland and the UK. The previously close relationship between these two allies and the deliberately coordinated actions they took leading up to the agreement were critical to the success of the peace process. British-Irish unity also simplified American policy making because the US was not pulled between competing actors or forced to mediate between them.

However, in the aftermath of the Brexit referendum, the UK-Ireland relationship was at its lowest point in decades. The two countries had sharp disagreements over important policy choices, most notably how to interpret the Belfast/Good Friday Agreement in this new context. They also had difficulty presenting a united front when dealing with Northern Ireland's dueling political parties, who have often favored short-term political gains over long-term stability. This put the US between two allies who were both actively lobbying US policy makers to different ends. It also meant that Irish American remobilization came at a moment of greater contestation

---

[5] For example, British Cabinet Secretary Robin Butler would eventually tell Joseph Small, the Irish Ambassador to London, that "the granting of the American visa was, with benefit of hindsight, on balance, beneficial" (see https://www.thejournal.ie/gerry-adams-us-visa-5632405-Dec2021/).

than at any point in previous decades, as traditional roles between the three countries were in flux. In short, the stakes for Irish American lobbying vis-à-vis US foreign policy were greater than they had been in decades, but so too were the opportunities.

Second, though the strategic alliance between the US and the UK remains, Brexiteers' willingness to upend longstanding political conventions put an indelible strain on the relationship. As we will note in the subsequent chapters, the US government took a dim view of Boris Johnson's government's admission that his 2020 Internal Markets Bill breached international law. It also viewed his threat to unilaterally amend the Withdrawal Agreement two years later with alarm. Indeed, many American policy makers were flabbergasted that the UK was abandoning established aspects of its own international legacy as well as the international regime it had helped to build. Each move provoked strong statements from Congress, the State Department, and other parts of the Biden Administration. In short, British behavior around Brexit constituted a new environment for Irish American lobbying focused on altering British policy.

Third, Brexiteers' emphasis on bilateral trade deals gave Irish America unique leverage during key points in Brexit negotiations. One of the key arguments Brexit supporters made in the run-up to the referendum was flexibility on trade. Instead of having to follow EU trade rules, which it often disagreed with, the UK could negotiate its own bilateral deals. A bilateral trade deal with the US was seen as a special Brexit prize. However, the constitutional requirement that any US trade deal be approved by Congress allowed Irish America to pressure its supporters in Congress to tie any trade deal to preservation of an open border between Ireland and Northern Ireland. These circumstances created an avenue for Irish Americans to pressure the UK government on behalf of Ireland in ways that had never before existed and that fundamentally altered the traditional balance of power between the UK and Ireland in terms of US foreign policy. The advantage was little anticipated and may never be relevant again, but for a time, it was powerful. And most importantly, Irish America was well placed to take advantage of it because of its high level of representation in and strong connections to Congress.

In addition to a changed opportunity structure, the Russian invasion of Ukraine in 2022 posed a new set of strategic considerations for the US in its approach to Europe and the UK in particular. The Biden Administration clearly saw a strong need for a collective response to Russian aggression. What was not clear in the immediate aftermath of the invasion was how the need for a united European front would affect the US response to the disputes between the UK and the EU, and between the UK and Ireland, which is not a North Atlantic Treaty Organization (NATO) member and has remained neutral since the 1930s. Although some worried that the UK's military might and diplomatic prestige might lead the US to abandon its defense of Ireland in the Brexit dispute, by the summer of 2022, the US sought to tie the war in Ukraine to the need for a negotiated solution to the ongoing arguments over Brexit and the Protocol. As we will demonstrate in this book, Irish America took advantage of these new dynamics to center the importance of the Belfast/Good Friday Agreement in US foreign policy.

## Irish America as an ethnic lobby

Irish America's resurgence since Brexit is also intriguing because it is a black swan of ethnic lobbies, distinct from other ethnic lobbies and even from itself in earlier periods. Considerable scholarly literature examines the influence of Armenian, Cuban, and Jewish ethnic lobbies on US foreign policy toward their respective "homelands."[6] This literature also identifies factors deemed critical to the success or failure of such lobbies, including the community's size, wealth, organization, level of concentration vs. assimilation, legitimacy, political activism, level of networking, and representation in Congress (see, inter alia, Rubenzer, 2008; Paul and Paul, 2009). Some of these factors were clearly in play in Irish American lobbying since 2016, but our study identifies other variables that explain the Irish American lobby's success regarding Brexit.

---

[6] Ethnic "homelands" are better understood as social constructions than historical facts. While some ethnic groups' "homelands" are uncontested, others are contested or otherwise subject to debate. Moreover, the definition of a "homeland" is often dependent on the time period an ethnic group uses to establish a claim to a particular territory.

For starters, Irish American activism has waxed and waned over the last few decades. However, the literature on ethnic lobbying tends to refer to groups in static terms, neglecting the extent to which external events may drive their potential for mobilization/ remobilization and influence (see Paul and Paul [2009], for example). The Irish American case study clearly shows the importance of variables borrowed from the study of collective action, such as changing opportunity structures in motivating and shaping ethnic group organizing and lobbying.

Irish American lobbying has also been crucial to the process of defining US strategic interests in this post-Brexit phase. Multiple scholars contend that ethnic groups are most effective at influencing US foreign policy when the interests of the ethnic group overlap with other national strategic interests (Rubenzer, 2008; Dewind and Segura, 2014). Given all the changing circumstances prompted by Brexit, this case study offers a fascinating opportunity to examine how ethnic lobbying can help shape the perception of what constitutes US strategic interests in the first place.

Finally, though the literature on ethnic lobbies tends to acknowledge that Irish America is powerful (Smith, 2000; see, inter alia, Paul and Paul, 2009), it does not describe how it wields its power. In its current form, Irish America does not rely on traditional lobbying tactics, such as raising money or fielding candidates for office. Instead, as we will demonstrate here, Irish America's success is manifested through informal pathways, relying on its networks, skills, positioning, unique opportunities, and an extraordinary amount of goodwill, including bipartisan support.

## Gauging influence

To chart Irish American mobilization and its impact on US policy toward the peace process, we used primary and secondary source data to identify key points of Irish American impact during Brexit negotiations. We began by tapping into networks cultivated over years of teaching and writing about the peace process, co-organizing events on continuing challenges related to the agreement, and running study abroad programs in Northern Ireland. Using these contacts, we identified people based in the US, the Republic of Ireland, Northern Ireland, and the UK more broadly who were involved in Brexit negotiations, lobbied for particular outcomes in the negotiations, and/or had a window into either process as it affected the Belfast/Good Friday Agreement.

Our largest group of interviewees—23—were Irish American or part of the Irish American lobby.[7] Two grew up in Ireland but are now American citizens. This group included members of the Ad Hoc Committee, the ABC, and the AOH. Many of these people were what we call eminent "formers"—that is, people who had previously served in Congress (as members or chiefs of staff), as special envoys to Northern Ireland, as Consul Generals in Belfast, or in other diplomatic posts relevant to Northern Ireland. A smaller number of interviewees in this category were also members of groups active during the Troubles, such as the Irish Northern Aid Committee (NORAID). This group also includes people who joined forces with one or more of these groups, but were not active members in any of them.

We also interviewed two Irish leaders—an ambassador to the US and a member of the Irish Senate—who were knowledgeable about the Irish government's approach to Brexit, and its efforts to work with Irish America. Both had a front row seat to how the Irish government managed Brexit and interfaced with Irish America. Finally, we interviewed nine people who worked in or for Northern Ireland, including business leaders, academics, and current and former staff in the Northern Ireland Civil Service (NICS), the Northern Ireland Office (NIO), and the Northern Ireland Bureau.

We concentrated on Irish American interviewees because they were best situated to explain why and how Irish America remobilized, what strategies/tactics the lobby employed, and how they saw the lobby's impact. However, we used interviews with people in Ireland and the UK to flesh out Irish American accounts and to "test" Irish America's reports of impact. Specifically, we wanted to know if our Irish and British interlocutors saw American influence in the same way as Irish Americans did. Most of our interviews were on the record, though we allowed interviewees to

---

[7] As we note in Chapter 3, Irish America is an ethnic lobby, but many of the people who associate with/belong to it do not have Irish ancestry.

go off the record at any time during the course of their interview.[8] We also interviewed people in high-level positions who could not go on record because of the nature of their jobs. We include them on our list of interviews, even though we could not quote them, because they were indispensable in providing background information and context, which in turn helped us frame our questions to others.

Our secondary sources of data span a variety of types of material. In addition to government reports, formal speeches, and parliamentary and Congressional records (hearings, resolutions, and so on), we used newspapers, blogs, radio broadcasts, and magazine and journal articles to create a detailed Brexit/Irish American timeline that helped us match key events in Brussels, Dublin, and London with Irish American actions in the US. For this part of our research, we relied on the BBC, the *Belfast Telegraph*, *The Guardian*, *The Independent*, the *Irish Times*, *Irish Central*, the *Irish Echo*, the *New York Times*, *Politico*, and the *Washington Post*, among many others.

## Key arguments

Our research leads us to make three main arguments. First, whereas Irish America had largely withdrawn from active engagement in the aftermath of the Belfast/Good Friday Agreement, Brexit compelled an enthusiastic remobilization of Irish America in defense of the peace deal. This remobilization defied predictions about the status and health of Irish America.

Second, Irish America may be a black swan among ethnic lobbies, but its success offers important correctives to the academic literature on the topic. Simply the fact that Irish American activism waned and waxed in the past few decades suggests that the scholarly literature on ethnic lobbies needs to consider the dynamic, external factors that contribute to ethnic (re)mobilization and influence. Likewise, whereas the scholarship argues that ethnic lobbies are most effective when their agendas align with US national strategic interests, the Irish American case demonstrates that ethnic lobbies can also reshape perceptions of strategic interests in moments of great flux. Most

---

[8] When individuals asked to go off the record, we quote them anonymously.

importantly, Irish America is unique in that it has been successful, despite lacking the main organizational elements considered crucial for ethnic lobbies to succeed. It does not constitute a voting bloc, have a campaign apparatus, conduct letter-writing campaigns, or lobby in the traditional sense that other ethnic groups do. Its particular path to influencing American foreign policy makes it an especially interesting and compelling case.

Finally, we argue that Irish America has been extraordinarily effective despite these gaps. It made sure its own government understood the threat that Brexit posed to the Belfast/Good Friday Agreement—no mean feat, given that many of the members of Congress who had championed the agreement were retired or had died. It then convinced the US government to put pressure on the UK government to withdraw from the EU in a way that prevented the reimposition of a hard border on the island of Ireland. The US position was reinforced by the Irish government and the EU, and together they were able to constrain the British government's approach to Brexit.

In the course of this book, we point to five traits that explain Irish America's effectiveness in the present moment. First, despite its internal diversity and its retreat after 1998, Irish America has maintained a coherent political culture and an almost "tribal" bond. Second, when it chose to act, it called on dense networks that had been nurtured over decades. Irish America's proximity to political power was a third trait that allowed its success. Though the days of machine politics are long gone, Irish Americans are still over-represented in Congress, and many others are former high-level government officials who can call on contacts inside government with ease. Fourth, Irish America drew on a Washington, DC institution—official St. Patrick's Day celebrations—to re-ignite its domestic and international networks. Irish Americans have long used St. Patrick's Day events to interact with key politicos and civil society leaders from Ireland and Northern Ireland in Washington, DC. During a week of events, these guests hobnob with members of Congress, the Executive Branch, and sometimes even the President. During Brexit, St. Patrick's Day events provided an especially important opportunity for Irish America to do its work. Indeed, no other small country has such routine access to the halls of American power as the Irish. Finally, Irish America has been able to win broad support for its issues because of the deep well of societal goodwill it has developed over nearly 200 years. Its political rise was fraught, but its ascendance is now celebrated as an American success story. Indeed, the Irish "brand" or ethos is attractive to many contemporary Americans. These traits helped Irish America open doors many other ethnic lobbies must work to unlock. This, in turn, meant that they could more easily and readily take advantage of political opportunities when they arose.

## Overview of the book

The remainder of the book is organized in the following manner. In the next chapter we provide a brief history of Irish America, tracing two distinct waves of Irish migration to the US and explaining the political differences that animated them. We overview Irish America's rise to political dominance in the 20th century and conclude with a review of Irish American influence during the Troubles and the march to peace that culminated in the 1998 Belfast/Good Friday Agreement. In Chapter 3, we review the literature on ethnic lobbying and demonstrate how the Irish American lobby's path to influence does not fit standard explanations for ethnic lobby success. We also identify traits that have made Irish America uniquely influential.

In Chapters 4 and 5, we discuss the Irish American lobby's remobilization and its efforts to influence the UK's Withdrawal Agreement with the EU. Specifically, in Chapter 4, we discuss the UK's rocky tenure as a member of the EU, trace the Brexit campaign to leave the EU, and explain the slow pace of Irish America's remobilization. In Chapter 5, we chart Irish America's reawakening and its efforts to ensure that the UK's Withdrawal Agreement with the EU did not lead to the reimposition of a hard border on the island of Ireland—a move it saw as inconsistent with (and a threat to) the Belfast/Good Friday Agreement.

In Chapter 6, we review a new threat to the Belfast/Good Friday Agreement—the Internal Markets Bill. We explain why the bill was a threat and how Irish America successfully confronted it. We also highlight an unexpected ally in these efforts—Donald Trump's then new chief of staff, Mick Mulvaney.

In Chapter 7, we cover new Brexit-related threats to the Belfast/Good Friday Agreement by Prime Minister Boris Johnson and the hard-right flank of his Conservative Party. We also discuss how US President Joe Biden's election, and more robust EU and Irish responses to Tory recalcitrance, created favorable ground for continued Irish America activism. This chapter concludes with the signing of the Windsor Framework in 2023.

In Chapter 8, we address Irish American activism relating to the UK government's efforts to quash investigations into crimes committed during the Troubles. Irish Americans have long been interested in uncovering human rights abuses by British forces in Northern Ireland's Troubles, and the British Legacy Bill, which proposed ending ongoing criminal probes, met with stiff resistance from Irish America. We also explain why Irish America's efforts to prevent the bill's passage were not as successful as its prior efforts to avert a hard border.

In Chapter 9, we turn to the question of Irish unity. For many people, Brexit created the most favorable conditions for reunification since the signing of the 1998 peace agreement. Indeed, working groups on both sides of the Atlantic formed to think through how reunification would work in practice. Although Irish America largely supports reunification, there is no agreement within the Irish American lobby on whether, or how, Irish Americans should engage with the issue. We review this internal debate and its implications for American involvement going forward.

In Chapter 10, we summarize our main argument, paying close attention to how Irish America wielded its influence and how different opportunity structures affected its level of success. As we note, the core traits that helped Irish Americans scramble up the political ladder in the mid- to late 1800s, carried forward to the contemporary moment. Yet, its ability to wield these core traits successfully depended on external factors that were not constant across the period we discuss here.

## *A note on terminology*

In Northern Ireland, terminology around the peace agreement will often "locate" you vis-à-vis one or the other community in Northern Ireland. In this book we try to avoid terminology that suggests proclivities for one side or the other, or a position on the constitutional question at the heart of the conflict. For this reason, we use the term "Belfast/Good Friday Agreement" to describe the agreement. This term captures the two distinct names given to the agreement. However, if an interview subject uses one or the other of these names, we quote them as they speak. In most cases, we also use the term "Ireland" to refer to the island of Ireland, not the country. However, we do use the term "Ireland" to signify the Republic of Ireland if it is used in a sentence that includes reference to other states (for example, the US or the UK) and/or the EU.

Finally, except in Chapter 2, where we discuss how Irish immigrants and their descendants climbed the political ladder starting in the late 19th century, we use the term "Irish America" very narrowly to refer to the small lobby of Irish Americans who worked to defend the Belfast/Good Friday Agreement from the threats posed to it by Brexit. As we note in Chapter 2, Irish America writ large—that is, people who claim Irish ancestry on the census—is a much larger group than the contemporary Irish American lobby, which is now a very small cohort of activists with deep connections in Washington, DC and in government.

2

# A Short History of Irish America

Irish America is a sizable if quotidian part of America's so-called melting pot. Like other waves of European migrants, Irish emigrés left poverty, famine, and limited opportunities to build new lives in America. Though many Irish emigrés would remain poor and "foreign" after decades in America, their descendants would move up the socioeconomic ladder, becoming fully assimilated within three or four generations. While assimilated, these greatgrandsons and daughters of Ireland continue to recognize their Irish roots. In 2021, 31.5 million Americans—9.5 percent of all Americans—claimed Irish ancestry on the US Census form (US Census Bureau, 2023).[1]

Though most Irish emigrés were fleeing desperate poverty, they brought distinct political sensibilities and skills with them and ultimately become an integral part of America's 20th-century political landscape. Irish émigrés in the 19th century often had no choice but to embrace ethnic politics because the political establishment was dominated by Dutch and Anglo-Saxon Protestants who saw them as inferior and had little inclination to welcome them into "respectable" society. Squashed together in crowded tenements

---

[1] US Census questions on ethnic heritage, first introduced in 1980, have not been consistent, which complicates efforts to track longitudinal trends in this identity. For example, the Census has classified subcategories (for example, "Scotch-Irish" and "Celtic") as Irish in some years and not in others.

in cities on the Eastern Seaboard, acting collectively was often the only way to improve their lot, even as it placed them in fierce competition with other migrants, both foreign (Italians, Poles, and Hungarians) and domestic (Black Americans heading north during the Great Migration).

In this chapter, we focus on Irish America's early forays into ethnic politics. Irish America writ large did not follow a traditional path to ethnic influence—most notably by forming a well-funded lobby. Instead, it succeeded by forming dense networks of ethnic patronage and harnessing them for survival and later political advantage.

For much of its history, Irish America's focus was domestic and often localized, but at key moments its attention was diverted to events in Ireland, particularly around Irish nationalism. Although the community was frequently divided over the best tactics to counter British colonization and exploitation in Ireland, by the late 19th century most of Irish America was unified in its support for Irish self-determination. Irish America's time in the political trenches, and the dense networks they formed in them, prepared them to shape American policy around Northern Ireland during the Troubles and again after Brexit.

The chapter proceeds as follows. We begin by asking a deceptively simple question: who is Irish America? To answer this question, we describe two distinct waves of Irish migration to the US and how their differences explain a key cleavage within the broad group of people who claim Irish heritage. Indeed, while we see truth in Trina Vargo's observation that there is "there is no monolithic Irish America" and as such "no [Irish] voting bloc," our work here demonstrates that the legacy of British colonialism still animates Irish Americans otherwise divided by class, political affiliation, religion and geography (Vargo, 2019: 5). This legacy in Northern Ireland provides a center of gravity for Irish America despite the centripetal forces in play.

We then turn to the structure of their ethnic politics—the hard scrabble up the political ladder, the consolidation of Catholic Churches in cities where the Irish lived, the building of machine politics in New York and beyond, and the path to Camelot. In the third section we focus on the post-Camelot era, when Irish America turns its attention to the then-brewing Troubles in Northern Ireland.

It was during this period that Irish America learned how to effectively influence American foreign policy vis-à-vis Northern Ireland.

## Who is Irish America?

Irish Americans historically have fallen into one of two mutually exclusive categories: "Scots/Scotch Irish" or "Irish Catholic." These groups emerged from two distinct migration waves, the first during the 1700s and the second in the mid-1800s after the Great Famine. Scholars have written extensively about the second group, but the quiet existence of the first explains an important feature of Irish America today. Irish Americans who came in the first wave tended to be Protestant and were geographically dispersed across colonial America. Those in the second wave were almost exclusively Catholic and initially concentrated in a few cities—Boston, New York, and Chicago. While descendants of both waves are counted among Americans who claim Irish ancestry on the census, they are not equally represented in the Irish American ethnic lobby we discuss in this book. This lobby and its political traditions are very much a product of the second wave. Many of its members were Catholic and some still live in East Coast cities associated with postfamine Irish migration. They also tend have more recent ties to Ireland and a more immediate stake in its future.

To be clear, the Irish American lobby is not a facsimile of its 19th-century ancestors. Most of the leaders we interviewed are two or more generations removed from the immigrant experience. Many grew up in suburbs and most hold/held powerful, well-paid positions in government or the private sector. Nor is the Irish American lobby we discuss here representative of the broader population of Americans who claim Irish heritage today. Indeed, the Irish American ethnic lobby that we focus on here is not particularly representative of Irish America writ large. Tobin Grant's (2014) analysis of survey data on Irish Americans between 2000 and 2012 indicates, for example, that "nearly half of Irish Americans are Protestant," while "only a third are Catholic." Moreover, a sizable minority of Irish Americans live in the South, not in East Coast cities often associated with Irish Americans. But, as we will demonstrate, the political skills developed by the second wave of Irish migrants laid important groundwork for the small but consequential Irish

American lobby that helped foster the 1998 peace agreement and defend it in the face of Brexit.

## Distinct migration waves

The Battle of the Boyne is central to understanding early Irish migration to the US (Dolan, 2008). The battle, which began on July 1, 1690 pitted William of Orange, a Dutch Protestant invited by Parliament to succeed to the throne, against James II, the sitting Catholic King of England. After James' defeat, William consolidated control of the island, marking the beginning of the Protestant Ascendancy in Ireland (Dolan, 2008).

William then consolidated Anglican dominance in Ireland by passing the Penal Laws, a series of restrictive statutes regarding religion, ownership of land, and employment. Although the bulk of the people affected by these laws were Catholic, Presbyterians[2] and other non-Anglican groups, often called dissenters, were also subjected to significant legal disabilities. The 1704 Sacramental Test Act, for example, forbade government officials from receiving communion from any church except the Church of Ireland. The Act effectively closed off government positions for Presbyterians who were otherwise aligned with the Protestant Queen Anne. The government also closed Presbyterian churches and schools, and refused to sanction marriages and funerals conducted by their ministers. Presbyterians were also prohibited from serving in Parliament, the judiciary, and other offices of the state until 1829. In response, many Presbyterians left for America.

There were also other push factors driving Irish emigration in play. In 1740, Ireland recorded one of its coldest winters on record. The "Great Frost," as it was known, destroyed much of the 1741 harvest. O'Grána (2015) estimates that 13 percent of the population died of famine-related starvation or illness. The famine prompted two types of migration (Engler, Mauelshagen, and Werner, 2013): the first was internal, with rural migrants moving to cities and towns in search of

---

[2] Most Presbyterians in Ireland were descendants of Scottish settlers who were granted small tracks of land to secure the colony for the British after the defeat of Ireland's local Catholic lords in the early 17th century.

food and work; the second was external, with migrants embarking for the American colonies.

Access to land was also an issue for Presbyterians (Dolan, 2008). Indeed, though the overall pattern after the plantation period was a transfer of land from Catholic to Protestant hands (O'Leary and McGarry 1993), Presbyterians were also displaced when Anglicans consolidated control of large estates and forced many off the land. A decline in the linen industry beginning in 1729 added insult to injury, robbing landless Catholics and Presbyterians of alternate forms of subsistence (Dolan, 2008).

Although the effects of the Penal Laws and Ireland's changing political economy were ultimately much worse for Catholics than Protestants, the majority of Irish emigrants who left during the 1700s were Protestant (Wokeck, 1989; Dolan, 2008). During the Great Frost, for example, most émigrés were Presbyterians in the northern part of Ireland (Wokeck, 1989). Several factors explain the disparity in emigration rates between Protestants and Catholics. Dolan points to the Gaelic belief that emigration was *deorai*, a shameful form of "involuntary exile" (2008: 9). The folk practices attached to Catholicism at the time also limited emigration. In particular, the centrality of sacred wells and other site-specific relics to worship practices made it difficult for the devout to leave (Dolan, 2008). Others give a nod to Presbyterians' relative economic advantage over their Catholic peers (Wokeck, 1989). Under an Anglican crown, Presbyterians may have been dispossessed, but they were better off than their Catholic counterparts and better positioned economically to migrate.

There were also pull factors aimed exclusively at Protestants. Colonial administrators in South Carolina and Georgia, for example, advertised free land specifically to Protestants in Ulster. Those who emigrated wrote letters back home encouraging their family and friends to follow in their footsteps (Wokeck, 1989). The same welcome was not extended to Catholics. Colonial administrators often forbade "native Irish" from homesteading and penalized settlers who used them as indentured servants (Dolan, 2008).

There were, of course, some Catholic émigrés during the 1700s, but most were single men. Without family, sacred sites, or physical churches to bind them to their faith, many lost their religious identity or joined Protestant sects after marrying. Others found their way to Protestantism during the Great Awakening, a religious movement that spread like wildfire across the southern colonies in the 1730s (Dolan, 2008).

Despite their different religious backgrounds and geographic dispersal, Irish émigrés in the 1700s saw themselves as having a common Irish heritage. As the historian Jay Dolan explains "religion did not define Irish Identity" in the first wave (Dolan, 2008: 40). The limited power of sectarian impulses was reflected in the largest émigré organizations at the time. Both the Friendly Sons of St. Patrick and the Shamrock Friendly Association accepted members from both religions (Dolan, 2008). In fact, the Friendly Sons chapter in Philadelphia, founded in 1771, required its presidency to alternate between a Catholic and a Protestant each year well into the 20th century (Smyth, 2020: 42).

Irish migration to the US came to a virtual standstill during the War of 1812. When it picked up again at the war's end, the Irish migration stream changed in three ways. First, the balance between Catholic and Protestant migrants flipped on its head. Whereas Protestants had dominated the first wave, Catholics would dominate the second (Dolan, 2008: 37). Second, unlike migrants from earlier periods who tended to arrive in the Mid-Atlantic region (Virginia, Maryland, and Pennsylvania) and head west, into the Appalachian Mountains, or south, down the Shenandoah Valley, newer migrants tended to stay in their initial ports of call, most notably in Baltimore, Boston, New York, and Philadelphia (Dolan, 2008). Indeed, by 1830, these cities were burgeoning industrial centers in desperate need of low-skilled workers. The south, by contrast, had few industrial centers, and the persistence of slavery meant limited demand for agricultural labor. By 1870, 72 percent of Irish Americans lived in seven states—Massachusetts, Connecticut, New York, New Jersey, Pennsylvania, Ohio, and Illinois—all of them north of the Mason–Dixon line (McCaffrey, 1975: 63). Finally, the second wave began abruptly, in response to the Great Famine in the 1840s, and its impact was thus concentrated and visible. During the Famine alone, estimates suggest two million Irish fled to America (Holan, 2017). Irish immigration continued after the Famine at a pace of approximately 50,000 a year from 1860 to 1890 (Cooper, 2017).

## Ireland's Great Famine and its consequences in America

The sense of a common, ecumenical Irish heritage would erode in the wave that began with the Great Famine as greater class and political cleavages between new arrivals and established Irish Americans were mapped onto the extant (but largely dormant) religious divide. By the 1850s, many of the descendants of Irish migrants from the first wave had built wealth and earned a measure of political status. The more than one million Irish who fled the famine between 1846 and 1850 and the two million who followed them over the next 25 years stood out compared to earlier migrants. Many arrived emaciated and destitute and crowded into tenements where they became a distinct group, separated from prior Irish immigrant communities and newly arriving immigrants from other European countries. Consolidated Irish Americans of both religions were wary of having their reputations tarnished by the new arrivals. New émigrés reciprocated by spurning established Irish American organizations for newer associations like the AOH (founded in New York City in 1836) that spoke to their circumstances. The result was that class and geographic differences within Irish America, which had not neatly overlapped religious differences before the Famine, began to reflect religious difference. To be established and of means was to be Protestant, while to be a new arrival and poor was to be Catholic.

Irish migrants in the second wave were also more likely than their predecessors to embrace anti-British sentiment and to equate it with their Catholic faith. Although Catholics would not outnumber Protestant émigrés until the 1830s, the 1800 Act of the Union, which among other things abolished the Irish Parliament, invigorated Irish anger toward Protestants in Ireland and the Protestant crown in England (O'Leary and McGarry, 1993). The Great Famine would add fuel to the fire. As O'Leary and McGarry (1993: 78) note:

> Although much of the contemporary Irish population is held to have believed that the potato-blight was sent by God, its surviving descendants held the English government responsible for the Famine. The folk-memory of the catastrophe was most vigorously sustained by the migrant Irish and descendants, and their "diaspora nationalism," especially in North America.

Not surprisingly, those who migrated to America were suspicious of Irish Americans who were Protestant, even though some of them also supported Irish home rule. Their worldview—crafted through struggle and deprivation back home—created a religious wedge in their new home.

As the 19th century progressed, the descendants of 18th-century Irish émigrées adopted the term "Scots Irish" to distinguish themselves from the new arrivals. Although the term was not new—it was often used to describe Ulster Presbyterians who were descendants of the Scottish planters who came Ireland in the 17th century—it took on a more politicized meaning in 19th-century America (Dolan, 2008). It created a carve-out for established Irish Americans who wanted personal and political distance from new migrants. Moreover, because the category emphasized Protestant and Scottish rather than Gaelic roots, it would ultimately separate Ireland's first-wave migrants from its second-wave migrants and the Irish political machine they built.

This rupture between 18th- and 19th-century migrants also explains many of the "classic" features we associate with Irish America as a whole. Although Irish Americans can be found all over the country, most people in the US associate Irish America with the cities in which second-wave migrants settled (for example, Boston and New York) rather than the places to which first-wave migrants moved (for example, Savannah, New Orleans, and Southern Appalachia). Indeed, the state of Kentucky is arguably as Irish as Boston. Kentucky's signature music—Bluegrass—is a first cousin to Irish music, and county names like McCracken, McCreathy, Magoffin, and Menifee leave little doubt who homesteaded the state.

This rupture also explains why Irish America is seen as almost exclusively Catholic and "green" (meaning Irish Nationalist). While Protestants and Catholics from the first wave supported versions of Irish Nationalism, their consolidated descendants were more interested in domestic politics. Conversely, for migrants in the second wave, especially those who fled a famine they blamed on the British crown, Irish politics remained an immediate and visceral concern. As Tony Smith notes: "Irish Americans repeatedly sought to involve Washington in conflict with London, hoping thereby to secure Ireland's independence" (Smith, 2000: 48).

There are countless examples of Irish nationalism stateside. In 1866, for example, the Fenian Brotherhood planned an elaborate and far-fetched plot to invade Canada, hoping it would force the UK to abandon Ireland or provoke war between the US and the UK (McCaffrey, 1975: 121). On the eve of the Easter Rising in 1916, the group Clan na Gael funded a mission to Germany to secure weapons for Irish fighters. Though the supporters of the physical force tradition were neither a majority of Irish America nor particularly effective, they developed a strong political ethos that bled into wider Irish American culture. As McCaffrey observes: "The Irish were the first Americans to use ethnicity as a political tool to manipulate American foreign policy in support of a European freedom movement" (1975: 113).

## *Whither Irish migration?*

The second wave of Irish migration would eventually slow down as the 19th century progressed. Starting in the 1880s, American-born adults of Irish descent began to outnumber first-generation Irish Americans (Meagher, 2005: 95). Though Meagher (2005: 98) estimates that two million Irish arrived from 1870 to 1920, Irish immigration dropped to the tens of thousands in each decade after 1930 and to less than 10,000 per decade by the 1970s (Blessing, 1980). The Immigration and Nationality Act (or Hart-Celler Act) of 1965 ended the national origins quota system in US immigration, which had previously permitted up to 18,000 Irish immigrants per year. The new system, which imposed a quota on immigration from the Western Hemisphere as a whole region, reduced legal Irish immigration even more, to under 2,000 per year.[3] In the early 21st century, American immigration to Ireland actually exceeded Irish immigration to the US for the first time (Dolan, 2008: 283–284). Despite the declining numbers of new immigrants, Ireland's "unfinished" history continues to animate small but influential corners of American politics.

---

[3] The overstaying of visas creates a sizable community in the US of illegal or undocumented immigrants from Ireland living in the US.

## A determined scrabble up the political ladder

In this section we look at Irish America's ascent up the political ladder. As we will demonstrate, the success of the Irish American ethnic lobby was marked by three traits: a heavy reliance on personalities, dense local organization, and carefully tended patronage networks.

### *What is it about the Irish?*

In many ways, it is surprising that Irish Americans became a political force in the 20th century. They faced immediate and stiff resistance from the Anglo-American establishment. Indeed, Noel Ignatiev (1995) argues that when second-wave Irish migrants arrived in the US, the Anglo and Dutch establishment did not consider them white.[4] Landlords refused to rent to them, employers wouldn't hire them, and newspapers caricatured them as half-human simians. This was possible, Ignatiev argues, because in antebellum America whiteness was not just a marker of skin color but also of citizenship. It was what allowed people "the right to elect and be elected, to be tried by a jury of their peers, to live wherever they could afford, and to spend, without racially imposed restrictions" (1995: 3).

Until the Civil War, and for some time after it, second-wave Irish immigrants were not allowed any of these liberties. It took years for famine migrants to apply for naturalization, and they had to fight the bigotry of an establishment that did not want to offer them the franchise. The Irish only "became white" when they chose to aggressively distinguish themselves from Black Americans rather than build solidarity with them.[5] The New York Draft Riot in 1863

---

[4] Ignatiev argues that the category of whiteness was not a stable category in the 1800s. As he explains, "coming as immigrants rather than as captives or hostages undoubtedly affected the potential racial status of the Irish in America, but it did not settle the issue, since it was by no means obvious who was 'white'" (1995: 41).

[5] Most scholars of Irish migration agree that the Irish faced intense discrimination, but some disagree with Ignatiev's contentions that that Irish were not initially seen as white and that they only became white by attacking Black workers rather than building solidarity with them. O'Malley (2023) argues, for example, that Ignatiev ignores important differences between the

provides a good example here. Over five days, Irish mobs attacked Black residents and destroyed their property.

For much of the 18th and 19th centuries, being Irish was also seen as culturally incompatible with being American. If Americans were enterprising, forward-looking, intelligent, law-abiding, and even-keeled, the Irish were deemed their opposite—lazy, superstitious, ignorant, sexually licentious, and prone to violence (Whelan, 2005; Franchot, 2022). Anti-Catholicism and nativism were also key features of American politics for much of the 19th century (see McCaffrey, 1975). Irish immigrants encountered multiple waves of anti-Catholic agitation, including the Know-Nothing Movement in the 1850s and periodic no-popery campaigns throughout the 19th and early 20th centuries. These efforts were designed to exclude Catholics from political life and sometimes resulted in mob violence against them.

Despite their exclusion, and perhaps because of it, the Irish endured. Indeed, those who arrived after the Great Famine had particular advantages over other Catholic immigrant groups, like Poles, Italians, Germans, and Hungarians. First, the Irish spoke English, meaning they did not need to learn a new language while also adjusting to a new culture. Second, they had a long history of communal organization. Because they had never been able to depend on the crown or its institutions in Ireland, the Irish knew how to organize and provide for their own basic needs. As Meagher comments: "From rural secret societies like the Whiteboys or Ribbonmen to O'Connell's mass protests to the Land League's boycotts, Irish peasants were schooled in the importance of group solidarity and its potency as a political weapon" (2005: 184).

Third, they had learned how to resist the British, and, at times, to extract concessions from them. In the 1820s, for example, Daniel O'Connell, "The Great Liberator," organized mass rallies—a first in the Western world—on behalf of Catholic emancipation. These rallies

---

experiences of Irish and Black Americans, effectively blurring class and race as analytic categories that capture unique and unequal forms of oppression. Dolan (2008) argues that Irish migrants' reliance on the Democratic Party, which was then segregationist, explains why the Irish failed to build bridges with Black Americans.

often had tens of thousands of participants. The Catholic Association O'Connell founded was one of the first modern mass-membership organizations. In 1829, facing the threat of mass insurrection, the British government blinked, passing the Catholic Relief Act, which removed legal barriers to Catholic education, employment, and participation in politics.[6] After the success of the Emancipation movement, O'Connell pivoted to a campaign to repeal the 1800 Act of Union and restore Ireland's home rule parliament, again mobilizing the Irish Catholic population and rallying tens if not hundreds of thousands of participants. The Great Famine arrived before the Repeal Movement could achieve success, but the Irish learned important lessons from these experiences, and those who survived brought these lessons with them to America. As McCaffrey (1975: 138) argues:

> The Irish may have arrived in the United States technologically impoverished, but they came politically experienced. Before crossing the Atlantic, they had already confronted Anglo-Saxon political, social and economic ascendancy in the United Kingdom ... The Irish arrived in the United States already familiar with the rules of the Anglo-American political game and with considerable confidence in their ability to manipulate the rules to achieve power and influence.

## Church and politics

Irish America's political power was also built through the Catholic Church. Although the Church wasn't political, it facilitated organization in Irish neighborhoods. The number of Irish Americans who regularly attended mass rarely exceeded 50 percent, but church was where children to went to school, parents socialized, and arrivals looked for help (Dolan 2008).

The Irish also helped build the Catholic Church in the US and, in so doing, gained power within it relative to other Catholic immigrant

---

[6]  On the same day that the Catholic Relief Act received royal assent, the king also signed an act to raise the property requirement for the vote, disenfranchising 80 per cent of Ireland's population.

groups. Dolan (2008: 110) notes that on the eve of the Great Famine, most neighborhoods in New York did not have parish churches, and those that did had little more than a "mass house." However, in less than 50 years, the Irish who arrived would help expand the footprint of the Church and take over its hierarchy.

The number of Catholic parishes grew in large part because the Irish population grew rapidly after the Great Famine. Wherever they settled, Irish migrants demanded a parish church if one did not exist and helped refurbish ones that did, often by combining the few small coins each family could spare. Irish American parishes also expanded what the parish did. In this regard, they followed the lead of Paul Cullen, the Archbishop of Dublin, who had helped create the notion of a "practicing Catholic" as a someone who attended Mass weekly, took the sacraments in church, baptized their children at church, and held funeral masses instead of (or in addition to) private wakes (Dolan 2008). Parishes also opened schools and provided other services for families. In short, the Church became a center of gravity in Irish Catholic life, thwarting the centripetal forces of poverty and immigration.

Given the importance of the Church to Irish Catholics, it is not surprising that the Irish would take over the Catholic hierarchy. Dolan (2008) notes, for example, that the Irish never accounted for more than 50 percent of the country's Catholic population, but dominated positions of power in its churches. In New York, for example, more than two thirds of the city's parishes were majority Irish, while in the diocese of Boston, it was 90 percent. From 1875 and 1924, 80 percent of priests hailed from Irish American families (Dolan 2008). Even in the 1970s, when only 17 percent of Catholics were Irish, 35 percent of priests and 50 percent of bishops were Irish (Greeley, 1973).

Irish America's ability to build power within the Church was reproduced in the political realm. As in the church, Irish American politics was vertically organized but also dependent on a strong web of horizontal connections on the ground—knitting Irish Americans to one another into mutual forms of obligation.

## *From Tammany Hall to Camelot*

After the War of 1812, Irish Americans aligned with the Democratic Party. The reason for this was simple. The other major party at the time (the Whig Party) was nativist. The Whigs opposed Irish migrants on the grounds that they would "break strikes and drive down wages" (Kenny, 2013: 42). They also questioned whether the Irish could put American interests above those of Rome. The Democratic Party, by contrast, courted Irish Americans. During the Great Famine, for example, the Democratic Party's platform described America as a refuge for immigrants, and its politicians promised to make naturalization easier as well (Kenny, 2013).

Irish America's political consolidation within the Democratic Party mimicked its church-building work. The hierarchy embedded in the Catholic Church, with devout parishioners at the bottom, parish priests in the middle, and a bishop at the top, was transferred almost wholesale to party politics. Neighborhoods were informally run by block captains, who reported to ward bosses, who in turn reported to the city boss (often the mayor). The system also ran on patronage. Mayors delivered jobs and other resources downward, to ward chiefs, who worked with block captains to distribute accordingly. In return, residents showed up at the polls and voted for Irish American candidates up and down the ballot.

The most common form of patronage was a city job. In Irish tenements, work was unstable and often sporadic (Dolan 2008). A city job came with steady paycheck that could lift a family out of poverty and tenement housing. Because each job affected a family, this patronage had positive knock-on effects for the wider community and feedback effects for the machine.

In cities like Boston, New York, and Chicago, the Irish moved up the economic ladder, becoming policemen, fire fighters, and teachers. In New York City, the Irish were almost half of the police department in 1860 and remained so well into the 20th century (Watkin, 2002). By 1900, approximately a third of all first and second-generation Irish Americans in New York City worked in the public sector (Trounstine, 2008: 156).

Another form of patronage involved assisting residents with naturalization. Tammany Hall,[7] perhaps the most infamous example

---

[7] Tammany Hall, formally known as the Society of St. Tammany, was a so-called benevolent organization in New York City that worked as a parallel, informal political operation. It supported Irish American political candidates running for office and helped Irish American politicians

of Irish machine politics, created "naturalization committees" to help Irish Americans and other immigrants become citizens (Dolan 2008). They helped illiterate migrants fill out naturalization forms and offered loans to those who couldn't afford the fees. The result was more votes for the machine. Tammany politicos also used bribes to encourage city offices to hire Irish applicants.

Not surprisingly, non-Irish people resented the machine's corruption. Tammany Hall boss George Washington Plunkitt was soundly mocked when he told journalist William Riordon that there was a difference between "honest" and "dishonest" graft. Dishonest graft, he argued, was "blackmailin' gamblers, saloonkeepers, disorderly people," while honest graft was "my party's in power in the city, and it's goin' to undertake a lot of public improvements" (as quoted in Riordon, 1963: 1).

Corruption notwithstanding, some scholars argue that machine politics also had positive effects (Golway, 2014). Historian Terry Golway argues, for example, that Tammany Hall's benefits "outweigh the corruption" (as cited in Fresh Air, 2014). Corruption was an antidote to the Anglo political establishment's efforts to prevent Irish integration. The wealth Tammany Hall produced and shared allowed Irish Americans to assimilate into American society.

By the 1880s and 1890s, Irish Americans had elected one of their own as mayor in Chicago, New York and Boston, among other cities (Meagher, 2005: 117). Their entry into city-level politics would also open doors down the road to higher-level political office, including state houses, state governorships, Congress, and ultimately the White House. As D.W. Brogan observed in 1954, the Irish were "the providers of a professional political class" (1954: 96–97).

Al Smith provides a good example of this Irish American upward economic and political mobility (Dolan, 2008). Smith was born in 1883 on the Lower East Side to an Irish mother and an Italian father. His rise through the ranks started with a Tammany Hall job in the Office of the Commissioner of Jurors. Within a decade, he had won a seat in the New York State Assembly, where he served for 11 years, acting variously as the chamber's minority and majority leader. His

---

deliver resources to Irish American neighborhoods. The term "Tammany Hall" refers to a specific place, but is also a stand-in for Irish machine politics in urban centers across the US.

next position, as Sheriff of New York County (appointed through Tammany Hall), allowed him to launch a successful gubernatorial bid. He would ultimately serve four (nonconsecutive) terms. For his final act, Smith ran for President in 1928 against Herbert Hoover (Dolan, 2008).

Although numerous Irish Americans could be found in Congress and multiple state houses by the early 1900s, it would take several decades for an Irish American—John Fitzgerald Kennedy—to win the presidency. Despite Al Smith's prodigious political talents and national name recognition, he lost to Herbert Hoover by a landslide. Many scholars blame the loss on anti-Catholic bias. During the campaign, the Protestant establishment repeatedly questioned whether he would put fealty to Rome (as Catholicism was pejoratively described) above loyalty to the US (Kenny, 2000).

The role of anti-Catholicism also permeated the election between Richard Nixon and John F. Kennedy. Carty (2001) argues that Kennedy faced anti-Catholic sentiment not just from nativists, who saw Catholicism as a threat to Anglo-Saxon Protestant hegemony, but also from liberals who supported his civil rights record, but worried he would not defend the separation of church and state (see also Moats Miller, 1990). However, unlike his predecessors, Kennedy was able to withstand the attacks from outside his party about divided loyalties. And he neutralized the threat from inside the liberal fold by promising to execute American laws without the fear or favor of the Catholic Church (Dolan 2008).

Camelot[8] was the apogee of Irish America's rise to political power. As Nathan Glazer and Daniel Patrick Moynihan noted, on the day Kennedy was assassinated in 1963, "the President of the United States, the Speaker of the House of Representatives, the Majority Leader of the United States Senate, the Chairman of the National Committee were all Irish, all Catholic, all Democrats" (Glazer and Moynihan, 1963: 287).

---

[8] The term "Camelot" is often used to describe Kennedy's time in the White House. The National Park Service (2021) credits Kennedy's widow, Jacqueline Kennedy Onassis, with coining the term to describe her husband's presidency. As the Park service notes, the term likens Kennedy to the fictional King Arthur, lending his presidency an almost mythical aura.

However, it is worth noting that even during Camelot, Irish American power was largely confined to the domestic sphere. Its influence did not extend to foreign policy matters regarding Ireland. Three factors explain why. First, Irish America was divided on matters of foreign policy. Irish American leaders disagreed, for example, on the utility of Ireland joining NATO and the extent to which they could use this as leverage in relation to the UK government on Northern Ireland (see Arthur, 1997).

The second was Ireland's policy of neutrality in the Second World War, which Arthur argues "antagonized successive American administrations" (1997: 50). Arthur points to a 1950s National Security Council memo discussing the possibility of bringing Ireland into NATO as an example. Although some Irish American politicos saw dangling Irish membership in NATO as an opportunity to force concessions from the British regarding partition, the memo concluded that ending partition was not a "price worth paying" (1997: 50).

The final obstacle was the so-called "special relationship" between the US and the UK. Winston Churchill first coined the term in a 1946 during a speech in Fulton, Missouri to celebrate the two countries' partnership in the Second World War and to emphasize its promise for the future. In geopolitical terms, the special relationship meant that the UK was the principal international ally of the US. As a result, even during the early years of the Troubles, the US foreign policy establishment supported the UK government's perspective on Ireland/Northern Ireland and was loath to back Irish American calls to change it.

## Consolidation post-Camelot

It was only in the 1980s that Irish America began to have some impact in the realm of foreign policy. The primary reason was the advent of the Troubles. The most violent years of the conflict were in the 1970s, and many Americans saw the aftermath of car bombs on their televisions. Hamill (1972) argues that Irish Americans had a particularly visceral response to the carnage. Many faulted the British government for the descent into violence, and some reclaimed their Irish identity as a result. Smyth argues that the Troubles also encouraged young Irish Americans to think in ethnic terms and join Irish American organizations (Smyth, 2020).

By the time the hunger strike by IRA prisoners began in October 1980, Irish America was watching. The very public deaths of the ten young Republican prisoners galvanized Irish Americans. The Irish Northern Aid Committee (NORAID), which fundraised for Irish Republican causes in the US, raised $250,000 in the first half of 1981 (more than double the half-year amounts in the previous seven years). Although Irish Americans were divided on how to respond to the conflict, they agreed it merited a US response, thus increasing pressure on the American foreign policy establishment.

Personality also played a role, particularly in Congress. In the 1980s, Irish American politicians worked together even when they hailed from different parties. Their shared heritage made bipartisanship easier and paved the way for political cooperation. The classic example is the relationship between Republican President Ronald Reagan and Democratic Speaker of the House Tip O'Neill. Their warm relationship allowed Irish Americans to bring their concerns through the Democratic Speaker to a Republican President, who could in turn bring them to the UK Prime Minister Margaret Thatcher.

Finally, it is worth noting that the special relationship between the US and the UK began to attenuate in this period. Although the UK government had come to see the special relationship as a permanent feature, Arthur (1997) argues that the relationship was never as idealistic as the British imagined it to be. And, when American and British interests began to diverge, the relationship adjusted accordingly. This became evident in the wake of the collapse of the Soviet Union (McKercher, 2017: 8). As the lone superpower still standing, US policy makers became more unilateralist. In the context of Irish interests, this meant that the Cold War adherence to "spheres of influence," where Ireland was deemed to be within Britain's sphere of influence, gave way to a more horizontal understanding of power. This reset allowed the US to emphasize transborder relationships, more ad hoc alliances, and human rights, which had been shunted to the side during the Cold War.

This reset set the stage for the US to begin pressing the British for concessions on its policy in Northern Ireland. And as Arthur notes, the 1985 Anglo-Irish Agreement, forged shortly before the Cold War ended, inadvertently helped the Irish Americans. In particular, the agreement's acknowledgement of Irish interests in what happened in Northern Ireland redefined the conflict as regional, thereby "call[ing] into question the UK government's claim to be sole arbiter" (Arthur, 1997: 54).

## Key Irish American actors

Taken together, these changes allowed Irish American activists to make headway in foreign policy discussions relating to Ireland. However, Irish American activism was still hampered by the longstanding divide between those supporting a physical force approach—now represented by pro-Republican groups supporting the IRA—and constitutional Nationalist groups who preferred peaceful means (Smyth, 2020). Four of Irish America's most influential groups during the period put the divide into sharp relief.

In Congress, the so called "Four Horsemen"—Speaker of the House Tip O'Neill, Congressman (and later Governor) Hugh Carey, and Senators Ted Kennedy and Daniel Patrick Moynihan—took a strong stance in favor of constitutional nationalism. Although Kennedy and Carey had been more militant in the early 1970s,[9] both moderated their views after engaging with Social Democratic and Labour Party leader John Hume, who was the leading voice of constitutional nationalism in Northern Ireland.

NORAID, by contrast, openly supported the IRA and courted the ire of the US government as a result. In 1981, for example, the Department of Justice successfully forced the group to register as a foreign agent and to list the IRA as its "foreign principal" (Guelke, 1996). Two years later, four of the group's members were convicted of gun-running for the IRA in federal court. Prominent Irish Americans also kept their distance. When NORAID's founder, Michael Flannery, was named Grand Marshall of the New York St. Patrick's Day Parade in 1983, the state's governor, Hugh Carey, and senior senator, Daniel Patrick Moynihan, boycotted the festivities (*The Journal*, 1983).

The AOH vacillated between constitutional nationalism and militant approaches. As a cultural organization, the group was well

---

[9] In 1971, Kennedy and Carey co-sponsored a resolution in Congress calling for the withdrawal of British troops from Northern Ireland that led to Congressional hearings on the issue.

positioned to move between the two approaches. However, when it engaged with militants, it kept the IRA at arm's length, choosing instead to work with political groups (Dumbrell, 1995: 112). However, some chapters dissented. At its annual convention in 1980, the Florida AOH publicly endorsed NORAID (Smyth, 2020).

In 1983, Texas millionaire Jim Delaney founded the Irish American Unity Conference to combat the factionalism in Irish America. Although the conference would ultimately adopt a posture that was more militant than not (Dumbrell, 1995), tacitly supporting the IRA and ardently defending reunification, it maintained a level of respectability that NORAID did not. The conference would organize numerous delegations to Northern Ireland that included American bishops, business leaders, local and state politicians, and members of Congress.

Although these groups disagreed vociferously on how to deal with the Troubles, they all worked to put the Troubles onto the political radar, meeting with members of Congress, sponsoring delegations to Belfast and Londonderry/Derry, and talking to the press about the ongoing violence in Northern Ireland. Their work gave the issue wider political currency and meant that members of Congress would hear about the Troubles when they went back to their districts (Guekle, 1996). These groups also made a point to talk to members of Congress without Irish ancestry, helping to build a political coalition that extended beyond shared lineage. They took a similar approach to party affiliation, courting members from across the partisan divide.

As we will demonstrate in the next section, while both sides lobbied Congress, Irish Americans supporting constitutional nationalism would ultimately prevail in the policy realm. They realized that American support for the IRA, especially its gun-running, weakened US influence with the British government and set out to contain stateside support for Republicanism. However, once the IRA signaled a willingness to enter into peace talks, Irish American leaders who had sought to rein in their supporters in the US changed course, agreeing to work with them on a plan for peace. The constitutional Nationalists' long-term principled denunciations of violence provided them with the legitimacy and credibility to encourage the US government to get involved in the peace process and take risks to move the process forward.

## Irish America and the Belfast/Good Friday Agreement

The role of Irish America in fostering the Belfast/Good Friday Agreement is well documented.[10] Here we focus on the factors (contextual and political) that allowed the Irish American lobby to successfully advocate for a peace agreement in Northern Ireland.

### *The 1970s*

Former President Jimmy Carter is not usually associated with peace in Northern Ireland, but scholars argue that a 1977 speech he gave on human rights in Northern Ireland generated early momentum (McLoughlin and Meagher, 2019). Read today, Carter's comments seem uncontroversial. He affirmed US support for "peaceful means" to resolve the conflict and indicated that the path to peace should "involve both parts of the community of Northern Ireland" (Carter, 1977). But his statement that the UK *and* Irish governments had a role to play in an eventual settlement was groundbreaking at the time.

The speech was Carter's, but Irish Americans and John Hume had a hand in its creation (Martin, 2016). In Carter's first year in office, the Four Horseman approached Carter's Secretary of State, Cy Vance, with a proposal that Carter make a statement about the Troubles. The implications were momentous. If he gave a speech on the conflict, Carter would be rejecting a well-established foreign policy stance—that Northern Ireland was an internal British matter—and embracing a new "moral" foreign policy that had few backers in the State Department and was certain to anger the UK government. Speaking about the conflict was not an aberration, but describing it as relevant to Britain *and* Ireland made it consequential. It pushed open the door to American involvement that had been firmly shut until then.

Democratic congressman Mario Biaggi also played an important role in the 1970s. In 1977 he formed the Ad Hoc Congressional

---

[10] See, among others, Wilson, 1995; Guelke, 1996; Mallie and McKittrick, 1996; O'Clery, 1997; Thompson, 2001; Lynch, 2004; Brundage, 2016; Cooper, 2017.

Committee for Irish Affairs (ACCIA) over the objections of his party's leadership. Biaggi used the Committee to highlight Catholic oppression and introduced bills offering economic assistance for Northern Ireland on the condition of British withdrawal. He was also willing to work within the firmament of the IRA and its American supporters. Indeed, he put the Congressional spotlight on British security forces' treatment of IRA men and Catholic civilians, and, echoing Carter, described many of their actions as human rights abuses. Though none of Biaggi's proposed bills succeeded, he drew attention to the issue and prompted the US State Department to cover human rights abuses by official entities in Northern Ireland in its annual Report on Human Rights Abuses beginning in 1979. He also succeeded in attaching an amendment to the State Department's Appropriations Bill that banned the sale of American arms to the RUC on the grounds that it abused civilians.[11] Johnson argues that Biaggi's efforts helped "broaden the political dialogue to include paramilitary groups" (2007: iv) who would ultimately have to be part of an eventual agreement.

## The 1980s

In the 1980s, new political actors joined the fray. In 1981, 24 members of Congress formed the Congressional Friends of Ireland Caucus. Though its members—most notably three of the Four Horsemen[12]—had been advocating for addressing the Troubles for years, the caucus enhanced and institutionalized the power of the moderate wing of the Irish American lobby (Weinraub, 1981; McLoughlin and Meagher, 2019).

Across the Atlantic, Margaret Thatcher moved into Downing Street. Unlike her predecessor, she took a strident approach to the Troubles. Her refusal to negotiate with the IRA's hunger strikers rejuvenated Sinn Féin's political prospects in Northern Ireland. In

---

[11] Cooper (2017: 99–100) notes that O'Neill, as Speaker of the House, allowed Biaggi's amendment to go forward in order to establish the principle that arms should not be provided to either side (RUC or IRA) in the conflict.

[12] Carey left Congress in 1974 and was serving as Governor of New York when the Caucus was formed.

1981, for example, Sinn Féin dropped its policy of abstaining from elections and won five seats in the Northern Ireland Assembly election the following year. And in 1983, Gerry Adams ran for and won a seat in Westminster.[13]

To thwart an emboldened Republicanism, John Hume worked with Irish Taoiseach Garret Fitzgerald to create the New Ireland Forum. Its goal was to provide a space where constitutional Nationalist parties could develop ideas for resolving the Troubles. To increase the likelihood that the UK government would take the Forum seriously, Hume reached out to the Four Horsemen for support. The Horsemen delivered, issuing a statement on St. Patrick's Day, 1983, signed by 28 Senators and 53 members of the House of Representatives, recommending the initiative and arguing that it was far superior to the British government's plan for the Assembly (Wilson, 1995).

In its final report in May 1984, the New Ireland Forum recommended three potential solutions: a unitary state; federalism; or joint British/Irish sovereignty. The Friends of Ireland Caucus again endorsed its efforts, this time introducing a resolution (H. Con. Res 310) that passed the House with 59 co-sponsors. At a press conference in November 1984, Thatcher offered praise for the efforts, but rejected all three of the political options, derisively replying "That is out!" in response to a reporter's query about her views on each one.

At Hume's request, the Four Horsemen turned to President Reagan for support. So did William Clark, Reagan's former National Security Advisor and a member of the AOH. Clark was close to the former Irish ambassador Seán Donlon, who with Tip O'Neill asked the President to broach the issue with Thatcher at an upcoming meeting in December. Reagan did not bring the idea up directly, but when Thatcher raised it herself, he encouraged her to develop options she could support (Cooper, 2017). At O'Neill's urging, Reagan also dangled an invitation to speak before a joint session in Congress. No UK Prime Minister had had such an honor since Winston Churchill in 1952 and such an occasion would help cement her legacy. Reagan encouraged Thatcher to make progress on the conflict before she returned. In February 1985, Thatcher

---

[13] Sinn Féin runs candidates, but does not take its seats in Westminster.

addressed Congress and, at the instigation of Tip O'Neill, praised the Taoiseach and said that she was prepared to cooperate with the Irish government to find a political solution to the conflict. On that visit, Secretary of State George Schultz advised Reagan to tell Thatcher he was "concerned that unless there is the appearance of progress at the next Anglo-Irish Summit, a radicalization could occur in Irish-American opinion which would endanger the current bipartisan support that our Northern Ireland policy enjoys" (memorandum from Schultz, quoted in Cooper, 2017: 169).

According to Wilson, both Clark and Donlon believed Reagan's pressure was integral to breaking Thatcher's intransigence on the issue (Wilson, 1995). Certainly, there was considerable pressure on Thatcher to give in from within her own party. Indeed, many believed her "out, out, out" reaction to the Forum's proposal had undercut constitutional Nationalists and played into the hands of Sinn Féin. However, Thatcher herself said on multiple occasions that the Americans factored significantly in her support for the Anglo-Irish Agreement. Her long-term advisor Lord McAlpine recalls Thatcher telling him that it was "pressure from the Americans that made me sign the agreement" (McAlpine, 1997) and that she had done so to put the UK "on side with the Americans" (O'Clery, 2015).

Irish Americans also kept the heat on through local politics in the 1980s. In 1984, for example, New York City's comptroller, Harrison Goldin, created the so-called MacBride Principles, which laid out fair hiring/employment practices for companies doing business in Northern Ireland. Goldin modeled MacBride on the Sullivan Principles, which set out similar guidance for companies doing business in South Africa. The comparison was intentional. Putting Northern Ireland, then governed by direct rule from Westminster, in the same league as an apartheid regime put the morality of the conflict into sharp relief (O'Dowd 1985). Over the next decade, numerous city and state governments adopted the McBride Principles (McManus, 1997), and in 1999, they were formally adopted into US law.

## The 1990s

Irish America continued to press for peace after Reagan left office, but its relations with his successor, George H.W. Bush, were cooler than they had been with Reagan. Bush held firm to the standard State Department view that the conflict should be solved on the other side of the Atlantic. During the 1992 presidential campaign, Democratic presidential candidate Bill Clinton took advantage of the gap that was emerging between the Bush administration and Irish America (O'Grady, 1996). His interest was initially about political survival. As O'Grady notes, Clinton looked to Irish America only after he lost the Connecticut primary to his rival, former California Governor and Irish Catholic Jerry Brown.

In response, Clinton worked to shore up the Irish American vote for the upcoming primary in New York—a state with a sizable Irish American population. He started by signing on to three Troubles-related proposals that Jerry Brown had already adopted—appointing a special envoy to Northern Ireland, granting a visa for Gerry Adams, and investigating alleged human rights violations by British security forces. Clinton also agreed to attend a forum organized by John Dearie, a New York Assembly member from the Bronx, who had organized similar events for presidential candidates in 1984 and 1988 (O'Grady, 1996). At the forum, Clinton leveled the playing field with Brown by publicly supporting his proposals (O'Grady, 1996). With his Irish credentials established, Clinton had a fighting chance against Brown, and would best him in New York two months later. Shortly after, Clinton won the backing of key Irish American politicians in Congress, who created a political action committee, Irish-Americans for the Clinton-Gore ticket. The committee was chaired by Connecticut Congressman Bruce Morrison, who would prove influential in implementing Clinton's Northern Ireland agenda in Congress (O'Grady, 1996).

After the Downing Street Declaration was released in December 1993, Clinton's willingness to keep his campaign promises was put to the test. The declaration, released jointly by Irish Taoiseach Albert Reynolds and the UK Prime Minister John Major, was the result of multiple sets of secret negotiations between Adams and Hume, the UK and Irish governments, and the IRA's central command and British security services (O'Grady, 1996). The declaration signaled a framework for future negotiations (Arthur, 1994). Reynolds and Major acknowledged that Northern Ireland's place in the Union was secure, but reaffirmed the people's right to change that status by democratic means. The declaration also stated that Britain would welcome peace talks and would include Sinn Féin if they "committed themselves to exclusively peaceful means" and showed that "they abide by the democratic process" (Major and Reynolds, 1993).

In response, the National Committee on American Foreign Policy organized an event for the major parties to meet in the US to begin discussions. The Committee also sent invitations to key players, including Gerry Adams. The event put Clinton in a quandary because the State Department had deemed Adams a terrorist, making him ineligible for a visa. The UK government also opposed the visa because the IRA had yet to announce a ceasefire. Bruce Morrison and other Irish Americans pressed Clinton to forge ahead, arguing that the visa was necessary to get talks going and that talks would lead to a ceasefire, not the other way round. They argued that granting Adams a visa would also moderate the IRA by showing it what was available if they ended their violent campaign.

Clinton granted Adams the visa in January 1994. Three months later, the IRA announced a three-day cessation of hostilities, and five months later it declared a ceasefire. Gerry Adams made his first visit to the US two months later in October (Phoenix, 2018). Over the next five months, Adams would be given three additional visas. On each visit, he met high-level policy makers and in March 1995 he was invited to the White House as part of its St. Patrick's Day festivities. Although the IRA would break its ceasefire in 1996 by bombing the London Docklands, Irish Americans kept up their engagement and persuasion. Sinn Féin eventually signed the 1998 Belfast/Good Friday Agreement.

Clinton's other substantive move was to appoint George Mitchell, then a Democratic Senator from Maine, in several high-level, Northern Ireland-specific roles. He started by asking Mitchell to organize a conference on investment in Ireland and sweetened the pot with a contribution of $10 million to the International Fund for Ireland (IFI). Clinton then appointed Mitchell as US Special Advisor to the President and Secretary of State for Economic Initiatives, a partial fulfilment of his campaign pledge in 1992 and a key agenda item for Irish American groups (O'Grady, 1998). So, when peace talks stalled over the UK government's refusal to talk with the IRA prior to their decommissioning, Clinton tapped Mitchell to lead a study on decommissioning. Mitchell's group—the International Body on Arms Decommissioning—recommended having decommissioning and all-party talks occur in tandem (International Body on Arms Decommissioning, 1996). In supporting the conclusions, Clinton again bucked the UK government and his own State Department to move things along. Clinton's final appointment of Mitchell in 1996 was as chair of the all-party talks that successfully negotiated the 1998 Belfast/Good Friday Agreement. Mitchell proved an adept negotiator, getting the agreement to the finish line in 700 days. Throughout the process, Irish Americans and President Clinton would nudge, cajole, encourage, and incentivize the parties to continue their negotiations and come to an agreement.

## A history carried forward

Irish America has been a formidable political force since the 1850s. Its strength lies in five traits the burgeoning lobby adopted early and carried forward right up until the 1998 agreement. First, Irish Americans built a strong political identity. That identity was forged out of the Great Famine in Ireland and the systematic discrimination they faced in their new homeland. Learning to survive primed them for politics from the start.

Second, Irish America would develop dense political networks, first for survival and later for influence. These networks gave new arrivals a hand up, tied them together, and ultimately opened political doors for them. Irish Americans used these networks to run and win local, then state, and finally federal elections.

By the mid-1980s, Irish Americans third key strength was apparent. They were often in (or near) the rooms where important decisions were made. When Reagan discussed the Anglo-Irish Agreement with Prime Minister Thatcher, for example, Irish Americans shaped the contents of the conversation he had with her. Likewise, in 1994, Irish Americans in Congress were able to convince a then green President to buck his own State, Treasury, and Justice Departments and the UK government, and grant Gerry Adams a visa.

That Adams would eventually meet that president at a St. Patrick's Day event demonstrates the fourth source of their power. Irish America's peculiar institutions pay political dividends. It's trite but true—St. Patrick's really is an American holiday. But it is also a work day where serious diplomacy happens—at catered Irish breakfasts, at whisky tastings, and at black tie galas. Indeed, Kevin O'Malley, former US Ambassador to Ireland, described these events as "full-on substantive" (MacKinnon and Quinn, 2020).

Finally, Irish America's ascent up the political ladder has won them the affection they were initially starved of upon their arrival. They are often pushing on an open door. It is this threshold where Irish America helped nurture peace and, as we will demonstrate in this book, where it protected that peace when Brexit threatened to rip it apart.

In the next chapter we turn to the Irish America's work as an ethnic lobby. As we will demonstrate, the lobby's continued success defies the conventional wisdom about what makes ethnic lobbies successful.

3

# Irish America as an Ethnic Lobby

I have friends across town.

Paul Quinn,[1] 2015

In 2019 two books on Irish America hit bookstore shelves. *Shenanigans* by Trina Vargo, former Congressional staffer for Senator Ted Kennedy, pulled few punches describing her frustrations working with the Irish American establishment to fund her US-Ireland Alliance and the now-inactive Mitchell Scholarship Program. But Vargo also made some important observations about contemporary Irish America, notably that it was not a "monolith," particularly "cohesive," or even a "voting bloc." As she put it, claims about "Irish American political clout and donations ... don't withstand scrutiny" (Vargo, 2019: 5–7).

Caitríona Perry, BBC's Washington correspondent, made similar points in her book on Irish American influence. Drawing from dozens of interviews with prominent Irish American figures, Perry too contended that Irish American power and influence is "fading" (2019: 238).

These analyses were not incorrect, especially for the moment they described—the 20-year period after the 1998 peace agreement. And

---

[1] Irish American lawyer and long-time board member of the Ireland Funds, previously called the American Ireland Fund. Interview with Kimberly Cowell-Meyers.

both books seemed to be driven to encourage people to think in new ways about how Americans might relate to a newly prosperous and relatively peaceful Ireland in the future. But the trajectory they describe does not anticipate the re-emergence of the Irish American lobby in the period that followed Brexit and its subsequent successes in shaping US foreign policy.

Instead, Irish American leaders paid close attention to how the UK's withdrawal negotiations could hurt the Belfast/Good Friday Agreement. To ensure their concerns were heard, they formed new groups, including the Ad Hoc Committee to Protect the Good Friday Agreement in 2019, the American Brexit Committee in 2016, and the American Irish State Legislators Caucus (AISLC) in 2021. Together with Irish Americans in Congress and diplomats for the Republic of Ireland, they worked to protect the agreement and its dividends on both sides of the border.

There is a sizable scholarly literature that considers the influence of ethnic groups on US foreign policy toward their ancestral (or otherwise constituted) homelands, including work on Armenian, Cuban, and Jewish American lobbies, among others (see, inter alia, Ahrari, 1987a; Uslaner, 2002; Rubenzer, 2008; Paul and Paul, 2009). This literature identifies a variety of factors seen as critical to their mobilization (levels of assimilation, cohesion, and so on) and effectiveness (size, fundraising capacities, depth of alliances, and so on). As Brexit loomed, Irish America lacked many of these features; indeed, it barely looked like a lobby at all. That it would ultimately play an important role in preventing three Tory Prime Ministers from undermining key elements of the Belfast/Good Friday Agreement is not well explained by the scholarly literature.

Multiple scholars contend that ethnic groups are most effective at influencing US foreign policy when the interests of the ethnic group overlap with other national strategic interests (Ahrari, 1987a; Uslaner, 2002; Dewind and Segura, 2014). But, as we will demonstrate later on, Brexit raised questions about what US interests should be going forward. Indeed, as the UK crafted a withdrawal agreement with the EU, it sparked intense debates between three of the US's closest allies about Brexit's effect on Northern Ireland, compelling the US to navigate new dynamics. In fact, during UK/EU negotiations, the EU adopted most of Ireland's position on how Brexit should unfold vis-à-vis Northern Ireland, forcing the US to choose between its oldest ally and the largest trading bloc in the world. Irish American lobbying helped shape how US policy makers would come to see the situation—and that view did not ultimately favor the UK government's position.

Our case study offers a fascinating opportunity to examine how ethnic lobbying can help define US strategic interests and shape the perception of which countries' interests (in this case, US-Irish or US-UK?) converge and diverge. In addition, our case study provides a window into a phenomenon that the scholarly literature on ethnic lobbies rarely considers: ethnic resurgence. Although there is some discussion in the literature on why ethnic lobbies form and decline, scholars largely tend to treat ethnic lobbies and the groups they represent in static terms. Doing so neglects the extent to which ethnic lobbies can rejuvenate themselves as the Irish Americans did.

As we demonstrate here, Irish America is also interesting because it influences policy through pathways other than those typically discussed in the ethnic lobbies literature. We argue that, as in earlier periods, Irish American influence relating to Brexit stems from its coherent political culture and tribal bond, strong networks of skilled activists, unique positioning in key political roles, quirky institutionalized opportunities, and an abundance of societal goodwill that translates into a general predisposition toward their key policy stances among policy makers. Some of these features appear in places in the ethnic lobbies literature, but attention to them is insufficient, given the key role they play in this case. Thus, Irish American lobbying in the context of Brexit can offer new ways to think about how ethnic groups influence outcomes.

## What is an ethnic identity?

According to Esman (1994: 15), an ethnic group is a set of people who claim a connection to one other through "common descent or fictive kinship." People in an ethnic group often share customs, styles of dress, and language (see also Smith, 2000; Paul and Paul, 2009). Being part of an ethnic group can also provide a shared identity for its members. And unlike "collective identities that are more instrumental to the individual," ethnic identity often "taps deeper layers of socialization, experience, emotion and pride" (Esman, 1994: 15).

However, the mobilization of ethnic groups for political purposes is not guaranteed. It usually requires a shared grievance and/or a shared goal. As Esman observes, many ethnic groups "forego political action because they harbor no major grievances, because they are reasonably satisfied with the status quo, because they prefer to remain relatively inconspicuous or because they consider themselves too few or too weak to make a political impact" (Esman, 1994: 17). When they do mobilize, ethnic groups work to "impress ethnically defined interests on the agenda of the state" (Esman, 1994: 27).

In the US, ethnic identity is often tied to the immigrant experience. As a consequence, when they lobby the government, their goal is often to affect US foreign policy toward their ethnic homeland (Rubenzer, 2008: 172; see also Scott and Osman, 2002). However, as Glazer and Moynihan (1963: 313) note, the ability to get an ethnic group to focus on the mother country, "rarely survives the 3rd generation in any significant terms." Sociologists refer to this as "'late ethnicity' or 'late generation ethnicity'" (Kennedy, 2017). This concept certainly describes contemporary Irish America. Its ethnic formation occurred in the late 19th and early 20th centuries, and its ranks are no longer being replenished with new arrivals. Even though 31.5 million Americans indicated they had Irish ancestry on the 2020 Census (Moore, Vazquez, and Dolan, 2021), a coherent Irish American identity is no longer a given. As Tony Smith observed shortly after the Belfast/Good Friday Agreement was signed:

> One should not confuse their [Irish American] numbers with their strength ... actual ethnic support is shallow (being Catholic or working class appear to be far more critical than being of Irish descent when it comes to voting) and even the majority of Catholics may be more concerned with class or religion than US foreign policy towards Ireland. (Smith, 2000: 117)

When we started this project, we found ourselves trying to reconcile Smith's (and others') observations about the shallowness of Irish American ethnic identity with the burgeoning resurgence of Irish America we were witnessing post-Brexit. It was, as political scientists say, a puzzle.

On the one hand, we agreed with the assertions of Vargo (2019) and Perry (2019) that Irish America is not a monolith and that the Irish American experience occurs along a spectrum. Many Irish Americans have assimilated to the point that their Irishness is a distant phenomenon, something they dust off in time for St. Patrick's Day. For others, it may be little more than a recognition that their last name is Irish.

Yet, through our connections to Irish American groups in DC, and our work in Northern Ireland, we met many Irish Americans who embrace their ethnic identity, culturally and/or politically. And while foreign policy toward Ireland may not be the sole defining issue on which they cast their ballots, these Irish Americans follow developments in Ireland, Northern Ireland or the UK closely. Moreover, a smaller subset within this group is actively engaged in lobbying on behalf of foreign policy objectives that affect Northern Ireland and its peace process.

## What makes an ethnic lobby possible?

To unpack this puzzle—to explain why some Irish Americans continue to be engaged in events in Ireland and Northern Ireland despite the centripetal forces at work—we turned to the literature on interest groups and a subset within it on ethnic lobbies.

Ethnic lobbies may be distinct from other interest groups by the nature of their ethnic bond, but they face the same challenges in terms of organizing and maintaining themselves as other groups do. Collective action is not a given. Many scholars have followed Mancur Olson in arguing that it isn't rational to sacrifice time, energy, or resources for the sake of the group, especially if you can benefit from the actions of the group without giving of yourself (Kennedy, 2017). Instead, groups tend to form only when the collective action problem can be overcome.

Collective action can be more difficult for ethnic groups than for other types of interest organizations because ethnic lobbies often ask individuals to sacrifice their time, energy, and resources for issues in their ancestral homeland with which they may have only a distant connection (see Paul and Paul, 2009). However, these limitations are often overcome because ethnic identity has a particular psychosocial pull on its members (Paul and Paul, 2009). What makes some groups have a greater sense of attachment to the collective is not especially well developed in the scholarship on ethnic lobbies in the US. Not everyone in a given ethnic group experiences their ethnicity in the same way, if at all. Anglo-Americans, for example, don't see their English heritage as an "ethnic" identity, and nor do they identify with a common set of cultural practices or religious/linguistic identifiers that would set them apart from other ethnic groups (Smith, 2000: 22).[2] In fact, much of the scholarly literature on ethnic lobbies examines what lobbies do more than it does why they do it, or why some involve themselves in this work while others do not.

When scholars do talk about what makes ethnic groups more likely to organize, assimilation is often considered a determinative variable. But assimilation functions as a double-edged sword for ethnic communities (Paul and Paul, 2009). Higher levels of assimilation are important because ethnic groups need to understand how politics work in their new homeland to organize effectively (Ahrari, 1987a; Smith, 2000; Uslaner, 2002). Yet, too much assimilation may weaken the connection back to the homeland and undermine the group's sense of cohesion. Irish America's trajectory in politics confirms this broad pattern. As Irish Americans made their way up the socioeconomic ladder, they were able to create a political machine that paid political dividends. But as they consolidated their place in America, their political power as an ethnic lobby waned. Ahrari (1987a: 156) argues, for example, that by the mid-1980s, Irish Americans were so assimilated that it "constrained their ability to effectively focus on foreign policy objectives" related to the Troubles.

Ethnic cohesion is another variable cited as key to ethnic mobilization. It is commonly fostered by "an underlying core of memories, experience or meaning [that] moves people to collective action" (Esman, 1994: 14). Paul's (2002) work on Armenian, Serbian, and Kurdish groups in the US shows that the existence of a common historical trauma makes mobilization of ethnic interest groups more likely. Ahrari (1987b) and Smith (2000) also point to the importance of trauma for unifying ethnic groups. Just the presence of ethnic enemies or threats to their ancestral homeland can motivate

---

[2] However, DeConde (1992) is very clear that their ethnic bond has privileged certain foreign policy outcomes for centuries.

individuals to join ethnic organizations (Paul and Paul, 2009: 113). Paul and Paul refer to this idea as salience and contend that ethnic groups mobilize when their identity is strong and political activity is salient to them. People with Norwegian, Swedish, and German heritage, for example, rarely pressure the US government to take specific actions regarding their respective homelands because they lack a strong or salient identity and their countries of origin do not have controversial relations with the US. Irish Americans, in contrast, continued to have a coherent political culture, fostered by trauma from British colonization, the Great Famine, partition, and later the Troubles. As *The Economist* notes, historically "Irish American politicians harped on the feeling this inspired, of struggle and two fingers to the bloody establishment, long after Ireland was free and most Irish Americans comfortably middle class" (*The Economist*, 2019). Though Irish Americans today have no direct experience with the Great Famine or partition, politically active Irish Americans were able to tap into this historical current during the Troubles because they saw the violence unfolding on their television screens as a contemporary manifestation of similar historical abuses.

However, these biases retreated, and became latent after the 1998 peace agreement as Irish America "moved on." As former Consul General in Belfast Barbara Stephenson explained in our interview, Northern Ireland was "pushed to the back burner" after the agreement was finalized. And, as Brian O'Dwyer, former Grand Marshall of New York City's St. Patrick's Day Parade, explained to us, "it was hard to get anybody terribly interested in it. Because the issues were not clearcut and not easily solveable, they were not easy to organize around." Anti-Britishness didn't go away for many Irish Americans, but became latent until Brexit revived it.

In short, levels of assimilation and cohesion are not especially helpful variables for understanding why Irish American activism has waxed and waned because its state of assimilation and ethnic cohesion has remained largely constant.

## Why some ethnic lobbies are more effective than others

Irish America is commonly referred to as one of the US's most powerful ethnic lobbies by scholars and policy makers alike (Smith,

2000; Paul and Paul, 2009). However, the reasons for their influence, are not particularly well described in the academic literature. In particular, many of the variables identified in the literature to explain success do not apply to the Irish American case.

One such variable is population size. It stands to reason that larger groups would have more voters and elected officials would be more likely to respond to their concerns. However, this relationship is not borne out by the facts. As Paul and Paul (2009) note, some of the smallest groups by population size are commonly considered the most influential. Cuban Americans, who are often described as one of the strongest ethnic lobbies in the US, made up only 0.5 percent of the population in 2005. American Jews are also considered a powerful ethnic lobby, despite comprising only about 2 percent of the total population. And Armenian-Americans, another powerful ethnic lobby, represent even smaller proportion of the population at 0.15 percent.

However, there is a difference between how large a group is overall and how large it is in any given political constituency. Groups that are small nationally may have much larger numbers in particular districts, allowing them to influence electoral outcomes. In short, population concentration can be just as important as total numbers.

In their work, Paul and Paul (2009) create an index of dispersion across Congressional districts and find that groups that make up at least 1 percent of more Congressional districts are considered more influential by policy makers than those that are even more dispersed. By this measure, Irish Americans should be a dominant lobby in the US. Indeed, by their account, in 2000, Irish Americans made up 25 percent of the population in four Congressional districts, 10 percent of 252 districts, and 5 percent of 383 districts (of the 438 total districts) (Paul and Paul, 2009: 110). Yet, as we noted earlier, for many Irish Americans, their ethnicity doesn't tend to drive their political behavior, especially in terms of domestic politics. In a similar fashion, the largest ethnic groups in the US—Germans and English—are actually the least likely to be organized as ethnic lobbies.

Population size as a variable then functions in a similar way to assimilation, which contributes to or detracts from a group's ability to organize. Yet, though population size matters because more ethnic group members means more votes and Irish America is one of the largest ethnic groups, Smith argues that he could not find "a single quantitative study that demonstrates the impact of this community on foreign policy through voting since WWII" (Smith, 2000: 95). At the very least, this gap suggests that Irish America uses other means to influence US policy.

Another variable that should predict success is the education, civic skills, and political engagement of the ethnic group. Groups with higher levels of education have the "communications and organizational capacities that are so essential to political activity ... Citizens who can speak or write well or who are comfortable organizing and taking part in meetings are likely to be more effective when they get involved in politics" (Brady, Verba, and Shlozman, 1995: 273, as quoted in Paul and Paul, 2009: 125). Prasad and Savatic (2023) find that immigrant groups that come from democratic countries are more likely to be able to mobilize effectively as an ethnic lobby, which they argue flows from the group members' experience and understanding of how to advocate within the democratic process. And Rubenzer and Redd (2010) even find that the size of the ethnic group matters less to decision makers than how politically active or engaged their members are, especially how likely they are to vote. Smaller groups with more political skills and thus a greater propensity to vote are more valuable to elected officials than larger groups that don't turn out.

As we noted in the previous chapter, Irish America's scrabble up the political ladder was possible because Irish America developed and deployed its political skills from inside the political system. But having political skills in pocket does not mean that groups will always use them, or help predict when they will use them or be successful at doing so. Indeed, it took almost three years for Irish America to re-engage after the Brexit referendum.

Another variable that scholars identify as crucial to ethnic lobby success is its wealth. As Loomis and Cigler (1995: 25) argue, money is "the mother's milk of politics." Smith (2000: 108) agrees, noting that "ethnic money buys political influence" and "political influence solicits ethnic money." The wealthier the ethnic group, the wealthier their organizations are likely to be. Paul and Paul (2009) find support for this claim: though the groups may be small, two thirds of the ethnic groups active in the foreign policy-making process have an average income higher than the national median. In their quantitative analyses of the influence of ethnic lobbies, the average wealth of an ethnic group is a statistically significant factor in their success. One exception is for ethnic group lobbying related to military engagement or other international interventions (Kustra and James, 2022); in this context, wealth is not determinative.

However, the main link between the wealth of the ethnic group and the influence of their lobby is the ability of the group to make campaign contributions. Political action committee (PAC) money is a central aspect of lobbying, and for good reason. According to the Center for Responsive Politics, the candidate who spent most in the 2022 elections won 93 percent of the time in the House and 82 percent in the Senate ("Did Money Win?," no date).

To be fair, ethnic-oriented PAC money is wholly dwarfed by the contributions of other groups like business, real estate, labor, and healthcare. Whereas the American Israel Public Affairs Committee (AIPAC)-associated PACs and SuperPACs raised some $36 million in the 2022 election cycle ("Pro-Israel Summary," no date), miscellaneous business groups gave approximately $428 billion, healthcare industry groups $284 billion, and the real estate industry $273 billion in 2022 ("PAC Dollars to Incumbents, Challengers, and Open Seat Candidates," no date).

However, this differential does not mean that ethnic lobbies' PACs are insignificant in terms of influence. For some ethnic lobbies, for example, PAC money can garner attention to their issues, particularly when it is used to target members of Congress on key committees, such as the Foreign Affairs Committee in the Senate and the International Relations Committee in the House. As Tony Smith argues: "Small ethnic communities, some almost utterly lacking in voting strength, may nonetheless find politicians willing to represent their interests ... Contributions based on ethnic lobbying are ... a critical part of the process" (Smith, 2000: 101). Paul and Paul (2009) find donations made by ethnic-oriented PACs are significantly related to the perception of ethnic group success in all of their empirical tests.

However, Irish Americans don't currently lobby in this way. There is only one Irish American PAC today—the Irish American Democrats—and their fundraising is miniscule. In 2020, when Joe Biden, an ardent Irish American, ran for President, the Irish American Democrats PAC only raised $72,400 ("PAC Profile: Irish American Democrats," no date). By comparison, in 2024 the Ireland Funds raised $1.2 million for their philanthropic activities from Irish

American donors in a single night. Though Irish Americans have given significant campaign cash in the past, campaign donations simply aren't the main source of Irish American influence. In fact, by the time the 2020 election season kicked into high gear, Irish Americans were already deeply involved in lobbying members of Congress to prevent a hard border without having made sizable campaign contributions.

Another variable identified by the scholarly literature is the presence of a well-organized lobby. In fact, Smith (2000) argues that an ethnic community only becomes a seriously viable political force when it has an organization whose chief purpose is to influence decision makers to adopt policies favorable to the group's interests. AIPAC is widely considered the model for ethnic groups with influence (Uslaner, 2002). Its size, budget, and operational capacities allow it to engage in multi-pronged lobbying. As Esman (1994: 36) argues, formal organizations are "the indispensable weapon for political struggle ... [they] aggregate material and human resources, prepare for the purposeful deployment, provide for the division of labor, maintain infrastructure for communication and facilitate the socialization of individuals into the movement" (see also Haney and Vanderbush, 1999). Statistical analyses back up these findings. Paul and Paul (2009), for example, found that organizational strength is significantly related to the success of ethnic lobbies in all their tests. Yet, here too, Irish America stands out in the sense that it has no overarching political organization, further highlighting the puzzle that motivates our analysis.

Charismatic leadership is another variable that scholars identify as critical to ethnic group success. The classic example of a charismatic ethnic leader is Jorge Mas Canosa, the founder and leader of the Cuban American National Foundation (CANF). In the early 1990s, journalist John Newhouse called him "the most significant individual lobbyist in the country" (1992: 77). Indeed, he likened CANF to a parallel state for Cuban exiles and described Canosa as their Castro.

While most ethnic lobbies lack figures like Canosa, strong leadership can also involve stirring ethnic communities through other means. Paul's (2002) work on ethnic elites demonstrates that leaders can also use religious symbols and historical memories of trauma and persecution to mobilize the grassroots. She finds that the choices and tactics of leaders are central to when and how followers are mobilized, and determine, at least in part, the effectiveness of the ethnic group. Likewise, Prasad and Savatic (2023: 835), argue that the very "existence of diasporic interest groups is likely the result of a top-down process driven by political entrepreneurs."

Although leadership has been an important feature of Irish America since its machine politics days, the leaders behind Irish American activism on Brexit functioned in very different ways. There was no one charismatic figure behind the activism we discuss in this book. Instead, the leadership by groups like the Ad Hoc Committee to Protect the Good Friday Agreement, and their peers in Congress, was focused on swaying elite decision makers rather than winning broader, popular support (within or outside of Irish America writ large).

Scholars also attribute success of ethnic groups to their ability to take advantage of allies and coalition building (Ambrosio, 2002a, 2002b). This is a tactic that is common to marginalized groups who don't have the numbers to make policy happen on their own. For example, women-friendly public policy actors in a variety of contexts have depended on the actions of male allies and/or "critical actors" (Schlozman and Tierney, 1986; Childs and Krook, 2009). Smith points out that the most powerful ethnic groups are those with "the capacity to find at least some allies" (Smith, 2000: 88). Ambrosio (2002a) notes that Jewish Americans, for example, formed a short-lived strategic alliance with Turkish Americans to encourage US foreign policy positions that were favorable to Turkey (closer ties to the West) and Israel (a regional counterweight to Islamist regimes). Other ethnic groups have found common purpose with human rights or free trade groups.

Alliance building is not a particularly strong feature of Irish American lobbying. Although Irish America has periodically used human rights framing to criticize British military operations in and around Northern Ireland, for example, it has not made sustained alliances with human rights organizations like Amnesty International. In fact, its most enduring alliance has been with various Irish governments.

Finally, scholars explain success of ethnic groups in US politics as stemming from having members of the ethnic group in policy circles or in government positions in Congress or the Executive Branch.

Smith refers to this as the "surest way [for ethnic groups] to have a voice" in policy-making (Smith, 2000: 122). This is easier for some groups than others, which may contribute to why some groups are more effective than others; Jewish-Americans and Cuban-Americans, for example, are or have historically been over-represented in Congress, while Black and Hispanic groups are under-represented. As we demonstrate in this book, this variable does help explain Irish Americans' success during the post-Brexit period. Irish America has an ethnic caucus in Congress, for example, and many Irish Americans felt they had hit the jackpot when Biden was elected. Indeed, he proudly described himself as not just "Irish American" but "Irish," and is sometimes described as the "most Irish president of all presidents" (Fiona Fitzsimons, as quoted in Beard, Padilla, and Garrison, 2023).

However, as we noted earlier, just having an ethnic heritage is not the same as actively identifying with the group. Thus, descriptive representation within Congress or the Executive Branch does not necessarily or tidily translate into foreign policy gains for the group. Irish America has long recognized this. This is why, for example, the Ireland Funds invited Vice-President Mike Pence to give an address at its first Washington gala of the Trump Administration in 2017, presenting him with a copy of his Irish family tree and a photograph of the registrar of the school his grandfather attended in Ireland. The strategy was to trigger his ethnic identity and to find a toe-hold for the group in the otherwise unfamiliar Trump Administration. These overtures did not move Pence firmly into Irish America, but they helped limit the damage of this otherwise uninitiated group in the White House.

When we review these variables for their explanatory power vis-à-vis Irish America's recent remobilization, we come up short. To be sure, some features deemed important in the ethnic lobbying literature do help explain Irish America's success in the post-Brexit era, including possessing political skills and having members in high-level government positions. But other variables identified as important for success do not apply, including having well-funded PACs, making campaign donations, and building coalitions with other groups. That the scholarly literature on ethnic lobbies has such a mixed record on explaining Irish American influence makes our case all the more curious and worthy of examining.

## Effectiveness in the foreign policy context

Scholarship on ethnic lobbying also identifies features of the foreign policy context that contribute to ethnic lobbying success. First, scholars argue that certain types of issues in foreign policy are better targets for ethnic lobbying groups than others (Haney and Vanderbush, 1999; Paul and Paul, 2009; Milner and Tingley, 2015). Smith (2000: 122) argues that it is "far more difficult to gain access to the President and effectively influence his policies than it is to lobby members of Congress, where the threshold of entry is far lower and a much closer working relationship can be established." For example, ethnic lobbies are far more likely to affect foreign aid decisions on issues like military procurements or immigration policy, which Congress controls, than on issues like treaties, which are the purview of the President. Indeed, in the case of trade, lobbies can only try to affect change on the back end, after a president sends a trade deal to Congress for ratification.

Second, scholars often argue that ethnic groups are more successful at influencing US foreign policy when their interests overlap with existing US strategic priorities (Ahrari, 1987a; Uslaner, 2002; Rubenzer, 2008). Organski argues that regardless of other factors, "strategic considerations, rightly or wrongly, dictate what countries receive substantial American support" (Organski, 1990: 6). This is, in fact, a common retort to claims that AIPAC has captured US foreign policy in the Middle East. Protecting and supporting Israel has been a US strategic priority since 1948, so the Jewish American lobby is not taking US foreign policy anywhere that the political establishment was not already willing to go (this may change in light of Israel's devastating war on Gaza that began in 2023). Rubenzer (2008: 171) calls this "strategic convergence." Dewind and Segura (2014) argue that the absence of strategic convergence may also explain why some ethnic groups from countries with strained relationships with the US do not engage in lobbying—their mobilization simply is unlikely to make any difference to US foreign policy.

The importance of strategic convergence is reasonable if we think of US national interests as fixed (see Morgenthau, 1951). However, defining what constitutes "US interests" is complex and subject to interpretation. Actors may all agree on the fundamentals of US national interest, but disagree on what that means in terms of specific foreign policies. Moreover, the definition of national interest may become an object of ethnic activism. After all, most groups attempting to persuade US foreign policy makers to act do so by framing their campaign as benefiting US (rather than specific ethnic) interests. As Peter Trubowitz argues, "the national interest is an arbitrary construction reflecting the wishes of that section of society which succeeds in getting Washington to act as the dominant social forces see fit" (Trubowitz, 1998, as described by Smith 2000: 140). Dewind and Segura explain that the perception that ethnic and national interests converge can result from the "shaping of national interests in the give-and-take of democratic processes, including lobbying" (Dewind and Segura, 2014: 6). Similarly, Rubenzer (2008) argues that strategic convergence can be an indication of the success of ethnic lobbies as much as it is a condition of their success. As we will demonstrate in the coming chapters, Irish American efforts to protect the Belfast/Good Friday Agreement began by taking advantage of the lack of consensus in the US foreign policy establishment on how to approach Brexit.

Third, scholars also often argue that ethnic lobbies are more successful when they advocate for policies that are generally supported by the American public. In these cases, Ambrosio (2002b: 12) argues that ethnic groups can benefit from a "reserve of public sympathy and moral legitimacy." This congruence with public opinion and sense of sympathy for past injustices would explain, for example, why AIPAC has been more successful historically than the Arab American lobby, whose agenda overlaps less with that of the general public (see Uslaner, 2002). However, as the protests on college campuses and elsewhere in 2024 indicate, this sympathy is in flux as a consequence of the Israeli war on Gaza.

Public ignorance or naivety on international affairs can also ease ethnic lobbies' efforts to (re)define the country's strategic interests. As Thomas Ambrosio notes: "On many issues that ethnic lobbies care about, the average American either does not know enough to form an opinion, or cares so little that the issue has no significant political impact with the wider populace" (Ambrosio, 2002b: 11). This means that interest groups, specifically ethnic lobbies, have a lot of room to shape how the issues are understood not just by foreign policy decision makers, but also the public. If most people do not have a strong opinion on a given policy that an ethnic lobby cares deeply about, the group may encounter little resistance in shaping the outcomes because policy makers see no electoral downsides to doing as they ask (see Ambrosio, 2002b, 11). Smith (2000: 94) argues, that groups are most influential "when special interests are focused and the public is inattentive." Indeed, "a lot of members of Congress regard a vote on an ethnic issue as almost a throwaway vote" (Greve, 1995).

As we will demonstrate in the next few chapters, Irish Americans were able to effectively define the stakes of Brexit because so few Americans, including many members of Congress, knew what it meant for the Belfast/Good Friday Agreement. Irish America took good advantage of this information vacuum by providing policy makers with expert information from trusted sources that would allow members of Congress to adopt their position (Lindsay, 1994: 36).

Fourth, ethnic lobbies are also widely seen as more effective when they operate without a strong or well-organized opposition. Turkish Americans, for example, have faced stiff opposition at different historical moments from Greek and Armenian Americans. Arab American foreign policy objectives have likewise been stymied by the prowess of the Jewish American lobby. Although Irish America never had to contend with a British American lobby, let alone a British American voting bloc, it did have to face an American foreign policy establishment that has long been "unmistakably English" in orientation (DeConde, 1992). US-UK shared views were forged out of two world wars and led to the so-called special relationship we described in the previous chapter. The power of that relationship checked the influence of the Irish Americans for much of the 20th century (DeConde, 1992).

However, as we explain in the coming chapters, after Brexit, the UK government was slow to explain its position on Brexit to the American government. In contrast, the Irish government and its diplomats set about lobbying members of Congress almost immediately. The British were also slow to recognize the threat that Irish American remobilization posed to their efforts. By the time the UK government approached the US for support, it found that its arguments were gaining little traction because Irish and Irish American lobbying had already shaped the position of key officials in Congress and the Executive Branch.

Fifth, ethnic lobbies are more effective when they support policies that reflect the status quo (that is, advocating for the continuation of an existing policy or developing a new policy for which there is precedent: Haney and Vanderbush, 1999; Paul and Paul, 2009). In a similar vein, Lindsay (2002) argues that ethnic lobbies are more successful when they do not advocate for significant change. This finding is borne out in the Brexit case. Irish America's goal—to protect the integrity of the Belfast/Good Friday Agreement— represented a continuation of the status quo, which enjoyed broad, bipartisan support. Indeed, the Agreement is widely seen as one of the US government's biggest foreign policy achievements since the Second World War.

## Explaining Irish America's resurgence as an ethnic lobby

Though the ethnic lobbies literature frequently describes Irish America as powerful, it also acknowledges the conundrum we pointed to in Chapter 1 (Paul and Paul, 2009). After the 1998 Belfast/ Good Friday Agreement, the Irish American lobby could not even convince its own rank and file to focus on the issues Northern Ireland faced after the peace. Smith's (2000) contention that Irish American activism hinged on the continuation of conflict in Northern Ireland rang true for 20 years.

Irish America's remobilization after Brexit defies prediction. So too does its ultimate success in protecting the agreement from the threats Brexit posed to it. To explain this puzzle, we cannot rely solely on the variables identified in the ethnic lobbies literature; rather, we point to two explanations for its success.

### *The seeds of success updated*

First, Irish America still manifests the five traits that allowed its ancestors to climb the political ladder in the late 1800s and early 1900s. To begin with, Irish Americans still have a strong political culture and shared sense of identity. Despite being economically, politically, and ideologically diverse (Newhouse, 2009; Perry, 2019), their ethnic ties still bind. As *The Economist* notes, this political culture is so strong that "Generations after most Irish Americans lost touch with the old country, it is still evident—indeed especially evident—on the right and left today" (*The Economist*, 2019).

The Irish understand this well. When we interviewed former Irish Ambassador Daniel (Dan) Mulhall, for example, he told us:

> Unlike other European diasporas, say Scandinavian, Swedish, German, Italian, Greek, the Irish diaspora continues to have a genuine interest in the affairs of Ireland ... Whereas when I was in Britain, I found that people born in Ireland, were Irish, and had an Irish identity of some kind. Their children, sometimes had a degree of Irish identity. Beyond that, Irish identity didn't seem to travel down the generations in the way it does in America, where it can travel across four or five, six generations. And that's the unique nature of Irish America in my view—that it persists. And it persists I think, because Irish Americans have always felt themselves to have a cause that they wanted to advance.

Ciarán Quinn, Sinn Féin Representative for the US and Canada, concurred with Mulhall's emphasis on the durability of Irish American identity:

> People think the political connection between Ireland and the US is transactional. They think it has to do with Irish American political leaders or American political leaders pandering to a section of the electorate. I don't think that's where the main influence comes from. It's actually a lot stronger than that, and it's to do with history and family and identity.

Consider, for example, President Biden. Even though his closest familial connection is five generations in the past (more than 165 years ago), he embraces his Irish roots (Beard, Padilla, and Garrison, 2023). We can see something similar in the Congressional Friends of Ireland Caucus. The caucus devoted time and energy to Northern Ireland's politics even when they arguably had more pressing issues to deal with, from a global pandemic to the Russian invasion of Ukraine.

As Colm Quinn explained in the *Irish Times* when discussing a 2019 Congressional delegation to Ireland and the UK:

> The United States' approach to Ireland, a country that doesn't fit the bill of a traditional ally (no defence ties, no oil, no large consumer market) might confuse outsiders. Politicians signalling support for Ireland doesn't carry the same political weight as say, support for Israel does [but] ... one look at the makeup of the House Speaker's delegation shows that long-standing family ties with the US still give Ireland a special seat at the table. (Quinn, 2019)

Second, even though Irish machine politics are a thing of the past, Irish American political networks are still densely organized. When Paul Quinn, a long-time board member of the Ireland Funds, was asked by Senator Ted Kennedy to help his sister, Jean Kennedy Smith, win the nomination as US Ambassador to Ireland in the 1990s, he could rely on his connections and their collective skill set to help frame the campaign. As he explained it, "I have friends across town."[3] In our interview with Irish American lawyer and lobbyist Erik Huey, he described Irish American political networks as "high-minded, well-connected, dedicated, and tireless." When we asked him to explain Irish America's success in lobbying against a hard border, he pointed to a "core group of 30–50 people in and around the [Washington] Beltway that are very good at whisper campaigns."

Third, Irish Americans are frequently in the rooms of power. Though there is no ethnic register of politicians, Irish Americans tended to be well represented in Congress in the last decades of the 20th century, at one point having two separate ethnic organizations of Congress members (the Congressional Friends of Ireland Caucus and the Ad Hoc Congressional Committee for Irish Affairs). Likewise, President Biden, who was a member of the Congressional Friends of Ireland when he served in the Senate ("Congressional Friends of Ireland: Celebrating 40 Years 1981–2021," 2021), surrounded himself

---

[3] Kimberly Cowell-Meyers, unpublished interview with Paul Quinn, 2015.

with staff who understood Northern Ireland politics, including Jake Sullivan, his National Security Advisor, and Dr. Amanda Sloat on the National Security Council. This density of expertise meant that the White House and Congress tended to speak with one voice on Brexit. They were joined by the Ad Hoc Committee to Protect the Good Friday Agreement, whose members also had deep experience in Northern Ireland. Indeed, the organization is headed by two former members of Congress and includes retired ambassadors, former special envoys, and other diplomats familiar with Northern Ireland. The eminent status of its members meant they were often brought on in an unofficial capacity as important conversations unfolded.

Fourth, contemporary St. Patrick's Day festivities, which stretch over a week, give Irish Americans ample opportunities to influence policy makers and draw attention to the issues the lobby cares about with leaders from Ireland, the UK, and Northern Ireland. For decades, the Irish Taoiseach has had a formal meeting with the President of the United States on or near to St. Patrick's Day. The Taoiseach is also routinely honored with a luncheon hosted by the Speaker of the House—one of the hottest ticket items for members of Congress and Irish America in the calendar year. No other country in the world with a population of five million people has such access or occasion to mingle, connect, and lobby. As Leahy notes:

> And every single one of them [the other nations of the world] would give a generation of their first born for the opportunity and access enjoyed here by the Irish Taoiseach [during St. Patrick's week] ... US interest in Ireland has yielded concrete benefits for Irish people, North and South, in their daily lives. And that's before you even consider the economic dividends. If you think all this has nothing to do with green ties and bowls of shamrock in Washington, you need to revisit your understanding of how the worlds of politics and diplomacy work. (Leahy, 2022)

Even before Biden was in office, Ed Luce wrote in the *Financial Times* in 2019: "No one who sampled Washington's manic schedule of St Patrick's day events ... could miss the formidable display of Ireland's influence" (Luce, 2019). This specific holiday and the events surrounding it foster a unique institutionalized opportunity for Irish America to reconnect with policy makers, communicate priorities, and reaffirm their ties.

Finally, Irish America, perhaps more than any other ethnic lobby, is pushing on an open door: there is goodwill toward Ireland, and Irish soft power abounds. Henry McLeish argues that Ireland and "everything Irish" holds "a special place" in "US politics, especially in Washington DC and the US Congress" (McLeish, 2020). Stella O'Leary, who founded the Irish American Democrats PAC, made a similar point, perhaps with some hyperbole, telling author Caitríona Perry: "There is nobody on Capitol Hill, no Congressional member, who'll close their door to an Irish request – none. They've no reservations about it. They don't ask questions. They say 'Come on in and tell me what you have on your mind,' and so forth'" (Perry, 2019: 68). In our interview with former Irish Ambassador Dan Mulhall, he explained what the open door looked like in the diplomatic arena:

> We do well in Washington, because the odds are stacked in our favor on this issue. As one American member of Congress said to me, the British can win most arguments in Washington except the Irish argument. So, the odds were stacked against them ... the turf I was playing on was favorable to an Irish point of view.

Part of this goodwill also stems from the fact that Irish Americans are seen as campaigning to preserve a peace agreement that is widely viewed as a seminal US foreign policy achievement. In our interview, William Tranghese, Congressman Richard (Richie) Neal's Chief of Staff for decades, described the agreement as "the most successful foreign policy achievement in a generation," a sentiment echoed by his boss in the press (Wall, 2022d). As McLeish (2020) observes, "pride in America's role in shaping and delivering the 1998 peace deal" still fuels engagement on the issue.

It also helps the Irish American lobby that the Belfast/Good Friday Agreement has broad bipartisan support. The Congressional Friends of Ireland, for example, have long been careful to present a bipartisan front, having members from both parties co-chair the caucus. The Ad Hoc Committee to Protect the Good Friday Agreement has similarly mirrored this structure by having two former members, a Democrat and a Republican, serve as co-chairs. The extent to which the peace process draws bipartisan support can even be seen in the efforts the Bush and Obama Administrations made to sustain it (McGurk, 2019). Even in the currently polarized political environment in the US, Irish American issues enjoy a high degree of consensus, bringing otherwise opposing figures like Mick Mulvaney and Brendan Boyle to work together (see Chapter 6).

## Opportunity structures

In addition to these five traits, a second broad explanation for Irish America's successful remobilization is the changing opportunity structures Irish America found after Brexit. Social movement scholars, for example, often point to opportunity structures to explain why movements emerge and why some are more successful than others. Opportunities for mobilization are dynamic features that are out of the control of movements, but can be harnessed by them (McAdam, Tarrow and Tilly, 2001). Groups challenging a sitting government, for example, may be more successful if that government faces external shocks, such as a market collapse or a natural disaster.

We argue here that Brexit upended the special relationship between the US and the UK. Though the bond remains in place, Brexit certainly put it under pressure. Suddenly, the US was faced with key allies in sharp disagreement, and it was by no means clear which view the US would or even should support. Domestic political changes also put the US position on Brexit into question. While the Obama Administration had quietly opposed Brexit, it supported efforts to avoid disrupting the Agreement once it passed. Even before Trump came into office in January 2017, he suggested Brexit could be good for Britain. But, he never articulated a clear and unwavering stance on the issue, leaving room for considerable doubt about what US policy was on the issues. As a result, there was room for Irish America to define US interests and to lobby for that definition.

Opportunities also opened up for Irish Americans after the US midterm elections in 2018. Democrats won a majority of seats in the House of Representatives, and the new Speaker of the House,

Nancy Pelosi, appointed Congressman Richie Neal (D-MA[4])—an Irish American, who was also co-chair of the Friends of Ireland Caucus—as the chair of the Appropriations Committee. With the appropriations gavel in hand, Neal was able to use a bilateral trade agreement as a bargaining chip when the UK was hammering out its various withdrawal agreements.

Finally, Irish Americans' efforts to protect the Belfast/Good Friday Agreement were made considerably easier because they overlapped with those of the Irish government and the EU. Indeed, the EU decided early on to defend Ireland's concerns about a hard border and it maintained a strong position on this throughout the negotiations. So, when Irish Americans joined the fray, they had considerable political power behind them.

In short, these opportunities allowed Irish America to deploy its talents to shape a common understanding of US strategic interests in a moment when its allies were in conflict with each other. With its interests clarified, the US government was then able to articulate and defend a clear policy preference in its conversations with the UK government.

However, as we demonstrate in the coming chapters, the internal strengths of the Irish American lobby did not encounter the same political opportunities when it lobbied against the UK's 2023 legacy bill, which effectively stopped most historical inquiries into Troubles-related murders. As we discovered, the Conservative Party was more willing to buck pressure to stop the bill because investigations were seen as dangerous to Tory power, and by some as a threat to the peace agreement. And Irish America had, in that case, fewer opportunities to connect British policy to American consequences than it did on Brexit.

In the next chapter, we will provide context on Brexit and chart Irish America's gradual reawakening. Though Irish America was slow to re-engage, its existing networks were easy to mobilize once key leaders decided it was time to act.

---

[4] In the US, members of Congress are identified by their party and state. D stands for Democrat and R for Republican. States are identified by their two-letter mailing code.

# 4

# Brexit and the Problem of Northern Ireland

In many ways, Irish America's involvement in lobbying to preserve the Belfast/Good Friday Agreement in the wake of the 2016 Brexit referendum is an improbable tale. As indicated in previous chapters, though Irish America was a force to be reckoned with during the Troubles and in the march to eventual peace in 1998, it had lost its vitality by the time the Brexit referendum occurred in 2016. There are several reasons for this retrenchment, including population decline and dispersion, organizational collapse, a lack of leadership and the changing nature of the conflict. But British withdrawal from the EU held risks for key parts of the Belfast/Good Friday Agreement and threatened wider understandings that had facilitated the process, such as the centrality of bilateral cooperation between the UK and Ireland. It also triggered an unlikely and unanticipated revival of Irish American lobbying in the years after the referendum.

To chart Irish America's improbable path back to influence, we divide our discussion into the following sections. In the first and second sections, we provide a brief history of UK/EU relations and discuss the politics that led to the 2016 Brexit referendum. In the third and fourth sections, we discuss what Brexit meant for the Belfast/Good Friday Agreement and map the state of Irish America at the time of the referendum.

## A brief history of European unity and the UK

In 1973 the UK joined the European Economic Community (EEC), the predecessor to the EU. While many countries join the EU with great fanfare, Britain's entry is described with diffidence. Scholars and commentators use words like "awkward" (George, 1990), "complex" (Schütze, 2022), and "reluctant" (Moss and Clarke, 2021) to describe the entry. In fact, polls in the early 1970s indicate that the public was evenly divided on the issue, and there were no civil society campaigns clamoring to join the EEC (Mortimore, 2016). When Prime Minister Ted Heath led the UK into the EEC in 1973, he did so without holding a referendum on the issue. Britain's conflicted feelings are probably best illustrated by the fact that when the country first asked to join in 1963, its relationship with other European powers—particularly France—was so poor it had to wait ten years for the application to be accepted.

Scholars point to a variety of reasons for British diffidence. A primary factor is that the UK came out of the Second World War with a different understanding of its respective place in the world than did other European countries. Whereas the rest of Europe viewed European integration as a necessary means to prevent another war between France and Germany, the UK still considered itself a global power, superior to continental European states and distinct from them. When Labour leader Clement Attlee became Prime Minister after the war, for example, he derisively described the countries interested in European integration as "a group of nations in which we have just saved four of them from the other two" (Thody, 1997: 4). The UK preferred to function as "a bridge between Europe and the US, and Europe and the Commonwealth" rather than a part of Europe itself (Kenealy, 2016).

Domestic politics also complicated British participation in efforts at European integration. The Labour Party, which was in power when European integration began, wanted to nationalize its coal industry, which would be prohibited by European supranational organizations (Kenealy, 2016). Labour, in fact, remained skeptical of the European project well into the 1990s. The UK's approach to governance also animated its caution. Its leaders preferred an intergovernmental approach to coordination rather than a supranational one (Schütze, 2022).

These divides were put into sharp relief when France's Foreign Minister Robert Schuman spearheaded the creation of the European Coal and Steel Community (ECSC) in 1950. The so-called Schuman Declaration proposed putting French and German coal production under a supranational governing body so that neither country could use its energy resources to wage war against the other and, in the process, drag other European countries into war. The UK declined to join.

In 1957 the UK again declined to join forces with its European neighbors in the establishment of the EEC. Instead, it tried to compete with the EEC by establishing the European Free Trade Area group. After four years of lackluster growth, Britain finally applied for membership in the EEC in 1963. However, the French President Charles de Gaulle vetoed the request, pointing to Britain's economic woes at the time, its limited agriculture outputs (in comparison to the then six Member States in the EEC), and its overly close alliance with the US. De Gaulle also feared that a recently signed defense agreement between the US and UK governments would place the EEC under American influence (Adityo, Harapan, and Marihandono, 2019). When the UK applied in 1967, de Gaulle vetoed the application once again. It was only in 1972, after de Gaulle was out of power, that the UK's application was approved.

From the start, the UK membership in the EEC (and later the EU) was conditional in a way that other Member States' relationships were not. Schütze (2022) notes, for example, that the UK's decision to join the EEC was largely economic and it remained deeply suspicious about supranational decision making. And, as integration moved into new arenas, Britain fought against such moves or secured opt-outs on mechanisms for further integration. In 1984, for example, Margaret Thatcher's government negotiated an annual rebate on UK contributions to the EEC. In 1992, the UK received an opt-out from the Economic and Monetary Union, which would establish a single currency (the euro) and a set of rules for financial institutions in Member States. Five years later, in 1997, the UK opted out of the Schengen Agreement and the treaty on "Visas, asylum, immigration and other policies related to the free movement of persons." The opt-outs continued into the early 2000s. In 2007's Lisbon Treaty, the UK secured a partial opt-out on the EU Charter of Fundamental Rights and a full opt-out on provisions around police and judicial cooperation.

Large portions of the British public remained skeptical about the value of EU membership. Although initially embraced by business elites seeking opportunities in economic integration, the Conservative Party was divided on compromises required by that integration, particularly the limitations it placed on the UK's ability to set its own economic policy. Prime Minister Margaret Thatcher, who led the UK into the European Exchange Rate Mechanism in 1990, developed a wariness of European integration, and intense internal disagreements over these issues would ultimately contribute to her and successor John Major's downfall.

For its part, the Labour Party initially viewed the European project negatively, as a vehicle for expanding the interests of capital. Throughout the 1970s and 1980s, it opposed ascension at party conferences and campaigned on platforms to withdraw the UK from the EU. It changed course in the mid-1990s under Tony Blair, who viewed European regulation as a way to deliver on his party's social goals.

Division in British public opinion on Europe also contributed to the creation of the United Kingdom Independence Party (UKIP), a far-right anti-EU party in the 1990s, which rose to win first place in UK elections to the European Parliament in 2014. Pressure from UKIP explains in part why the Conservative Party included a plank calling for a referendum on EU membership in its election manifesto in 2015. Prime Minister David Cameron, whose party won a small majority in that election, then opted to call a referendum in 2016.

## The march to Brexit

There is no one reason the UK ultimately decided to leave the EU, and no brief review, as we do here, can capture the full complexity. As such, we only focus on the broad outlines of the story.

In a philosophical sense, Brexit was a totalizing event. People in the UK responded to it both rationally and emotionally, understood it as an economic and a cultural process, and saw it as saying something broader (whether positive or negative) about the UK and its people. Support for Brexit cut across party lines and typical left-right political divides (Fieldhouse et al, 2019) and left British society polarized around identities as Leavers and Remainers with deep affective biases (see Duffy et al, 2019). Indeed, five years after the referendum, more British people saw themselves in terms of their Brexit identities, as Leavers or Remainers, than as members of political parties. Two thirds of these Leavers and Remainers described their identities as very or extremely important to them, whereas only one third of party supporters saw their party identities as very or extremely important (Hobolt and Tilley, 2022: 40). Overall, Brexit was more than the sum of its parts. O'Reilly (2016) likens the moment to the "Great Transformation"—a term Karl Polanyi used to describe the disruptive move from feudalism in prior centuries to a market economy in the 19th century in Europe. When the referendum took place, the post-Second World War neoliberal order was collapsing in on itself; Brexit's clarion call to "take back control" was a response to it, albeit driven largely by those on the right of the political spectrum. And as is clear by now, many of the political elites who favored the movement to leave the EU not only made stunning political miscalculations about how Brexit would unfurl, but also had huge blind spots about how it would affect Northern Ireland. As we will note in the following chapters, these miscalculations would carry forward into their negotiations with the EU on a withdrawal agreement.

## *Economic factors fueling Brexit*

A variety of scholars note that Brexiteers were spread across Britain's usually intractable class divides. O'Reilly, for example, describes Leave voters as a "contradictory coalition" (2016: 811) that included homeowners with no mortgage *and* tenants in council or other subsidized housing. This unexpected pairing is largely due to the fact that deindustrialization and the shift toward a finance-based economy affected working class *and* elite Britons. For the working class, deindustrialization led to the decline of organized labor, wage stagnation, and growing informality in work. This, in turn, meant that working class people no longer had a "springboard up into better jobs" (Warhurst, 2016: 823).

These changes also created a chasm among elites, especially between the wealthy and the very wealthy. In the business sector, this divide pitted firms committed almost exclusively to short-term gains—in executive compensation and shareholder returns—against those who still saw their role as contributing to the wider public good, however unequally their profits might be distributed downward in the form of wages, pensions, and so on (Morgan, 2016). Though the latter group saw Brexit as bad for Britain's competitive advantage over the long term, the former group viewed Brexit as an opportunity for new, short-term profits. In the context of the Brexit referendum, this gap meant that David Cameron could not rely on 100 percent support from the business community to campaign and vote for remain (Morgan, 2016).

## Cultural factors fueling Brexit

Cultural factors also played a role in how citizens viewed the Brexit referendum. Anti-immigration sentiment picked up in the UK after ten states joined the EU in 2004, a move that opened Britain's doors to tens of thousands of new migrants each year (The Migration Observatory, 2025). Anti-immigrant sentiment gathered further steam in the wake of the Syrian Civil War in 2011, as millions fled to Europe. Immigrants became a central issue for Brexit voters in two ways—their potential effect on the availability of social services and the meaning of Britishness.

Two of the largest pro-leave groups, "Vote Leave" and "Leave. EU," depicted immigrants as overburdening already-weakened public services, including the National Health Service (NHS) and affordable housing (Gietel-Basten, 2016) and faulted the EU for the presence of immigrants. Whether these claims were true or not, the pro-leave/anti-EU narrative resonated with an existing sense that British public services were declining and provided a foreign culprit to blame.

Immigrants were also depicted as a threat to a particular notion of Britishness that is white and Christian. The Vote Leave campaign often highlighted increasing immigration flows from countries with sizable Muslim populations already in the queue to join the EU. Turkey was held out as a prominent example, even though the country had yet to meet the great majority of its requirements for joining the EU (Gietel-Basten, 2016). Pro-leave advocates also pointed to the then ongoing Syrian Civil War, in which nearly five million Syrians had been displaced from their homes, to hint (both subtly and not so subtly) at the racial and religious changes continuing membership in the EU might portend.

Although the UK had only accepted about 4,000 Syrian refugees by the end of September 2016 (Refugee Action, 2016), UKIP produced an incendiary poster suggesting that Syrians would overrun Britain's borders if the referendum failed. The poster showed a photo of hundreds of Syrian refugees lined up at a border post underneath a large red slogan—"Breaking Point." Although the picture was taken at a crossing on the Slovenian border, over 1,000 miles away from Britain, nothing on the poster indicated the distant location. Commentators decried the poster, comparing it to Nazi propaganda singling out Jews (Tharoor, 2016); even the Vote Leave's co-chair, Michael Gove, condemned the poster. But by then, the impression had been made—remaining in the EU would allow immigrant "hordes" to flood the country.

*Political miscalculation*

No Brexit origin story, however brief, can ignore the political miscalculations and in some cases malevolence that informed the process. The EU had long been a sticking point for the Conservative party's right flank, known collectively as Eurosceptics. By the time the Conservatives came to power on their own after the 2015 general election (that is, without needing a coalition with the Liberal Democrats), Eurosceptics had become a vocal minority that punched above its weight within the party. Indeed, in advance of the 2015 election Euroscepticism was so influential that the party included a commitment to hold a referendum on EU membership by 2017 in its election manifesto ("Conservative Party Manifesto," 2015). It was a remarkable addition given that the majority of the party supported remaining in the EU (Hobolt, 2016).

After his party won the election and the legislation calling for the referendum became law, Prime Minister David Cameron did his best to maneuver around the referendum commitment and stave off support for leaving by bargaining for numerous concessions from Brussels. Although he was successful—winning regulatory concessions for London's financial sector, the right to limit welfare assistance going to EU migrants in Britain, and an exemption from treaty requirement to build an "ever closer union"—Eurosceptics panned his efforts (Hobolt, 2016). *The Sun* described the deal as "a steaming pile of manure" and called the EU concessions "the square root of diddly-squat" (see Greenslade, 2016).

Cameron finally agreed to hold a referendum, reckoning it would fail, but would give him leverage over the Eurosceptics threatening to defect to UKIP (Morgan, 2016). As we now know, Cameron badly miscalculated his fellow party members' views on Brexit and those of the wider public. When the vote tallies came in, confirming a Brexit victory, Cameron resigned.

In the end, it was domestic politics, primarily in England, that drove the Brexit result (Prosser, 2016). Support for the Leave campaign (51.9 percent overall) was concentrated in England (53.4 percent) and Wales (52.5 percent), with Northern Ireland and Scotland voting to remain (55.8 percent and 62 percent respectively). The insular focus on English interests tracked with how unprepared mainland politicians were to deal with the complexities Brexit heralded for Northern Ireland.

## Whither Northern Ireland?

One of the most notable things about the Brexit vote is how little Northern Ireland figured into the debates about it (see Cowell-Meyers and Gallaher, 2021). This is especially remarkable given how prominently Northern Ireland figured in debates about Brexit's implementation. This is not to suggest, of course, that politicians never mentioned the potential impacts before the vote—they did. Chancellor George Osborne and Theresa May spoke out about the negative fallout Brexit would have in Northern Ireland. So did former Prime Ministers John Major and Tony Blair (McCormack, 2019). But for a variety of reasons, worries about how Brexit might hurt the people of Northern Ireland or its broader peace process never resonated in the rest of the UK.

Several factors explain why. First, Sinn Féin's longstanding refusal to take its seats in Westminster meant that there were fewer Northern Ireland voices to articulate what Brexit would mean on the ground for everyday citizens. The negative impact from Sinn Féin's absence was made worse by the fact that the Northern Ireland voices that did participate in debates—most notably, members of the DUP—publicly supported the leave position, as did the Secretary of State for

Northern Ireland, Theresa Villiers. The absence of a counternarrative from Sinn Féin or the Northern Ireland Office (NIO) gave the mistaken impression that Northern Ireland supported Brexit.

General ignorance about Northern Ireland in the rest of the UK also played a role. It would be hard to underestimate just how little the rest of the UK knows about Northern Ireland or its peace process.[1] Indeed, the average citizen would likely not have understood the ramifications without a campaign to educate them (McCormack, 2019). Even elites, including Members of Parliament, frequently misrepresented the Belfast/Good Friday Agreement and the treaty obligations it imposed on the UK in speeches to the House of Commons (see Cowell-Meyers and Gallaher, 2021).

And yet, shared EU membership by the UK and Ireland was crucial to the success of the Belfast/Good Friday Agreement. Although the primary social cleavage in the conflict has always nominally been religious—Catholic and Protestant—these religious differences have functioned more like an ethnic divide. In other words, Catholics and Protestants see themselves as peoples with unique histories, heritage, and worldviews. This divide was also mapped onto the constitutional question. Nationalists/Republicans, who are mostly Catholic, wanted Northern Ireland to be part of a united Ireland, while Unionists/Loyalists, who are largely Protestant, wanted it to remain a part of Great Britain. And because these groups functioned like ethnic groups in a zero-sum environment, the answer to the question of Northern Ireland's status was seen as crucial to group survival.

In this context, the beauty of the agreement was that the constitutional question—what country Northern Ireland should ultimately belong to—did not have to be answered at the time of signing. All parties agreed that the decision would belong to the people and would be undertaken via peaceful means—a referendum.

---

[1] Polling data show that majorities from Great Britain are unconcerned with Northern Ireland in general and would not be concerned if Northern Ireland were to leave the UK (see, for example, https://www.whatukthinks.org/eu/questions/how-would-you-feel-if-northern-ireland-left-the-uk/, https://d3nkl3psvxxpe9.cloudfront.net/documents/Internal_Ireland_Mar20.pdfhttps://lordashcroftpolls.com/2018/06/brexit-the-border-and-the-union/#more-15616).

However, until such a time, the agreement allowed people to define themselves as British, Irish, or both, to have one or both passports, and to travel freely across the border between the Republic of Ireland and Northern Ireland. Moreover, the Assembly was structured with a first and a deputy first minister who must be selected from the largest party on each side of the conflict divide to ensure that both sides had an equal say in government. The agreement also set up East-West and North-South bodies to ensure cooperation on the island and across the Irish Sea. As Brendan O'Leary (1999, p 68) notes, the agreement contained "imaginative elements of co-sovereignty" not typically found in peace agreements.

What made all this possible was the two countries' joint membership in the EU. Being in the EU meant, for example, that border infrastructure could be dismantled once the security situation was resolved and goods, people, capital and services could flow freely between Ireland and Northern Ireland, as they did elsewhere in Europe. This, in turn, meant that cross-border business flourished, and production and supply lines became increasingly integrated. Shared regulations on goods and services affected many practical aspects of daily living as well, so that products looked the same and professionals needed similar qualifications in the UK and the Republic, minimizing the differences between being Irish in a Northern Ireland that was still in the UK and Irish in the Republic. The EU has also contributed approximately €3.3 billion to facilitating conflict resolution at the local level through its PEACE Programmes since the 1990s. Joint membership also paid foreign policy dividends, encouraging the UK and the Republic of Ireland to interact with each other on an equal footing (see Hayward and Murphy, 2012).

Brexit brought a lot of the issues that had been smoothed over by the Belfast/Good Friday Agreement back into sharp relief. As Barbara Stephenson, former Consul General in Belfast, explained:

> What happened as part of the Good Friday Agreement is some of these identity issues where it was all-in, one-or-the-other, were mitigated by having the EU there because both parts of the island were under a whole series of rules and regulations that were common because they were part of the EU. One of the risks of Brexit is that as Britain moves away from that homogenizing influence, it

is causing the salience of Catholic or Protestant identity to rise again.

She continued:

> Up until Brexit, you could often avoid wrestling with thorny issues like British rule or Irish rule, but Brexit brought to the foreground a whole series of issues—is it time for a referendum? What is the future of Northern Ireland?—that had been muted and softened, pushed to the back burner.

Brian O'Dwyer, Chair of the Irish Chamber of Commerce in the US and the 2019 Grand Marshall of the New York City St. Patrick' Day Parade, echoed this point, explaining the consequences of Brexit for the peace process this way:

> The border was very much evident before the peace accord. As you went into the north there were these monumentally ugly towers that were built from which the troops looked down upon you, covered with steel plating. Just eyesores on top of everything else. Then you were confronted by armed troops as you passed the border. After the Good Friday Agreement, that all came down. And, basically the only thing you felt in crossing the border was that your cell phone carrier changed. That of course has changed [with Brexit]. All of a sudden people are beginning to think about the border and the distinctions between being in the north and in the republic.

## Irish America on the back foot

Few people expected the public to vote in favor of leaving the EU in 2016. When it did, Irish America was unprepared. In fact, the general impression of Irish America was that it was an ethnic lobby that had peaked with the peace process in the 1990s and was in decline for multiple reasons.

## Demographic changes

Principal among these factors was that Irish America was shrinking; the population claiming Irish heritage on the US Census dropped from 44.4 million in 1990 to 34.7 million by 2010 (see Census Bureau, 2012). Irish immigration, long in decline due to American immigration reform in the 1960s, totaled just over 1,000 per year, meaning that Irish America would never replace itself demographically (see Lobo and Salvo, 1998). No longer the marginalized ethnic group of the past, Irish American social status and physical mobility also left them with less common experience to organize around. By 2010, the Census indicated that Irish Americans were:

> better educated, more affluent and more likely to work in white-collar jobs than are US residents as a whole. They are also more likely to be homeowners rather than renters, which helps explain why the Irish population is noticeably higher in suburban counties than in cities like New York, Philadelphia and even Boston. (Sullivan, 2018)

Irish America was also dispersed across the US, representing the least concentrated ethnic group of all 48 groups Paul and Paul tracked in their study published in 2009 (Paul and Paul, 2009). Irish America was more divided religiously and politically than it had been in centuries, with half of all Irish Americans claiming to be Protestant and a third Catholic in the General Social Survey from 2000 to 2012 (see Grant, 2014). Polls also showed American Catholics, many of whom would be Irish American, almost evenly divided between Trump and Clinton supporters in 2016 (Newport, 2020). As Colm Quinn noted in the *Irish Times* in April 2019, "White Catholics, of which Irish-Americans are included … have broken for the Republican candidate in every presidential election of the 21st century. In the 2018 midterm elections, the White Catholic vote went 54–45 in favour of Republicans even as the Democrats experienced a landslide victory in the House" (Quinn, 2019). When House Democratic Caucus Chairman Joe Crowley lost in the Democratic primary in New York City's 14th Congressional district to Alexandria Ocasio-Cortez in 2018, it seemed to signify the collapse of Irish American power in the city and more generally.

In addition, by 2016, several key Irish American statesmen like Senator Ted Kennedy and Daniel Patrick Moynihan had died or retired, and others had moved on to other areas of concerns. Jim Walsh, a former Republican Congressman from Central New York and a key player behind the Adams visa, told us that the Irish American lobby was "aging." Trina Vargo, a long-time aide to Edward (Ted) Kennedy, and the founder of the US-Ireland Alliance, also cited age as well as the lobby's failure to build a second generation to take up the mantle:

> There's this generation of Irish American politicians that were senior, that ran [Congressional] committees, like [Ted] Kennedy, [Daniel Patrick] Moynihan, and [Chris] Dodd who are deceased or no longer in politics. The political leaders, directly involved with the Northern Ireland peace process in the 1990s, is dwindling. The mid-1990's were a high point in the relationship in many ways—the peace process, World Cup, Riverdance, U2 ... Demographics are changing in the US, Irish America is in decline, and no one wants to put the necessary resources into building this relationship for future generations. There is a window, and it's closing fast.

Susan Davis, the former chair of the US Ireland Business Summit and board member of Irish American Republicans, agreed with this sentiment that Irish America at the time did not have a second generation to pick up the Brexit issue: "They are mostly a small group of people on the East Coast, and it's been a generational advocacy. And, I think with every generation, Irish America is being diluted. People in their twenties, thirties, and forties don't see themselves as Irish."

A senior Congressional staff member expressed similar views as Vargo and Davis when describing the state of Irish Americans in Congress in 2020: "We don't have younger members who are interested in this ... Most of the people we've dealt with have been on the older side. I'm hard pressed to think of a younger person whose played a leadership role and wants to be a leader in the future."

Even people across the Atlantic saw Irish America as past its heyday. An official from the UK government told us that the perception among some British officials is that Irish America is "stuck in the past." Another British official offered a similar, if more colorful assessment, telling us that many people describe Irish America as "stale, male, and pale."

In short, at the time of the Brexit referendum, Irish America didn't have the leadership or deep, multigenerational bench of actors in place to focus minds on the issues that they had had in earlier eras.

## *Organizational changes*

Organizationally, Irish America was also in decline. In fact, by 2005, of the extant Irish American interest groups, only the Irish American Unity Conference and the Irish National Caucus had registered lobbyists (see Paul and Paul, 2009). There were PACs, but only the Irish American Democrats were still active, according to the FEC (Irish American Republicans raised their last campaign dollars in 2006). In 2016, Irish American Democrats raised $25,000, although they raised $72,000 in 2020 ("PAC Profile: Irish American Democrats," no date) and gave $47,000 to federal candidates. In elections that cost between $6.5 billion (2016) and $8.9 billion (2022) nationally, the dollars raised by Irish American groups was largely insignificant ("Cost of Election," no date). Other traditional Irish organizations were also diminished. Membership in the AOH, for example, was aging and shrinking. Though it still had about 30,000 members in 2022, it had lost something approaching 20 percent of its members over the previous decade (Wall, 2022a). Even with 30,000 members, only 1 percent of Irish Americans would be members in this moment. Moreover, though the Congressional Friends of Ireland Caucus was still in existence, its membership had declined from 90 members at its heyday to 30 or so in the 2010s.

## *'The Troubles were over'*

Compounding the situation was the sense that the comprehensive settlement of 1998 had resolved the main motivating issues that had engaged Irish Americans for decades; Irish Americans had moved on to other things with the end of the Troubles. Indeed, scholars of ethnic politics had been noting for years that if Northern Ireland remained peaceful, Irish America's ability to shape foreign policy would cease to exist (see Smith, 2000: 117). Our interview subjects also frequently mentioned the declining interest in Northern Ireland after 1998. As Joe Crowley, a former Congressman from Massachusetts explained: "It's done and over and people move on." For Crowley, it was a logical outcome: "It's because of the success of the Good Friday Agreement, because of peace, the removal of the physical border."

Brian O'Dwyer concurred. He told us that even though there were some outstanding issues to grapple with, most people had stopped paying attention to Northern Ireland well before Brexit: "After the Good Friday Agreement ... many people would look at me and say 'Isn't that all over?'" Moreover, the issues that remained weren't psychologically compelling: "There are no emotional ties to try to work on getting economic investment in Northern Ireland. That's nothing that gets anybody terribly excited." A senior Congressional staffer explained it to us this way:

> I've been on the hill [Capitol Hill] for a decade, and during that time, I didn't hear a peep from Irish America. They would come through on St. Patrick's Day. But, it's not like they had a serious policy ask as when [John] Hume was coming through in the eighties. The main policy ask has been around visa issues and work permits, which is not a top tier foreign policy issue.

In a similar vein, Danny O'Connell, the President of the Ancient Order of the Hibernians, also pointed to immigration as one of Irish America's biggest contemporary concerns, telling us: "From an Irish American standpoint, the biggest issue is the flow of Irish people to America ... Forget about the Morrison and Donnelly visas. We haven't had a positive flow [of people] from Ireland since 1967."

In 2022, when we interviewed O'Connell, he said the AOH's priority issue was lobbying Congress to allow Irish citizens access to E-3 visas, which are currently only reserved for Australian citizens. E-3 visas are two-year work visas reserved for those in specialty occupations, and unlike H1-B visas, allow spouses of E-3 holders to work without a degree. The AOH was also advocating for visas that would allow American retirees to move to Ireland in exchange for an equal number of E-3 (or other) visas allowing young Irish college graduates to come here. As O'Connell argued: "I'm not one of the people who want to live there. Have you ever been there in winter? But we need multi-generational migration. That's the most important thing for Irish America."

To be fair, O'Connell did tell us that he hoped Irish America would get motivated by Brexit, but he acknowledged some doubts, telling us: "At the AOH, we see a real void in Irish America. I don't want to offend anyone, but we're saying Irish America isn't where it was in the 1980s."

The only remaining issue for many Irish Americans was Irish reunification. We will pick this issue up in Chapter 9. Suffice it to say here that Irish unity is an outcome most of Irish America supports, but recognizes is not theirs to enact, although Brexit has animated Irish American engagement around this issue.

## *The changing nature of the conflict*

Another reason for the decline of Irish American engagement in the ongoing aspects of the peace process "after the Belfast/Good Friday Agreement was signed and before the Brexit referendum" was the changing nature of the conflict. For Mitchell Reiss, US Special Envoy to Northern Ireland from 2003 to 2007 and a current member of the Independent Reporting Commission, the antagonists are different today, and Irish America isn't well suited to nudging them along:

> The nature of the challenge has changed and that is the conundrum. It's not about getting the IRA to decommission its weapons, and have Sinn Féin pledge to purely peaceful means and support justice and politics. That's where they [Irish Americans] had huge leverage and were able to use it effectively. Now, you want to restore the DUP's confidence? Well, good luck with that. That's not really what they [Irish America] are built for.

Jim Walsh also emphasized that the actors in need of prodding were different after 2016. He observed that unlike the mid-1990s, Irish

Americans lacked the kinds of relationships with Unionists that it had had in the 1990s with the IRA and Sinn Féin. When we asked why, he told us: "Unionists see us as more green than orange." He also noted that efforts to forge relationships between Unionists and Irish Americans had often met with limited success. As an example, he cited Norman Houston's work as the long-time director of the Northern Ireland Bureau in Washington, DC:

> Norman Houston really worked hard to put Northern Ireland in front of the US business community, but it was a tough sell to get [Peter] Robinson, [Ian] Paisley [Jr.], and [Arlene] Foster to agree. Unionists look to Republicans and Nationalists look to Democrats. But the Unionists haven't cultivated relationships with spokespeople or business connections for investment opportunities.

As a result of these changes, the Irish American ethnic lobby that came into being after the Brexit vote differed from the lobby in the earlier parts of its history. Although many of the individual activists and leaders are the same, the lobby today lacks the mass basis and organizational depth that early activists had relied on. It also lacked the connections to groups on the Unionist side that were there in the 1990s. The newer lobby's means to influence are, as a consequence, somewhat atypical, given its history, although, as we will show in the coming chapters, they had important impact on the Brexit process.

## Irish America takes on Brexit

While Irish America was not ready to respond to Brexit in a coordinated fashion for several years, they quickly saw the core problem it posed for the Belfast/Good Friday Agreement—Brexit meant that the two countries now would need to reinstate a functional border between them. Moreover, reinstating that border would call into question the imaginative co-sovereignty that allowed both sides to peacefully co-exist despite no final answer on the constitutional question at the heart of the conflict.

For their part, Irish America was adamant that a land border should not be reimposed on the island of Ireland. They saw a land border as antithetical to the Belfast/Good Friday Agreement. Kevin

Sullivan, the Project Director of the Ad Hoc Committee to Protect the Good Friday Agreement, told us in 2020 that a hard border would "infringe on the integrity of the Good Friday Agreement." Former Congressman Joe Crowley made the same point: "Any creation of any land border would be regression in terms of the Good Friday Agreement." And Brian O'Dwyer explained to us, "for Irish America, the main thing is the preservation of the Good Friday Agreement. And, concomitant with that, is that the border is removed."

Irish Americans also worried a hard border could lead to a resumption of violence. Some argued that a reimposed border would give paramilitary remnants something to attack. As Kevin Sullivan explained:

> When we heard the Irish government say you might need a green card to cross the border, it's an administrative thing, everyone went, "Ohhhhh!" Our redline is you can't have a hard border with barriers. This will create something to attack, police will have to come in, we don't want this to spiral away.

Martin Galvin, former publicity director for NORAID and current AOH National Freedom-for-all-Ireland Chairman, made a similar point, noting that any border—land or sea—could lead to violence, though he indicated a land border would be much worse:

> Right now, we're in a situation where an overwhelming majority know a land border would be disastrous. But what has happened is that this has been played up as if this is somehow undermining Loyalists and Unionists. That the Irish sea border is a betrayal. There seems to be an unstated threat that if this isn't taken care of, there will be larger protests, maybe violence.

Ciarán Quinn, Sinn Féin Representative for the US and Canada, referred to this argument with considerable caution, emphasizing instead the risk of provoking civil disobedience rather than violence. According to Quinn, Sinn Féin has advocated for the Belfast/Good Friday Agreement and worked to communicate "that violence was the past and should never return." Suggesting a return to violence was likely could risk undermining the credibility of their claims about the embeddedness of the peace process. In addition, once violence becomes a means of resolving differences, "no one knows where the road ends up." Along these lines, a further risk with this argument was that if potential violence by dissident Republicans was used as a threat to deter the creation of a land border in Ireland, Loyalists may see the threat of violence as useful for their cause as well, which was a lesson some took away from the early phase of the Brexit negotiations.

Irish Americans following the situation were also cognizant of the benefits an open border had created for businesses and consumers on both sides of the border. It was one of the things that had normalized the peace. Instead of dealing with driving through checkpoints with armed guards, people cross the border with little beyond paint colors on the lines on the road, signage, and cell-phone service to indicate they have moved from one country to another. To reimpose a border would undermine something people in both countries (and people from Northern Ireland's Protestant and Catholic communities) took advantage of—freedom of travel and trade across the island.

Despite their fears, Irish Americans who were engaged on these issues did not see much of a role for themselves in the initial phase of negotiations between the UK and the EU that began in June 2017 and culminated in November 2018 with the first Brexit Withdrawal Agreement. For starters, most Irish Americans who were tracking the challenges thought the Irish government and the EU were making a strong and firm case against reimposing a hard border on the island. In an interview with journalists at the European Social Summit in Gothenberg in November 2017, for example, Prime Minister Leo Varadkar drew a proverbial line in the sand one month before phase 2 negotiations were to begin on a withdrawal agreement between the EU and the UK: "We've been given assurances that there will be no hard border in Ireland, that there won't be any physical infrastructure, that we won't go back to borders of the past. We want that written down in practical terms in the conclusion of phase one" (Elgot, 2017).

A month later, EU President Donald Tusk met with Varadkar in Dublin. At the end of their meeting, Tusk told reporters that the EU supported Ireland's opposition to a hard border on the island post-Brexit:

It is no secret that we discussed Brexit with a special focus on the border between Ireland and Northern Ireland. I came to Dublin to reassure the Taoiseach and all the Irish people that the EU is fully behind you and your request that there should be no hard border on the island of Ireland after Brexit. The Irish request is the EU's request.

And putting a proverbial cherry on top of the message, Tusk closed his formal comments by quoting an Irish proverb—"Ni neart go cur le cheile" (There is no strength without unity).

## *The Trump wild card*

Irish America was also relatively quiet at this point because President Trump, then in his first term of office, was viewed as a bit of a wild card on the issues of Brexit and Northern Ireland. Trump's lack of foreign policy experience meant no one knew exactly where he stood on the thorny issues raised by Brexit and were afraid to poke the bear. They had also heard little, one way or the other, from key actors in federal agencies normally expected to articulate administration positions on key foreign policy issues.

We witnessed the confusion firsthand in 2017 when we took a group of university students from the US and Northern Ireland to the US State Department. Several students asked the representative from the Bureau of European and Eurasian Affairs if the US government's policy toward Brexit had changed since Trump had come to power. The desk officer told us that his office had yet to receive any directives and were cautiously continuing apace. When we asked what was causing the delay, the staffer told us that many positions on the Europe desk were vacant, including the position he reported to, as well as the one to which that position reported.

While vacancies are common in the first year of any president, Gramer, de Luce, and Lynch (2017) argue that the Trump administration took a "dismissive attitude to diplomacy and the civil servants who execute it." Its goal, they argue, was to systematically hobble the institution by cutting budgets and staff. It is also fair to say that Trump did not seem particularly interested in the particulars of Brexit. Though he was a fan of Boris Johnson and other Brexiteers, he rarely spoke about specific debates, or did so only in the most general of terms. When we asked Mick Mulvaney, who was Trump's Chief of Staff from January 2019 to March 2020, what the President thought about the Backstop, he replied:

> It never made its way up into the Oval Office. Brexit came up in passing. The President may have had a briefing, but we never talked about the Backstop, etc. I talked to Pompeo about it. It was something I was interested in following. But we didn't associate it [the Withdrawal Agreement] with the national interest.

Irish Americans also knew that the Irish government was similarly cautious about interacting with the new administration, choosing to engage in soft, behind-the-scenes diplomacy. Then Irish Ambassador Dan Mulhall told us, for example, that he and his team met with a variety of folks in the Executive Branch to explain Ireland's opposition to a hard border. When we asked with whom he met, he mentioned people at the State Department, in the National Security apparatus (Fiona Hill and Robert O'Brien), and on the White House staff (John Kelly and Chris Liddell). When we asked what he hoped to accomplish in those meetings, Mulhall told us:

> During the Trump Administration, I didn't have much hope they would intervene in a way that will be positive from our point of view. But I thought it was important that they didn't intervene in any way that was negative. In other words, that they didn't try to weigh in supporting the British arguments against the European ones. And I think that, I think it's fair to say, that never happened.

Concern about Trump was not misplaced. In July 2018, after Prime Minister Theresa May announced her "Chequers Plan," a UK government White Paper that laid out the government's key principles in upcoming negotiations with the EU, Trump immediately criticized it. And he did so on British soil, during his first official state visit, which coincided with the White Paper's release. In an interview with *The Sun* tabloid, Trump complained that May had disregarded his advice because the plan embraced a so-called soft

Brexit; she "wrecked it" he told the paper (Dunn, 2018). He also said that the plan, if formalized, would "kill" a trade deal between the two countries. He closed by adding insult to injury, telling *The Sun*'s reporter that Boris Johnson, a Eurosceptic thorn in May's side, would be "a great Prime Minister" (Dunn, 2018).

Despite the headwinds, May soldiered on, announcing a formal Withdrawal Agreement with the EU on November 14, 2018. In December, her party held a vote of no confidence in her leadership. She won the vote by 200 to 117, but May's enemies refused to relent, calling another no-confidence vote in mid-January 2019, this time in Parliament. May narrowly won again, by 325 to 306, but her Withdrawal Agreement was doomed to failure. In fact, she was unable to win approval from Parliament for any particular course of action and was forced to request multiple extensions from the EU to continue negotiations. It was in the midst of these chaotic months that Irish Americans began to remobilize. We will turn to this phase in the next chapter.

5

# Irish America Remobilizes

This chapter recounts the re-emergence of the Irish American lobby in 2019 and the efforts it took to prevent the UK Withdrawal Agreement with the EU from re-establishing a hard border between Northern Ireland and the Republic of Ireland. Specifically, we cover the time period bookended by the collapse of Theresa May's 2019 Withdrawal Agreement, which included the Backstop, and the approval of Boris Johnson's 2020 Withdrawal Agreement, which replaced the Backstop with the Protocol.

As we will demonstrate, Irish America's key role during this time was to shape how the US understood its strategic interests in the context of Brexit, and then to make those views known to the UK. This was no mean feat. Brexit created a wedge between two of the US's strongest allies and, in so doing, called into question what kind of withdrawal agreement would be in the US's best interest.

The narrative of the Irish American lobby's reengagement makes clear that despite all the changes since the 1990s, it maintained the core traits that had facilitated its prior political successes. It still had a coherent political culture and well-networked members in and out of Congress. It was also well equipped to use St. Patrick's Day festivities in official Washington to its political advantage. And, its bipartisanship and general appeal ensured goodwill from power brokers across Democratic and Republican administrations.

## Strategy for re-engagement

As Irish America began to remobilize in this period, its lobbying involved a three-pronged strategy. The first was direct Congressional action. The most notable group in this regard was the Congressional Friends of Ireland Caucus. As noted in Chapter 2, the Caucus was formed in 1981 by three Irish American politicians—Senators Daniel Patrick Moynihan and Ted Kennedy, and Speaker of the House Tip O'Neill. Its goal was to encourage fellow law makers, successive presidents, and the diplomatic corps to actively facilitate peace in Northern Ireland. Although the group was started by members of the Democratic Party when it began, it quickly became a bipartisan group, and it remains bipartisan today. In 2019 the Caucus was co-chaired by Congressman Richie Neal (D-MA) and Peter King (D-NY). Of its 32 members at the time, 21 were Democrats and 11 were Republicans.[1] This group is not distinct from Irish America in the sense that they must be lobbied by Irish America to act. Instead, the members of the Caucus are typically either Irish American themselves or represent a more Irish American district than the average member of Congress.[2] They are also already well versed on the issues. Their membership indicates their commitment to furthering Irish concerns, particularly relating to the peace process. Given their familiarity and engagement, the Friends of Ireland Caucus became a primary mechanism for Congressional action around Brexit.

The second prong of the strategy involved creating a civil society organization specific to the issue at hand. Although there were a number of Irish American organizations in operation when Brexit occurred, none of them was set up for foreign policy advocacy. The largest Irish American group, the AOH, focuses on cultural issues, immigration, and to a lesser degree the narrow business interests of Irish Americans, though they often weighed in on human rights abuses during the Troubles. To strengthen its ability to engage in foreign policy, Irish America needed a new organization.

---

[1] The composition of the Committee is available through the subscription service Legistorm's archive.

[2] By our count, the 30 members of the Friends of Ireland Caucus in 2023 represented districts whose populations averaged 13.6 percent Irish-Americans. According to the 2019 US Census, Irish Americans were only 9.2 percent of the overall US population. The 27 members of the UK Caucus in contrast represented districts that averaged 8.3 percent Irish Americans.

And so was born the Ad Hoc Committee to Protect the Good Friday Agreement, which was founded in February 2019. The Committee began when Jim Walsh reached out to Kevin Sullivan, an alumnus of the Clinton Administration and the former chair of the Washington Ireland Program (WIP) to jumpstart an initiative of some sort. Sullivan then recruited Bruce Morrison. Both Walsh and Morrison were former congressmen and alums of the Friends of Ireland Caucus.

Walsh, Sullivan, and Morrison were old Washington hands. They had worked together for decades on issues related to the peace process, including supporting the so-called Adams visa. They had also kept abreast of the peace process well after many Irish Americans had moved on. In 2014, for example, they penned a letter to First Minster Peter Robinson and Deputy First Minister Martin McGuinness to express their concern that the peace process was at a stalemate. The letter was signed by former ambassadors, cabinet officials, key figures in the State Department, two former special envoys to Northern Ireland, board members of the Ireland Funds, and the founder of WIP, among other things. The group had also provided advice to Gary Hart, President Obama's Special Envoy to Northern Ireland, meeting with him regularly and arranging briefings for him with the wider Irish America community.

Throughout the Brexit period, the Ad Hoc Committee functioned as an eminent persons group, albeit an unofficial one. In addition to two former congressmen at the helm, the group included two former presidential envoys to Northern Ireland, five former US ambassadors, two former governors, the future National Security Advisor Jake Sullivan, and several current and former leaders of prominent Irish American organizations such as the Ireland Funds and the AOH. However, they are not a domestic political actor. Bipartisan, they make no campaign contributions, endorse no political candidates, and foster no letter-writing campaigns. Although the individual members are often quite wealthy, the group has no membership dues. It is not incorporated and until late 2024 had no website, email address, or physical address (not even a post office box). Despite all of this, the prominence of the group's members and the respect they command among members of Congress and the Executive Branch gave them access to policy makers.

As we will detail later on in this chapter and in subsequent chapters, the Ad Hoc Committee would meet with key actors in the UK, Ireland, Northern Ireland, and the US government. In terms of the UK government alone, the group would meet with four of the five Secretaries of State for Northern Ireland between the time the group was formed and the Windsor Framework was announced in 2023.[3] It also met regularly with the two Irish ambassadors stationed in Washington between 2019 and 2024—Daniel Mulhall and Geraldine Byrne Nason. Likewise, in Northern Ireland the committee met with leaders from the five main political parties as well as civic and business groups in Belfast and Derry. Stateside, the committee routinely met with members in the Congressional Friends of Ireland Caucus, as well as officials in the White House, the US State Department, and the National Security Council.

From its inception until the Windsor Framework was signed, the group held more than 20 meetings a year with political officials on both sides of the Atlantic, issued formal statements to the media, and letters to relevant actors. Although we focus on the committee's efforts to prevent a hard border in this chapter, their work continued up to and beyond the Windsor Framework (which we will cover in the following chapters).

The group's approach was succinctly summed up by its co-founder Jim Walsh in a press briefing October 2020 after a meeting with the Irish Foreign Minister, Simon Coveney, regarding UK government efforts to scuttle the Withdrawal Agreement. Scolding the UK government, Walsh told the press: "Building a green wall to protect the GFA is something we know how to do" (*Irish News*, 2020).

Though the main actor in pressuring Congress was the Ad Hoc Committee, the American Brexit Committee (ABC) also became active at approximately the same time. Though it was formed in 2016, it issued its first "Summary for Lobbying" in which it framed an agenda for pressuring Congress in February 2019. Larger and more mass-oriented than the Ad Hoc Committee, the ABC engages in more traditional and direct lobbying, in the sense of urging its members to contact their representatives and key members of

---

[3] The exception—Shailesh Vara—was only in office for less than two months.

Congress to press them on the US-UK trade deal, human rights, the legacy issue, implementation of the Belfast/Good Friday Agreement, and so on.

Much of the ABC's agenda overlaps with other parts of Irish America and the group often mentions its support for other actors like the Ad Hoc Committee, the AOH, and the Brehon Law Society in its communications. However, in contrast to the Ad Hoc Committee, the ABC is openly Irish Republican in orientation. For example, its website refers to Northern Ireland as the "last vassal colony in Europe," describes the "special relationship" as "largely a media fiction perpetuated to get the British government favors," and includes a list of British "destabilization actions" in Northern Ireland from 1972 onward.

Although the press in Ireland, the US, and the UK rarely mention the group in stories about Irish America's work around Brexit, the group lobbied for similar actions as the Ad Hoc Committee. As such, even if it was not the face of the contemporary Irish American lobby in the way that the Ad Hoc Committee was, the two groups buttressed each other's lobbying simply by walking the same path.

The third prong of Irish American strategy to emerge in this period was to change the rhetorical frame around discussions about how to enact Brexit. This strategy was aimed primarily at checking the actions of the UK government by linking protection of the Belfast/Good Friday Agreement during this period to the prospect of a bilateral trade agreement between the US and the UK. To be fair, during the period covered in this and subsequent chapters, successive UK governments maintained that their actions were intended to protect the agreement. However, as we will note later on, Irish America disagreed, sometimes vociferously, faulting the motives and/or potential effects of a variety of British positions over this period. Moreover, it used the potential trade deal as both carrot and stick. Indeed, a bilateral trade agreement with the US was a coveted prize for Brexiteers because they had often pointed to the prospect of one to blunt concerns about the costs of losing access to unfettered free trade in the EU market. In this context, the deal could be dangled as an enticement to encourage a policy position or a punishment to withdraw when an unfavorable policy position was considered. Irish America also used this rhetoric in its own internal conflict with pro-Brexit forces domestically. For example, they frequently cited the power of Congress to review and approve all trade negotiated by the Executive Branch as a way to check President Trump's sometimes enthusiastic embrace of Brexit. Irish Americans also used opposition to President Trump's stated goals on Brexit as a form of resistance to his vision of international affairs more generally (Kennedy, 2019).

## A "new Brexit sideshow"

Although Theresa May won her first two votes of no confidence, her withdrawal plan was in deep trouble by the time Irish America started gathering its forces. The first time she brought the deal to the House of Commons in January 2019, it failed by a wide margin, with 431 votes against and only 202 in favor. Her second vote of no confidence happened the next day.

Watching from across the Atlantic, Irish Americans were growing worried. The first moves they made were symbolic. On January 25, Congressman Brendan Boyle (D-PA), the only member of Congress with a parent born in Ireland, introduced House Resolution 88. The bill referred to the US as "one of the three guarantors of the Good Friday Agreement" and noted that Brexit "had raised concerns" about the Agreement's continued stability (US House, 2019). The resolution had 12 Democrat and three Republican co-sponsors, including many members and both co-chairs of the Congressional Friends of Ireland Caucus and the future US Special Envoy to Northern Ireland Joe Kennedy (D-MA) (Boyle, 2019).

The resolution was referred to committee, and though it was never brought to the floor for a vote,[4] Irish America was re-activated. In February 2019, the Ad Hoc Committee joined the fray, writing a letter to Taoiseach Leo Varadkar and Prime Minister Theresa May expressing its concerns about threats to the agreement. Sullivan penned the initial rough draft and then he, Jim Walsh, and Bruce Morrison reached out for support. In the end, the letter was signed by 40 high-profile people, including two former US senators, two former presidential envoys to Northern Ireland, five former US

---

[4] Because it was not brought to the floor for a vote, the bill died at the end of the session in December 2020.

ambassadors, two former governors, leaders of the Ireland Funds and the AOH, and the future National Security Advisor, Jake Sullivan. The committee also released a statement to the Irish and British press explaining its reasoning: "The recent decision by the Prime Minister and the Parliament to seek to re-open the withdrawal agreement and find an alternative to the Backstop has put the Good Friday Agreement into play. This alarms us."

Walsh and Morrison also gave interviews to Irish news outlets. And in stark terms, both laid out the stakes as Irish America saw them. Walsh argued that "a hard border will divide an already divided society even more. The GFA has kept the peace in Northern Ireland for over 20 years and it must be protected at all costs" (*The Irish Echo*, 2019). Morrison made a similar point:

> Peace is not inevitable in Northern Ireland. Stormont has already been mothballed for close to two years and the dissidents still have a capacity to cause trouble. A border defined by customs posts, checks points and infrastructure would reshape the economic, emotional and political landscape and resurrect the memories of the border when it was militarized during the Troubles. (As quoted in *The Irish Echo*, 2019)

Both leaders also signaled specific discontent with Brexiteers. Walsh was especially pointed in his comments, noting: "The Backstop is the insurance policy that protects the GFA and the GFA cannot be used as a bargaining chip as the Brexit advocates search for an alternative arrangement."

The Ad Hoc Committee also trumpeted its political re-engagement, announcing its plans to meet with high-level officials on both sides of the Irish Sea and the Atlantic, including "the Irish and British ambassadors in Washington and senior US State Department officials." The goal, the group noted, was to demonstrate that "Irish America was 'mobilized and vigilant'" (*The Irish Echo*, 2019).

Other commentators in Ireland took note of the Ad Hoc Committee's announcement. Writing in the *Business Post*, columnist Tom McGurk argued that the Ad Hoc Committee had kicked off "the opening chapter in a very significant new Brexit sideshow." As he explained:

> Throughout the long and winding road from the IRA ceasefire to the signing of the Good Friday Agreement, the input of the US was central. After initial resistance, London had finally to accept that Washington was going to be a player back then and had to be taken seriously. One suspects that is still the case. (McGurk, 2019)

The group's stature as an eminent persons group also meant that it could expect a formal response to its letter—something few ordinary civil society groups could ever dream of. Ten days after the letter was sent, the Ad Hoc Committee received a written response from Prime Minister May. She assured the group that she too believed in the importance of the Belfast/Good Friday Agreement, describing it as a "bedrock" and offering a solemn promise: "No Government that I lead will ever take risks with the hard-won relative peace and stability that these agreements have established." Members of the UK government's diplomatic staff also responded by organizing two meetings for the committee—the first with its Deputy Ambassador to the US, and the second with the Secretary of State for Northern Ireland, Karen Bradley (Lynch, 2019b).

The UK government would perhaps never again be quite this overt in acknowledging the importance of the role of Irish America, but after the Ad Hoc Committee's forceful statement, every Secretary of State for Northern Ireland who traveled to the US would request a meeting with the Committee. Indeed, Brandon Lewis would meet with the committee four times in 2022 alone!

## Putting trade on the table

The first time Irish America linked a bilateral trade deal to protecting the Belfast/Good Friday agreement occurred in 2019 at a February reception in Washington for the Irish Tánaiste, Simon Coveney. During the event, Congressmen Richie Neal (D-MA) and Peter King (R-NY), co-chairs of the Congressional Friends of Ireland Caucus, publicly warned the UK that it would need to keep a "soft" border if it wanted a trade deal with the US (William and Mace, 2019).

This link was reiterated in March when Richie Neal (D-MA), Chairman of the House Ways and Means Committee, and Congressman Joe Kennedy (D-MA), future US Special Envoy to

Northern Ireland, wrote a letter to Prime Minister May with 22 members of Congress from both political parties as co-signatories, warning that a post-Brexit trade deal might be "delayed indefinitely if we are obligated to respond to potential crises" in Ireland, referring to the chaos that a hard border might create (Lynch, 2019a).

That same month, Senator Chris Murphy (D-CT), a member of the influential Foreign Relations Committee, reinforced the message in person when he visited the UK. During a speech at the London School of Economics (LSE), Murphy (2019) referred to himself as part of the Irish American lobby and said he had made the trip in order to warn the UK that the special relationship between the two countries was "endangered by Brexit." He told the audience that President Trump's comments were "drowning out other perspectives coming from the United States," most notably Irish America's view that a hard border could "shatter the peace process." He also reminded the audience that it was Congress, not the President, who signed trade deals, noting that a hard border would "quell any interest in Congress to support a trade agreement with Britain" (Murphy, 2019). And in case Brexit hardliners were tempted to dismiss Irish America because of its relatively small numbers, Murphy expanded on his comments two days later in Dublin, telling the press "it only takes a minority of senators to stop a trade agreement" (Carswell, 2019a).

Given the special relationship between the two countries, it may seem odd that a member of Congress felt the need to spell out which branch of the US government has ultimate authority to approve trade deals, but several interviewees told us that the message was necessary. Ciarán Quinn, Sinn Féin's representative to the US argued, for example, that in 2019, "Brexiters seemed to think it [the US] was like a parliamentary democracy." As he explained to us in an interview:

> They had no understanding of how America worked. They thought because Trump had promised a trade deal, he could do it. That it was like he was a Taoiseach or a PM. So, they didn't understand that element of it. And, the whole episode of Brexit was driven by hubris and misunderstandings.

The timing of Murphy's visit also gave it resonance. By this stage, the UK House of Commons had rejected the Withdrawal Agreement three times, primarily over objections to the Irish Backstop (William and Mace, 2019). In doing so, Parliament also proved itself unable to agree to any alternative plan for withdrawal. With each rejection a no-deal Brexit seemed more and more likely, and so too did a hard border.

Given the stakes, Murphy's visit would be just the start of a more forceful Irish America. In mid-April 2019, Congressman Richie Neal organized a Congressional delegation (CODEL) to Ireland, Northern Ireland, and Great Britain, and invited the Speaker of the House, Nancy Pelosi. The speaker's inclusion was an important move because, as the leader of the Democratic Party in Congress and the leader of the House of Representatives, she was third in line of succession after the Vice President, but was arguably the second most powerful figure in American politics after President Trump. She had also, by that point, become a counterpoint in American politics to Donald Trump, with whom she clashed publicly and frequently. Dan Mulhall, who was the Irish Ambassador to the US at the time, explained the importance of her inclusion:

> First of all, the Speaker wasn't meant to travel to Ireland. It was meant to have been a visit by the Ways and Means Committee, chaired by Richie Neal. He invited Speaker Pelosi to go with him. And, on that trip, in Dublin, she was treated like it was a state visit.

Mulhall went on to explain what that looked like: "She was feted in Ireland, put up in the government guesthouse. She was given a state dinner at Dublin Castle. Second night we put on entertainment for her. She spoke to the Parliament. She got the full treatment."

However, the CODEL's first stop was London, and they received a more subdued welcome there. Indeed, though they met with a number of high-level officials, including the Chancellor of the Duchy of Lancaster David Lidington, Speaker of the House of Commons John Bercow, Labour Party leader Jeremy Corbyn, and the Chancellor of the Exchequer Philip Hammond, she did not meet with Prime Minister May, who was trying to get her withdrawal plan over the bar. One interview subject, who requested to go off the record about the visit, told us: "I think at the time, the Prime Minister, who was Theresa May, wouldn't see her [Pelosi] because she was probably afraid of annoying Donald Trump."

The CODEL's goals for the meeting appear to have been twofold. The first was to reiterate Congressman Murphy's comments to similar audiences in March. The second was to thwart competing messages from the Trump Administration. In 2018, for example, John Bolton, Trump's National Security Advisor, had met with the pro-Brexit European Research Group (ERG) and assured them that the US would quickly take up trade deal negotiations with the UK (Geoghegan, 2020). Although the Trump Administration had not adopted a consistent approach to Brexit even in 2019, often vacillating between positions, the ERG and Trump shared a political sensibility.[5] The CODEL needed to disabuse Eurosceptics that their shared sympathies with Trump were enough to carry the day; the President could not deliver a trade deal on his own.

During the visit, Pelosi made a number of points in formal meetings and later in interviews with the press. First, she reiterated Irish America's view that the peace agreement was something special that was not to be trifled with. Speaking at LSE, she described the agreement in transcendent terms:

> The Good Friday Accords ended 700 years of conflict. It's not just about that geography though. This is not a treaty only. It is an ideal. It is a value. It is something that is a model to the world, something we all take pride in ... And we don't want that model to be something that can be bargained away in some other agreement. (Pelosi, 2019)

---

[5] In the US context, Trump as often been described as wrecking normal politics and undermining democratic norms. In Britain, the ERG has been described in a similar fashion. Geoghegan (2020), for example, labels the group "cartel of Tory MPs" who "broke British Politics." Cusick, Corderoy, and Geoghegan (2019) refer to them as "a militant 'party within a party.'" Sabbagh and Barr (2018) call them a "shadowy group of Tories Shaping Brexit."

In the same speech, she also reiterated that while presidents can negotiate trade deals, only Congress can approve them, noting that trade legislation moves through the Ways and Means Committee, which she pointedly described as "the committee of jurisdiction for trade legislation." She also affirmed that the committee's chairman, Congressman Richie Neal, was not afraid to wield that power in defense of the agreement:

> First of all, let me say, it's very hard to pass a trade deal in the Congress of the United States. But, if there were to be any weakening of the Good Friday Accords, there would be no chance, whatsoever. A non-starter for a US/UK trade agreement. (Pelosi, 2019)

During her time in the UK and Ireland, she would also say such a deal would not get to "first base," it would not be "in the cards" (Carswell, 2019b). "Don't even think about that," she warned (Booth, 2019).

Pelosi was also willing to trek into the proverbial lion's den, sitting down with the ERG to which Bolton had made promises just a year earlier. There, she delivered the Irish American message. Although the group declined to share meeting notes, the press described the tenor of the meeting with stark language. Simon Carswell (2019b), writing for the *Irish Times*, called the encounter "forceful and at times heated," describing it as a "clash" and "a reality check." The BBC's John Campbell (2019) referred to it as a "stormy meeting." *Huffington Post*'s Ned Simons and Paul Waugh (2019) reported that Pelosi "had a terse exchange" with the group's then leader, Jacob Rees-Mogg.

Dan Mulhall, who was privy to chatter about the meeting in his role as the Irish Ambassador, confirmed that he had heard similar descriptions to those mentioned in the press:

> In London, she got some kind of a bum's rush in that, she had a meeting with some of the wilder elements of the Brexit tribe. And apparently, it was a very, very difficult meeting where they kind of insulted her and she sort of eviscerated them, as you could imagine Nancy Pelosi doing.

The CODEL also made sure to get their message across in pictures. When they got to Ireland, they insisted on going to the border. At the time, there was nothing to see there—no checkpoints had been established or cameras installed—but as William Tranghese, Richie Neal's long-time Chief of Staff, told us, the border carried great symbolic weight:

> We made it very clear to the parties, here and there, that we were going to the border to demonstrate how important the border issue was for our delegation. It re-emphasized the priority that the House was placing on this issue. I can't tell you how powerful that moment was. It was the focus of press attention the entire time we were there. Even before and during the planning of the trip, that visit to the border was always going to happen.

Although the CODEL did not result in an immediate change in UK policy, it laid some important groundwork. Most notably, it undermined a key argument Brexiteers had made to the electorate at large—that any damage from a no-deal Brexit and a reimposed border would be nullified by a trade deal with the US. As Congressman Brendan Boyle (D-PA), who was also part of the CODEL, pointedly explained to the *Irish Times*: "We very much attempted to disabuse them of that sort of conspiracy-type thinking" (Carswell, 2019b).

The delegation's efforts also sent an important message back home to the Trump Administration: Irish America's Congressional wing would stand firm in protecting the Belfast/Good Friday Agreement, no matter what the President thought. Their public stance stood in sharp contrast to the administration's muddled messaging, which was big on bravado and short on details. Indeed, *The Intercept's* coverage of the CODEL went with a headline that surely irritated the President—"Nancy Pelosi Takes Control of US Foreign Policy on Brexit with Stark Warning to UK" (Mackey, 2019).

## *Headwinds in a hot summer*

Irish America's rhetorical strategy linking protection of the Belfast/Good Friday Agreement with a bilateral trade deal would be a consistent theme from this point forward. But Irish America would face new headwinds (in London and Washington) as spring turned into summer.

The first gale came from Downing Street. In late March, Theresa May announced that she would put her withdrawal package up for a third vote. To win support, she promised her party's 1922 Committee, an informal caucus of raucous backbench Brexiteers, that she would step down after the vote, explaining in a formal statement on March 27, two days before the vote:

> And I have heard very clearly the mood of the parliamentary party. I know there is a desire for a new approach—and new leadership—in the second phase of the Brexit negotiations and I won't stand in the way of that. I know some people are worried that if you vote for the Withdrawal Agreement, I will take that as a mandate to rush on into phase two without the debate we need to have. I won't. I hear what you are saying. (May, 2019)

On March 29, the third vote on a pared-down withdrawal agreement was held. It failed by 58 votes. May had already resigned, but she stayed in office until July 24, when her successor—Boris Johnson—was selected by the party and invited by the Queen to form a government.

Boris Johnson began his tenure by announcing that he would deliver Brexit within his first 99 days. And, most disturbingly from Irish Americans' point of view, he signaled he would remove the Backstop from the Withdrawal Agreement, and if the EU refused to go along with that, Britain would go with a no-deal Brexit, which would necessitate a hard border. In late August, the EU formally rebuffed Johnson's demand to remove the Backstop, making the chances of a no-deal Brexit more likely (Rankin and Elgot, 2019).

A second front was emerging stateside. After Johnson was chosen to lead his party and one day before he met the Queen, President Trump praised Johnson at a Turning Point USA event, saying he was a "Britain Trump":

> Good Man. He's tough and he's smart. They're saying "Britain Trump." They call him "Britain Trump," and

there's people saying that's a good thing. They like me over there. That's what they wanted. That's what they need. He'll get it done. He's going to do a good job. (Forgey, 2019)

Just over a week later, Senator Tom Cotton (R-AR) and 43 other Republican Senators, including Chuck Grassley (R-IA), the Chair of the Senate Finance Committee, sent a letter to the new Prime Minister congratulating him on winning the leadership contest and pledging unwavering support for the UK. The group also pledged to advocate for a new US-UK trade deal, "irrespective of how Brexit occurs" (for the complete letter, see Cotton, 2019).

Though support for Brexit in the Republican conference was well established, many believed that Cotton's letter with his colleagues may have been connected to a grievance he had with the Irish government. Indeed, in 2018, he was the sole Senator to object to the E3 visa swap with Australia in 2018, which would have given Australia's surplus visas to Irish citizens.[6] Cotton's objection killed the provision, and he reportedly refused at the time to take calls from Irish diplomats and leaders (O'Dowd, 2018).

In mid-August, John Bolton also returned to London, where he met with Boris Johnson. After their meeting, he spoke to the press, further alarming Irish America by promising that the US government would support a no-deal Brexit and that the UK would be "first in line" for a trade deal. As explained to the British press, the US was prepared to do a "series of agreements" instead of one large agreement to speed things along. A "sector-by-sector" approach, he argued, could move "very quickly, very straight-forwardly" ("UK 'First in Line' for US Trade Deal, Says John Bolton," 2019).

## Back to the grindstone

Irish America responded to these threats in different ways. However, its various wings were united (if unequally forceful) on the message that Congress would not support a US-UK trade deal if a hard border

---

[6] The E3 visa plan remains an Irish American objective at the time of writing.

was reinstated on the island. The strongest voices came from Irish Americans in Congress. A day after Bolton publicly stated that the UK would be "first in line" for a trade deal with the US, Speaker of the House Nancy Pelosi issued a press statement reiterating Irish America's insistence that they would not sign off on a US-UK trade deal if a hard Brexit happened and was followed by a hard border. "Whatever form it takes, Brexit cannot be allowed to imperil the Good Friday Agreement, including the seamless border between the Irish Republic and Northern Ireland" ("UK 'First in Line' for US Trade Deal, Says John Bolton," 2019).

The Congressional Friends of Ireland Caucus also wrote to Prime Minister Johnson, making the same point:

> We will oppose any US-UK trade deal if the Good Friday Agreement is undermined. As you know, America is guarantor of that international peace accord. That is why we strongly oppose any unraveling of the historic treaty or a return of a physical border on the island of Ireland under any circumstances. (Sullivan, 2019)

The Ad Hoc Committee was busy as well, writing to Julian Smith, Johnson's new Secretary of State for Northern Ireland. The committee said a US-UK trade deal would not happen if a hard border was reimposed and reiterated its firm support for Speaker Pelosi: "All of Irish America will support the Speaker, right down the line" (as quoted in Borger, 2019).

Irish Americans in the US Senate also pushed back against the Cotton memo. Senator Chuck Schumer (D-NY) responded to the letter by making direct appeals to the US Secretary of State and the British Foreign Secretary (Mike Pompeo and Dominic Raab respectively):

> Much has been written and uttered recently about potential US/UK trade agreements after Brexit, including statements by officials of the United States government, that overstate the levels of support certain versions of such agreements would have in the Congress. While Britain is a unique and valued ally of our nation, as the Democratic leader of the United States Senate,

> which would consider prospective new bi-lateral trade agreements, I write to express my inveterate opposition to any prospective trade deal with United Kingdom that either undermines the landmark Good Friday Agreement or facilitates a return to a hard border. (Schumer, 2019)

Schumer also indicated the Senate would work in concert with the House to prevent such an agreement:

> In this, I stand shoulder-to-shoulder with the bi-partisan, bi-cameral supporters of the Good Friday Agreement (and opponents of a return to a hard border), especially including Speaker Nancy Pelosi, and will do all in my power to work in a bi-partisan way to prevent such pact from receiving the approval of Congress. (Schumer, 2019)

Former Irish American politicians also responded to Senator Cotton's memo. Gary Hart, who was the US Special Envoy to Northern Ireland between 2013 and 2017, wrote a letter to the US Senate Foreign Relations Committee, in which he focused on the possibility that a hard border could lead to a resumption of violence: "Virtually all knowledgeable observers believe such a policy has the distinct possibility of reigniting sectarian conflict and violence and thus abrogating the central purpose of the Good Friday Agreement" (O'Donovan, 2019a).

Irish American organizations outside of Congress also stepped into the fray. The AOH wrote to Senator Cotton after the letter was made public to complain that his letter failed to mention either the border or the Belfast/Good Friday Agreement.

Within the Trump Administration, advocates for Irish America also spoke up. By this point, some Executive Branch officials had already commented on the role of the Belfast/Good Friday Agreement in the Brexit process. For example, during Ed Crawford's April confirmation hearing as Ambassador to Ireland, he told the US Senate Foreign Relations Committee that "the US position was that the Good Friday Agreement should be upheld 'at all costs'" (*Belfast Telegraph*, 2019). President Trump had earlier acknowledged concerns about the border when he stood alongside Taoiseach Varadkar in March at the 2019 White House shamrock ceremony, describing the border as "very complicated" and "one of the most complex points" in the UK's withdrawal negotiations with the EU (Dallison, 2019). However, given the President's temperament and prior vacillation on the issue, the most that Irish Americans in his orbit could do was offer muted opposition to a hard border. And, sometimes, they were forced to backtrack. Vice President Mike Pence is a case in point. In early September on his first trip to Ireland as Vice President, Pence flew into Shannon Airport, where he gave a press conference with Simon Coveney, the Irish Tanaiste and Foreign Minister. In his remarks, Pence affirmed US support for the Belfast/Good Friday Agreement, saying: "We will continue to work closely with our partners in Ireland and the United Kingdom to support a Brexit plan that encourages stability and also one that keeps the strong foundation forged by the Good Friday Agreement" (Halloran, 2019). He also alluded to the potentially disruptive effects a hard Brexit would have on the border:

> I think the opportunity to better understand Ireland's perspective and unique needs, particularly with regard to the Northern Border, will make us even better equipped to hopefully play a constructive role that when Brexit occurs, it will occur in a way that reflects stability and addresses the unique relationships between the UK and the Republic of Ireland. (Halloran, 2019)

The next day, Pence walked back his comments, if clumsily. At a press conference after meeting with Varadkar, Pence reiterated his support for stability of the Belfast/Good Friday Agreement, but added: "As President Trump announced last week, when Brexit is complete, the United States will have a new trade agreement with the United Kingdom." He demurred when asked if preservation of the Belfast/Good Friday Agreement was a precondition for finalizing a bilateral trade agreement, telling the press: "Let me leave the details to others" (Lynch and McGee, 2019).

Others in Trump's orbit were more consistent. Trump's then Chief of Staff, Mick Mulvaney, was one such person. Two weeks later, he did some clean-up work at a commemoration of a 1916 Easter Rising Plaque at the Washington Monument (Lynch, 2019c). Though he did not specifically call out Pence's comments about a trade deal, Mulvaney reiterated the importance of the agreement: "We just want to make sure that the Good Friday Agreement is respected, that peace accords are kept and that things are worked out in such a way to peacefully see whatever happens, happens" (as quoted in Lynch, 2019c). While Mulvaney's public statement at the Washington Monument was not a line in the sand, it was nonetheless important because it sent a message that there were people in the administration who stood with Irish America.

## Averting a fall crisis

By late August, Boris Johnson was facing an internal crisis. The EU deadline for withdrawal, October 31, was fast approaching, and his party was split between those who wanted a withdrawal plan and those who preferred a no-deal exit. Johnson appeared to support a no-deal exit, but lost his majority in Parliament due to a series of expulsions and defections (Sullivan and Adam, 2019). As a consequence, he did not have enough party members behind him to win a vote on a no-deal option (Casalicchio and Cooper, 2019). He was also faced with a rebellion in early September that produced the Benn Act, a requirement that Johnson request an extension to the withdrawal date if Parliament had not approved either a withdrawal arrangement or a no-deal Brexit by October 19. In response, Johnson called for a vote on a new election, figuring his best shot at a no-deal Brexit would be to secure a sufficient Tory majority in the polls. He was rebuffed twice in as many weeks, the final time on September 10. It was bad timing for Johnson. It was the last day before his administration had scheduled a five-week suspension of Parliament, which was eventually declared unlawful by the UK Supreme Court, but not before it began (Witte and Adam, 2019). The British political system seemed to be in total chaos at this point, unable to make progress toward any form of withdrawal arrangement that could win the support of both the UK Parliament and the EU.

Irish America again turned up the heat. On September 24, Congressman Peter King (R-NY), one of the co-chairs of the

Congressional Friends of Ireland Caucus, and Tom Suozzi (D-NY) introduced a House resolution calling on the EU and the UK to agree to a Brexit deal that protected the Good Friday Agreement and avoided a hard border. The resolution also called on the UK to fully implement the Good Friday Agreement and the political parties in Northern Ireland to reopen the Stormont institutions. The resolution concluded with a warning—any bilateral trade deal would be contingent on the UK maintaining its commitments to the Good Friday Agreement. The resolution would garner 47 co-sponsors before it passed by unanimous consent as HR 585 in December 2019.

In a sign of America's growing clout in relation to the form of the final deal, important actors in Northern Ireland and the UK Parliament also reached out to Irish America for help. On September 2, for example, 22 civil and business groups in Northern Ireland sent a letter to Speaker Pelosi and other senior figures in Congress, requesting their continued fortitude on linking a US-UK trade deal to respecting the Belfast/Good Friday Agreement. The timing of the letter was strategic, given that Vice President Pence was still in Ireland at the time. The letter pleaded with Pelosi to ensure that Congress scrutinize any deal "very carefully to ensure full compliance with the 1998 Agreement": "We urge Congress to satisfy itself that the truly transformational foundations for peace and prosperity here, which were laid with the indispensable aid of the United States, are not undermined in any manner by decisions to be taken in Congress" (as quoted in Young, 2019).

Around the same time, the Labour Party sent its Shadow Secretary of State for Northern Ireland, Tony Lloyd to the US. While there, he met with the Ad Hoc Committee and members of the Congressional Friends of Ireland Caucus, including, notably, Ways and Means Committee Chairman Richie Neal. Though Lloyd was only the Shadow Secretary, his presence in the US sent a strong signal that Labour was also counting on the Americans to kill a no-deal Brexit.

Even an American novelist, Bonnie Greer, got into the mix. On October 4 Greer, a columnist for the *New European* newspaper, appeared on the BBC TV show *Question Time*. When the subject of Brexit came up, she sounded as if she were part of the Congressional Friends of Ireland Caucus: "At times, I hear people talking as if this country [the UK] owns Ireland. Ireland owes this country nothing. Ireland owes this country no concessions. It owes it no quarter. It owes it nothing" (as quoted in McKeone, 2019). She echoed Irish America's talking points on trade, continuing:

> We have to be more serious about this. The United States is Irish. Anybody thinks that they're going to get a deal through and have a trade relationship with the US that shafts Ireland, you've got another thing coming. It's not going to happen. It's not going to happen. I'm from Chicago, that's where I was born. Do you know what we do on St Patrick's Day? We dye the river green. People are very serious about Ireland in the US. Don't mess with it. Don't make it look bad. (As quoted in McKeone, 2019)

In early October, Boris Johnson made an abrupt U-turn, agreeing to meet with the Irish Taoiseach on October 10 to discuss areas of common interest. After their meeting, the pair made a joint announcement that surprised many in the press, given Johnson's past intransigence and Varadkar's comments a few days earlier that striking an agreement a month shy of the EU deadline would be "very difficult" (O'Carroll, Mason, and Rankin, 2019). The statement described both men as agreeing that "a deal is in everybody's interest" and that "they could see a pathway to a possible deal" (Sparrow, 2019).

A week later, on October 17, Johnson announced that he and the EU Commission President, Jean-Claude Juncker, had struck a deal to keep most of the original Withdrawal Agreement intact, but replace the Irish Backstop with the Northern Ireland Protocol. The Protocol would prevent a hard border on the island of Ireland by ensuring that Northern Ireland stayed in the EU Customs Union, which meant that customs checks would occur at Northern Ireland's ports of entry (BBC, 2019b).

It was a remarkable turnaround for Johnson, who, at the DUP party conference in 2018, had called the Backstop a tool to make Northern Ireland an "economic semi-colony of the EU" (Steerpike, 2018). Indeed, though his and other Brexiteers' intransigence regarding the Backstop had led to May's downfall, the new

Protocol tied Northern Ireland to the EU more tightly than the Backstop would have. In other words, while May's agreement had the Backstop as a fallback—the UK would remain in the Customs Union and Northern Ireland would stay in the Single Market only if the UK and the EU could not come to a future agreement that prevented a hard border—the Protocol left Northern Ireland in the Single Market and the Customs Union permanently, unless this was changed by a vote in the Northern Ireland Assembly. As Jonathan Powell, former Prime Minister Tony Blair's chief negotiator during the Belfast/Good Friday Agreement negotiations, noted on Twitter: "The funny side of the No 10 claim they have got rid of the backstop is that they have in fact transformed it from a fallback into the definitive future arrangement for NI with the province remaining in the Single Market and Customs Union" (Powell, 2019).

The agreement stunned some members of Johnson's own party. It also angered the DUP, which had signed a confidence-and-supply agreement with the Conservative Party in 2017 when May was Prime Minister as a way to protect against this very outcome. Indeed, for many Unionists, Johnson's agreement dealt a near-death blow to the Union because it created an internal border within the UK between Northern Ireland and Great Britain. After the agreement was announced, Nigel Dodds, then the DUP deputy leader, told the BBC that if Johnson had "held his nerve—and held out—he would, of course, have got better concessions which kept the integrity, both economic and constitutional, of the UK" (BBC, 2019a).

Given the uncertainty on the final vote, Irish America kept its eyes on the prize, continuing its pressure campaign stateside. For example, five days after the agreement was announced (October 22), the House Foreign Affairs Committee's Subcommittee on Europe, Eurasia, Energy, and the Environment held a hearing titled "Protecting the Good Friday Agreement from Brexit." The Committee's chairman, Bill Keating (D-MA), was a member of the Congressional Friends of Ireland Caucus. Dr. Amanda Sloat, then a Senior Fellow at the Brookings Institution and Dr. Henry Farrell, a professor at George Washington University, gave testimony. Sloat (who would go on to serve on President Biden's National Security Council) and Farrell both reiterated the stakes of a no-deal Brexit for peace in Northern Ireland ("Protecting the Good Friday Agreement from Brexit," 2019).

After new elections were held in December 2019 and the Conservatives won a large majority (365 seats compared to Labour's 203), the Withdrawal Agreement and the Protocol (formally known as the Agreement on the Withdrawal of the United Kingdom of Great Britain and Northern Ireland from the European Union and the European Atomic Energy Community) was approved by Parliament on January 23, 2020, a week shy of the January 31 deadline. As we will note in the next chapter, this would not be the last chapter in the UK's messy divorce from the UK. But, for a short time, Irish America could exhale. The Belfast/Good Friday Agreement was safe for now.

## Irish America's impact

This chapter documents Irish America's actions in nudging the British toward a withdrawal arrangement that avoided a hard border, and shows how forceful and extensive the American actions were. As we have demonstrated, one of the most interesting things about the Irish American lobby in the post-Brexit moment is how different it is from other ethnic lobbies in the US and even its own lobby in earlier periods. Irish America's influence in this period is not the result of greasing campaign wheels with donations or threatening to mobilize a voting bloc behind a primary challenger; rather, its power in this phase lay in the traits we laid out in Chapter 1, including its strong sense of identity, its dense political networks, its role in Congress, its use of St. Patrick's Day celebrations to affirm political positions/alliances, and its ability to tap into nostalgia for political ends.

All of these features factored into Irish American activism aimed at preventing a hard border. Novelist Bonnie Greer's comments on the BBC's *Question Time*, for example, demonstrated the influence of Irish American soft power to sway people without Irish heritage and the goodwill Irish American positions enjoy in the US. In fact, her comments showed she could articulate a pro-Irish American position as cogently as any member of the lobby.

Irish America's dense political networks, and its insistence on being bipartisan, were also on display. Some of our interviewees told us that in the early 2000s, the peace agreement risked becoming a Democratic achievement attached to Bill Clinton in much the same way that it had become a Labour achievement tied to Tony Blair in the UK. However, after Brexit, Democratic Irish Americans in Congress reached across the aisle to their Republican colleagues, ensuring that they moved in lockstep to preserve the agreement. They also quietly and successfully lobbied Republicans who were supporting Johnson. When reporters queried Republicans who had signed the Cotton letter, for example, several Senate staffers backtracked for their bosses, saying their members were not aware of the implications for the peace process when they had signed the memo (McKeone, 2019). And from that point forward, no group in Congress issued a statement in support of a US-UK trade deal without also referring to the need to protect the Belfast/Good Friday Agreement. Indeed, even the Senate UK Trade Caucus, which was founded in 2018 to advocate for expanding US trade with the UK, would qualify their calls for a bilateral trade deal with language about the need to protect the Belfast/Good Friday Agreement (see the Special Relationship Act, introduced by Senator Chris Coons [D-DE] and Rob Portman [R-OH], the co-chairs and founders of the UK Trade Caucus, in June 2022 and the UNITED Act in 2023). As Marian McKeone observed in the *Business Post* in mid-October 2019:

> The resolve of Congress to protect the Good Friday Agreement has hardened even as the White House continues to signal its desire for a speedy US-British trade deal. In recent weeks, Brexit and the prospect of a hard border that could undermine the agreement has galvanized the Irish caucus on Capitol Hill, and reignited a spirit of bipartisanship among Irish-American politicians that had not been apparent for some years. (McKeone, 2019)

Having Irish Americans in key leadership positions in Congress was important, most notably Richie Neal, who used his perch as the Chairman of the House Ways and Means Committee to organize a CODEL to Ireland and the UK in April 2019. His decision to invite the then Speaker of the House, Nancy Pelosi, elevated the delegation's status and impact. Indeed, everywhere the CODEL went, they had the ear of powerful people. Though the Prime Minister snubbed them, the ERG did not, and the CODEL was able to deliver hard advice to the group and lay out the consequences for not heeding it. Multiple interviewees commented on the CODEL's impact. The Irish Ambassador at the time, Dan Mulhall, called it "a genuine game changer."

Irish Americans in Congress also had a dense network of friends—other members of Congress not in the Congressional Friends of Ireland Caucus,[7] and so called "formers," including former ambassadors, special envoys, and consuls general. The Ad Hoc Committee is the most notable example of this wider circle of friends. Indeed, the Congressional Friends of Ireland Caucus often coordinated its efforts with the Ad Hoc Committee, creating the seamless green wall that Jim Walsh threatened to build when he and Bruce Morrison announced the Ad Hoc Committee's formation.

To be fair, it is important to acknowledge that the representatives we interviewed from the UK government were much more circumspect in describing Irish American influence than their Irish or American counterparts. Their reticence means we do not have members of the UK Parliament admitting they voted for one or the other of the withdrawal agreements because of Irish American influence. And we can only speculate on what was in Prime Minister Boris Johnson's mind when he reversed his position on a no-deal Brexit and negotiated the Protocol with Irish Taoiseach Leo Varadkar. However, such reticence is not surprising. Indeed, it would be rare for an American ally of the UK's standing to openly acknowledge they took particular decisions because of pressure from the Americans.

It is also important to clarify that Irish America (in and out of Congress) was not working alone. The Irish government came out

---

[7] Note that only one member of the 2019 CODEL, Steven Horsford, did not have family ties to Ireland; the Speaker of the House, Nancy Pelosi, has Irish grandchildren, and Representatives Richie Neal, Brian Higgins, John Larson, Joe Courtney, Suzan DeBene, Dan Kildee, and Brendan Boyle are all of Irish descent.

early and forcefully against a land border on the island of Ireland, and the EU backed their Member State. Irish America agreed with that perspective, and its role was to first make that position legible and to second build support for it in Congress. Our data confirm its success. Again and again, our interviewees highlighted the US threat to withhold a trade deal with the UK as the leverage that forced Brexiteers to abandon a hard border. Irish Americans in Congress, with the help of the Ad Hoc Committee, were relentless in making sure the Irish and UK governments, as well as media in both countries, knew that fact.

The Americans' role was not lost on others. As Ailbhe Rea succinctly explained it in the *New Statesman*, Irish Americans "represent a real-life obstacle to the new Prime Minister's hopes of a UK-USA deal" (Rea, 2019). The then Irish Ambassador to the US at the time agreed, telling us: "I doubt the Protocol would ever have been agreed but for the influence of Irish America on that debate."

Finally, we note that key groups in Ireland, Northern Ireland, and Great Britain, including the Shadow Secretary for Northern Ireland, civil society groups, and business leaders, sought out Irish American help. A senior Congressional staffer told us that people in Northern Ireland still see the Americans as powerful actors when it comes to Northern Ireland and often approach individual members of Congress and high-level committees:

> It's remarkable how many people we see who see the fulcrum of decision being in Washington. They really put a lot of emphasis on what members of Congress think. For years the North didn't have a government. Fighting, fighting, fighting, no one could be on the same page. There still is this mentality that the US needs to get involved.

In short, despite the lack of independent verification from British interviewees, the fact that so many actors behaved as if the US's opinion on the border mattered in the UK gives credence to our claim that it did.

Moreover, as this chapter demonstrates, Irish America's key role in this period was to shape *how* American policymakers understood US strategic interests vis-à-vis the UK's withdrawal from the EU. In so doing, they provided members of Congress and the US government with a coherent perspective from which they could forcefully articulate a position at odds with that of the Brexiteers.

6

# Facing Down the Internal Market Bill

When Boris Johnson's government succeeded in negotiating the new Withdrawal Agreement that replaced the Backstop with the Northern Ireland Protocol at the end of 2019, most Irish Americans believed that the greatest threats Brexit posed to the Belfast/Good Friday Agreement had been neutralized. Indeed, by placing customs check points for goods coming from Great Britain at Northern Ireland's ports, a hard border on the island of Ireland had been avoided.

However, in Northern Ireland, Unionists decried the solution, arguing that Johnson's withdrawal plan had created a border within the UK, separating Northern Ireland from the rest of the UK. They saw the separation as threatening Northern Ireland's economy, its access to the UK's internal market, and its very place within the Union. They also objected to the lack of democratic consent in the arrangement because Northern Ireland would continue to be governed by EU regulations it would have no role in crafting.[1] With the Conservative Party's overwhelming victory in the snap election in December 2019, the DUP's power to affect the Withdrawal Deal disappeared and the party began to seek new opportunities to influence the situation. As a result, the politics of Brexit continued

---

[1] The Protocol does include a provision for the Northern Ireland Assembly to approve the arrangement four years after it goes into effect.

to roil, even after the Withdrawal Agreement was ratified in January 2020 (Carswell, 2020; Haverty, 2024).

In this chapter, we pick the story up from the passage of the Withdrawal Agreement that included the Protocol (approved by Parliament in January 2020) and trace it forward, through the last year of the Trump Administration. We focus on the efforts by the Irish Americans to defend the Protocol from the Internal Market Bill announced in the summer of 2020 and to encourage the British to work with the EU in order to avoid collapsing the Withdrawal Agreement and defaulting to a hard border.

## The shift from the Protocol to the EU/UK trade deal

The "Agreement on the Withdrawal of the United Kingdom of Great Britain and Northern Ireland from the European Union and the European Atomic Energy Community" went into effect on February 1, 2020, with an 11-month transition period. During the remainder of 2020, the UK remained part of the single market and the customs union while it negotiated the future of its trading relationship with the EU. These talks on the UK-EU trade deal were of high stakes because if no deal could be achieved in 2020, the two former members of the same market and customs union would fall back on World Trade Organization rules and pay most-favored-nation tariffs. Though the average tariff on goods was 6 percent, some goods were taxed at a higher rate. For example, the EU's most-favored-nation tariffs on imported dairy products is more than 35 percent (Chatzky and Siripurapu, 2020). At the time, trade between the UK and the EU averaged $900 billion annually. If no deal was struck, these close trading partners would need to establish border checks for goods crossing between them, a scenario that would likely translate into backlogs, shortages, and higher prices for many consumer, food, and medical items.

Negotiations were predictably tense, with disagreements over fishing rights and quotas, government subsidies for businesses, and the role of the European Court of Justice (ECJ) in settling disagreements between the parties. Just as predictably, negotiations also came down to the wire—an agreement was signed one day before the deadline, on December 30, 2020.

However, as we noted earlier, at the start of 2020, Irish Americans were breathing easy, thinking that the worst potential outcome of Brexit had been avoided. Activity in the US quieted down after Parliament approved the Withdrawal Agreement in January. Irish Americans were pleasantly surprised when President Trump appointed a special envoy on Northern Ireland in March. Former Congressman Mick Mulvaney, an Irish American with what the *Irish Times* called "a long-standing interest in Ireland," would play an important role as a liaison between Irish America and the Trump Administration. His service was especially significant at a moment when relations between the White House and the House leadership were fractured, and Boris Johnson seemed poised to undermine the Protocol (Lynch, 2020).

## The appointment of Mick Mulvaney as special envoy

Several things about Mick Mulvaney's appointment as special envoy were curious. For starters, the post had been empty since President Trump took office in January 2017, and few thought it would be resurrected. Indeed, the State Department had announced in August 2017 that the post was being "retired" (Calamur, 2017). Second, by the time Mulvaney was appointed, Irish American organizations had largely given up on getting an envoy appointed. In 2017, for example, 32 members of Congress had written a letter calling for an envoy, and the following year Congressman Brendan Boyle had pressed Secretary of State Mike Pompeo about it in a Congressional hearing. The AOH had also sent a letter to Pompeo requesting an envoy (O'Hanlon, 2018), but after its efforts were ignored, Irish America moved on from the issue.

Third, it is worth noting that the push for an envoy was muted from the start. After Congressman Boyle's hearing, for example, Trina Vargo argued in the *Irish Times* that "one should be careful what one wishes for, particularly with a Trump administration … Donald Trump may be more pro-Brexit than the British prime minister" and "There is no reason to believe that a Trump envoy would be helpful" (Donlon, 2018). She also noted that the Irish government was not calling for an envoy at that time either (although the Irish Embassy would formally welcome the news).

Fourth, the Irish government was also quiet on the subject of an envoy. As Dan Mulhall, who was the Irish Ambassador to the US from 2017 to 2022, explained to us in an interview, the Irish government did not particularly want to call the Trump Administration's attention to the issues of Brexit out of fear that President Trump would comment on the wrong side of the debate: "I knew they [the Trump Administration] wouldn't weigh in in a positive way. I was fairly concerned they didn't weigh in in a negative way."

In short, when Mulvaney was appointed, there was no pressure on the Trump Administration to deliver a special envoy. Many Irish Americans were taken by surprise at the announcement. So, too, were politicians in Northern Ireland. Indeed, *The Times* reported that Colum Eastwood, head of the SDLP at the time, could point to no event or occasion that had prompted it (O'Brien, 2020).

As we discovered, the timing of the appointment and the choice of Mulvaney is better explained by events inside the Trump White House than by any external demands. In fact, it appears that Mulvaney was the driving force for his own appointment. On March 6, 2020 the press reported that Mulvaney was stepping down as Trump's Chief of Staff to take on the role of special envoy to Northern Ireland. The move was depicted as a knock down the totem pole. *The New York Times*, for example, alleged that Mulvaney had been fired from the Chief of Staff position and described the envoy appointment as a "consolation prize" (Baker 2020). However, Mulvaney indicated that plans had been in place for a long time for him to switch jobs and become the envoy (*Irish Echo* Staff, 2020).

In our interview, Mulvaney told us he had long sought the job. He explained that as early as 2018, he and Secretary of State Mike Pompeo had developed a plan for Mulvaney to serve as special envoy. Later that year, as Mulvaney's work as head of the Consumer Financial Protection Bureau (CFPB) was winding down, he told us that he approached President Trump about the envoy role. Trump had a different role in mind—Chief of Staff. As Mulvaney recounted in our interview, the President was unhappy with the way things were running in the White House and thought he would be an ideal replacement because he had "turned around" the CFPB: "He [Trump] told me—'You can do the Northern Ireland thing after, when you're done here. You fix this place, then you can do the Northern Ireland gig.'"

Mulvaney agreed to the deal and took the Chief of Staff position on December 14, with the expectation that he would stay in the White House for around six months. However, by the fall of 2019, efforts to impeach President Trump were underway, precipitating a delayed exit. As Mulvaney explained to us: "Everybody in the White House, most importantly the President and myself, agreed that having a Chief of Staff leave in the midst of an impeachment was probably not the best look."

The Senate voted to acquit President Trump in February 2020 and Mulvaney got his wish, becoming special envoy a month later. Mulvaney's account of this timeline is bolstered by the fact that he traveled on official business to Dublin, London, and Belfast in February 2020 without the President, essentially acting as a shadow envoy. Indeed, his visit would have been odd if plans were not in place for him to take on the role.

Though Mulvaney himself would not necessarily have been the choice of any Irish American group, in part because he was pro-Brexit, he identified as an Irish American, was a member of the Friends of Ireland Caucus during his time in Congress, and was closely involved with other Irish American and Irish figures. In Congress, for example, he worked across the aisle with Congressman Brendan Boyle to plant a ceremonial tree on the US Capitol grounds to honor Irish Americans on the 100th anniversary of the 1916 Easter Uprising. He also had personal connections to Ireland—his daughter was studying in Ireland at the time, even interning in the Oireachtas, and he was a close family friend of Mark Daly, the head of the Irish Senate.

Mulvaney was also a known entity in Ireland. Former Irish Ambassador Dan Mulhall told us that Mulvaney was regarded as a "friend of Ireland" by the Irish Department of Foreign Affairs. Indeed, though some British officials we interviewed claimed that Mulvaney was an unknown quantity at the time of his appointment, he was one of the first people Ambassador Daniel Mulhall met when he arrived in DC in 2017, having already been cultivated by the previous ambassador.

Mulvaney also worked on Irish American issues when he was Trump's acting Chief of Staff. In 2018 he lobbied for the Irish E3 visa legislation that would have transferred 5,000 unused Australian visas to Irish citizens had it passed (O'Dowd, 2018). He also arranged for a plaque to be installed at the Washington Monument commemorating the 1916 uprising (O'Donovan, 2019b), and in September 2019, he tweeted a call for the Brexit arrangement to respect the Belfast/Good Friday Agreement. He also told us that once he became envoy, he would have weekly conversations with William Tranghese in Congressman Richie Neal's office, who was the lead staffer for the Friends of Ireland Caucus.

A practicing Catholic, Mulvaney approached the role of envoy with some wariness of how he would be perceived. According to an interview he did with Ray O'Hanlon of the *Irish Echo*, his primary understanding of the role derived from a conversation with (former envoy) Richard Haass, who Mulvaney said characterized the role of envoy as an honest broker between two sides who benefit from having a "mutual friend" that can "help them work through things" (O'Hanlon, 2020). He had little opportunity to play that role because he was appointed at almost the same moment as the world slipped into quarantine in March 2020. In fact, it was during the American Ireland Fund gala dinner on March 16 that the US announced it was shutting down international flights, leaving Irish, Northern Irish, and British guests in DC for the St. Patrick's Day festivities scrambling to re-arrange their travel home during the dinner.

Despite the lack of opportunity to travel and engage during the pandemic, Mulvaney was widely seen by people we interviewed from Northern Ireland, Ireland, and the US as keeping the Trump Administration informed on the implications of Brexit for Northern Ireland and listening well. As a senior Congressional staffer told us: "Folks in the Irish American community are happy with him. He was a good contact for them in the White House. He would meet with them, be constructive." And Brian O'Dwyer told us: "I don't think anyone else [in the Trump Administration] cared about the issue. But, the fact that he really cared helped." Likewise, the then former Irish Ambassador Dan Mulhall told us in a 2023 interview that the fact that the Trump Administration did not weigh in to support UK positions over Irish ones on Brexit issues was attributable to Mulvaney, who "was very definitely on side with Ireland."

Separately, Mulvaney is also credited with representing these viewpoints to the British, who did not necessarily recognize the extent of his ties to Irish America or the Irish government. Instead, they saw him, not incorrectly in most respects, as ideologically aligned with them and coming from a sympathetic administration. In his capacity as a fellow ideological traveler, Mulvaney could explain to Brexiteers the difficulties of the UK position in Washington in ways that were difficult for them to dismiss. As Ambassador Dan Mulhall explained in our interview:

> Mick Mulvaney went over to Northern Ireland as special envoy, he met the Brexiteers in London, and he told them, "Look, I'm sorry, but I have to disabuse you. The President does not have the power to conclude a trade agreement with you, with anyone, without Congress. So, Congress are in control of a trade agreement like this. That was an important, important, penny that eventually dropped with the Brexiteers in London."

Though COVID-19 kept Mulvaney from fully playing the role he might have envisioned in more normal times, he served in the role during a period when the relationship between the EU and the UK deteriorated and US actors began to re-engage. At the start of 2020, as trade negotiations were in their infancy, the Trump Administration saw no real role for itself beyond encouraging its allies to find a productive way forward that averted a hard border between the Republic and Northern Ireland. As we noted in Chapter 4, Mick Mulvaney told us that while the State Department may have been developing plans and contingencies for a variety of outcomes, rarely did issues of Brexit rise to the level of the Oval Office.[2] However, things changed once the UK government began taking steps in mid-2020 that alarmed Irish Americans.

## The Internal Market Bill

The first such step was a UK government White Paper released in July of 2020, which would soon become the "Internal Market Act."

---

[2] However, he did tell the *Irish Times* in September 2019 that the White House was receiving briefings on Brexit daily and that President Trump was in regular conversation with Prime Minister Johnson (Lynch, 2019c).

According to the government, the bill aimed to resolve potential conflicts that could arise if the devolved governments of the UK were to create different economic regulations post-Brexit. It curtailed the powers of the devolved governments, thus keeping the internal market functioning across the separate regions of the UK.

Other actors outside government saw the bill as an effort to build leverage in the UK-EU negotiations by increasing the stakes if no deal could be reached (Lippman, 2020; Morris, 2020). The proposal was controversial in some parts of the UK, particularly Scotland and Wales. Indeed, the Welsh government has since taken the UK government to court over it. However, the part that drew international and internal condemnation (the House of Lords' own Constitution and EU Committees denounced it) was the portion that would have enabled the UK government to unilaterally override parts of the Withdrawal Agreement pertaining to the Protocol. When pressed about this on the floor of the House of Commons in September 2020, Secretary of State for Northern Ireland (SOSNI) Brandon Lewis offered a stunning answer, admitting that the bill as proposed would "break international law" by violating the Withdrawal Agreement, albeit "in a specific and limited way"! Concern over the breach of international law in the proposal prompted resignations from the head of the UK's legal department, the Advocate General for Scotland, the Prime Minister's special envoy for Freedom of Religion or Belief, and the Prime Minister's special envoy on Media Freedom.

While this was unfolding, the UK was also negotiating its trading relationship with the US. As we discussed in the previous chapter, a key claim of the Brexiteers was that leaving the EU would allow the UK to negotiate separate and better trade deals around the world. The prize deal among them would be a deal with the US—in 2019, the UK shared $270 billion in trade with the US (USTR Press Office, 2020). The UK also had a willing partner in the US. Indeed, the Trump Administration saw a free trade deal as "an opportunity to renegotiate the relationship in its favor: a chance to boost American jobs and economic growth" (Smith, 2019). When he met with Prime Minister Johnson in September 2019, for example, Trump had promised a "massive" and "magnificent" US-UK trade deal (see Bayliss, 2020). And though the US Trade Representative Robert Emmet Lighthizer was not himself known for being supportive of bilateral trade deals in principle (Lawder and Shalal, 2020), the two governments began negotiations on a new trade deal in mid-2020. From May until September, the US and UK held their only post-Brexit formal talks on the trade deal, holding four negotiating sessions before the talks were abruptly cut off, never to restart before 2025.[3]

## Irish America's reaction to the Internal Market Bill

The talks may have ended for any number of reasons, but their abrupt cessation coincided with the formal publication of the Internal Market Bill in September, which produced immediate denunciations from Irish America. Four Members of the House—Elliot Engel, Bill Keating, Richie Neal, and Peter King, the latter two co-chairs of the Friends of Ireland Caucus—immediately sent a letter to Prime Minister Johnson, denouncing the proposed legislation. Speaker Nancy Pelosi also issued strong objections and reiterated these messages when she met with UK Foreign Secretary Dominic Raab in Washington in mid-September.

Joe Biden, at that time campaigning for the presidency, joined the fray as well, warning that the Belfast/Good Friday Agreement could not be allowed to become "a casualty of Brexit" and that any future US-UK trade deal would be "contingent on respect for the Agreement and preventing the return of a hard border" (Smith, 2020). His campaign advisor and future Secretary of State Antony Blinken also tweeted[4] that: "As the UK and EU work out their relationship,

---

[3] In June 2023, the US and the UK agreed on "The Atlantic Declaration," a series of mini-deals providing for economic cooperation across a variety of sectors considered essential for economic security and technology protection, and pledging further talks on cooperation regarding minerals critical to electric vehicles. This was not the promised comprehensive trade deal the Conservatives had promised in their 2019 election manifesto. In October 2023, leaked documents showed that the USTR had developed a draft plan for negotiations for a "foundational" trade agreement that were to commence in October and conclude in the spring of 2024 before general elections took place in both the US and the UK (Lanktree and Bade, 2023). The Biden Administration quietly shelved these plans in December 2023 (Lanktree, 2023).

[4] https://x.com/ABlinken/status/1303463396227063808

any arrangements must protect the Good Friday Agreement and prevent the return of a hard border." While officially and publicly the Trump Administration demurred, with Secretary of State Mike Pompeo saying it was a matter for the UK government to handle, other efforts were afoot to communicate concern. Mick Mulvaney, who was now special envoy, quickly organized his first trip to the UK since his appointment, telling the press that he would discuss COVID-19, economic development, and "the Internal Market Bill and the Northern Ireland Protocol" (Lippman, 2020). The timing of Mulvaney's trip indicates the degree of concern. Although Mulvaney had previously explained to the press that he had not yet traveled to the UK and Ireland as special envoy due to quarantine measures, Daniel Lippman of *Politico* noted the same quarantine restrictions were still in place in Northern Ireland and the Republic when he took his trip in September 2020 (see Lippman, 2020).

Whereas Mulvaney was clear that the Trump White House did not have an official policy on the bill, he used his access to Brandon Lewis to explain the damage the bill could do to UK interests in the US. In our interview with Mulvaney, he recounted what he told Lewis.

> Brandon, there's not a lot of people here who care about Northern Ireland in Washington, DC. Maybe it's five or six people on Capitol Hill. But, those five or six people care a lot, and they pull a lot of weight. When you guys are sitting here talking about a UK-US free trade agreement as a cornerstone of your Brexit long term plan, I want to advocate for that in Washington, DC. But, when you guys cut a deal with somebody, and then unilaterally change it, that makes it really, really hard to deal with you going forward because we wonder if you keep your agreements.

Mulvaney's appeal to Lewis to adjust the government's policy was part of the pressure campaign Irish-America placed on the UK government to revise the Internal Market Bill in a way that protected the Protocol. And there is considerable evidence that American perceptions of the bill mattered to the British. Public statements by candidate Joe Biden and members of Congress were carried and debated in the British press (see Wintour and Boffey, 2020). Foreign

Secretary Dominic Raab was also dispatched to DC within days of the Internal Market Bill's introduction for what some press coverage referred to as a "charm offensive ... to reassure lawmakers about the plans" (Amaro, 2020).

Some of the British press also suggested that Raab and his team were coming to DC to counter the very proactive lobbying of the Irish diplomatic core. *The Guardian*, for example, reported that the then Irish Ambassador to the US, Daniel Mulhall, "has been working the corridors in Washington for the past fortnight." This coverage confirmed that perceptions in Washington were important to the British and that the British were concerned that the Irish were out-diplomating them in DC (Wintour and Boffey, 2020).

## The Biden effect

The success of a UK-EU trade deal was always dependent on the elimination (or significant revision) of the Internal Market Bill. While the UK government argued that the provisions of the Internal Market Bill that breached international law would only come into effect if there was no trade deal at the end of 2020, the EU was wary of striking a deal with a partner that might not honor it in the future.

However, the election of Joe Biden in November altered the calculus for Boris Johnson's government. Biden was far more supportive of the EU than President Trump had been, and his election signaled a significant shift in US foreign policy in favor of re-engaging with US international allies, particularly in Europe. Whereas the UK had been a useful bridge to the EU for the US in the past, being outside of the EU and at odds with the US would leave the UK isolated from important relationships and conversations (see Rahman, 2020). Biden also echoed prominent Irish American law makers in directly tying a future US-UK trade deal to preservation of the Belfast/Good Friday Agreement. This meant that he opposed reimposing a hard border and supported preserving the Northern Ireland Protocol, which the Internal Market Bill threatened to undermine.

By the time Biden was elected in November, the House of Lords had rejected the Internal Market Bill several times, and the government announced a delay on voting in the House of Commons. The move was depicted as a prudent response to Biden's election, with *The Telegraph* suggesting that voting on the bill risked "poisoning" relations with the incoming president (Crisp, 2020). The *Financial Times* also reported that "Senior figures in Westminster" were receiving "pressure from Biden" to alter the bill's provisions (Payne, 2020), and Raab was quoted in *The Guardian* as saying: "We listen very carefully to the concerns of our American friends. Particularly on the Hill in the Irish lobby they feel very invested in the Good Friday Agreement, we understand that" (Elgot, 2020). The Labour Shadow Attorney General also piped up, pointing to the reputational damage that comes with "being called out by the United States government" (Payne, 2020; Walker, 2020).

After Biden won the election, his first European phone call was to Boris Johnson. The press on both sides of the Atlantic described the call as more than a friendly overture between old allies. Numerous outlets suggested that Biden used the conversation to reinforce the message that preserving the Belfast/Good Friday Agreement was important to America. In its coverage, *The Times*, for example, asked whether: "The stance of the Biden administration may encourage ministers to be more flexible in their discussions with the EU" (Wright, 2020). Likewise, *Politico* suggested that "the Biden factor ... tips the scales further in favor of a deal being done" between the UK and the EU on trade (Rahman, 2020). *The Economist* was more direct, describing the content of the call as "an implicit threat": if Johnson did not revise the Internal Market Bill, "Britain would not get a trade deal with America" (*The Economist*, 2020).

There was also considerable internal pressure on the Johnson government to do a deal, especially from the business community that faced enormous uncertainty and objected to entering 2021 with no deal with either of the UK's two closest trading partners: the EU or the US.

## Finishing a difficult year

Irish American began 2020 with a reprieve from the threats Brexit posed to Northern Ireland. Yet, as the Internal Market Bill emerged, Irish America was in a good position to help thwart its passage in the UK parliament. Here again, Irish America's primary influence was to clarify what American interests should be in this context, which was an important move. The Trump Administration was ideologically aligned with Brexiteers, so it seemed unlikely Trump would push back on Johnson's threats to leave the EU without a deal.

Irish America was able to tip the scales in its favor here because Irish Americans in Congress continued to amplify the threat posed to the Belfast/Good Friday Agreement by the Internal Market Bill. Surprisingly, they discovered they could call on backup from inside the Trump administration. From his perch as special envoy, Mulvaney backed up Irish America's message and put their power to prevent a trade deal into sharp relief for recalcitrant Brexiteers. By the time Biden was elected, the British were already on the backfoot, and his strong Irish credentials meant that he could deliver his "implicit threat" with credibility (*The Economist*, 2020).

At the end of 2020, Irish America was able to deliver a consistent message from Congress and the White House. Fortunately, their message aligned with domestic (business) and international actors (Ireland and the EU). Seemingly bowing to pressure from all directions, the UK government agreed in early December 2020 to withdraw the most controversial parts of the Internal Market Bill, paving the way for the EU and the UK to announce a trade deal shortly thereafter.

# 7

# Irish America, Joe Biden, and the Path to the Windsor Framework

Joe Biden may have had a rough start to his presidency stateside, but he had a brief honeymoon on matters relating to Brexit. Indeed, after the UK government amended the Internal Markets Bill, its worst impulses on Brexit seemed to have been constrained. However, the reprieve would be brief. Relations between the UK and the EU began to deteriorate by the end of January 2021 and would kick off Irish America's most intense period of lobbying yet, crystallizing around protecting the Protocol from British actions to undermine it. This lobbying would span two full years.

## A tumultuous 2021

### The Biden Administration

The new Biden Administration offered a ripe audience for Irish American lobbying. President Biden, commonly referred to as the most Irish American president since John F. Kennedy, had extensive familiarity with the conflict in Northern Ireland. Though his family is also English, Biden was raised with a profound sense of Irish cultural identity and has tended to emphasize his Irish ancestry throughout his electoral career. As a new Senator whose wife and small daughter were killed in a car accident a month after his election, Biden's identity was also easily comparable to another Irish Catholic family touched by tragedy. As Biden explained in his 2007 memoir: "The Washington press corps ushered me to town as a kind of poor Kennedy cousin: I was Irish, Catholic, young, toothsome" (Biden, 2007: 107).[1]

As many observers have noted, Biden leaned into his Irish identity to maximize his appeal when talking about a wide variety of issues, including oppression, immigration, discrimination, working-class issues, and underdog politics in general (see Viser, 2021). As Eliot Wilson notes in *The Hill*, Biden's Irishness "places him in a narrative of warm-hearted, hardscrabble community" (Wilson, 2023). His foreign policy stances over his years in office have also affirmed his Irish perspective. When he was a member of the Friends of Ireland Caucus in Congress, for example, he opposed the US/UK Supplemental Extradition Treaty of 1986 that would have permitted suspected IRA members who had fled the UK for the US to be extradited, helping to force changes to the legislation. In 1990, he also proposed a resolution calling on the UK government to reopen the case of the Birmingham Six and encouraged President George H.W. Bush to press Margaret Thatcher on the issue. Documents from the Irish Department of Foreign Affairs indicate that the resolution "put significant pressure on the UK government" (Lynch, 2021b). In 2013 Biden was inaugurated into Irish America's Hall of Fame and in 2016 traveled to Ireland on an official visit as Vice President.

Not surprisingly, Biden carried his Irish American identity and sense of commitments forward as president. In November 2020, just after his election, he was asked by a BBC reporter if he could have a "quick word." Biden quipped, "The BBC? I'm Irish" (Borger, 2021). In his first press conference as president, he also emphasized

---

[1] Niall O'Dowd notes that: "When Biden's first wife Neilia and daughter Naomi were killed in a tragic road crash in December 1972, not long after he was elected to the Senate from Delaware, it was Senator Ted Kennedy who talked him out of quitting and who took care of his political duties until Biden was able to resume" (O'Dowd, 2022). Mariana Alfaro and Matt Viser observed in the *Washington Post* that "Ted Kennedy not only showed Biden the ropes—regularly trekking to Biden's office in Dirksen Senate Office Building—but embodied for Biden the way the Senate should run" (Alfaro and Viser, 2022).

the Irish American culture of grievance and resentment against the British, telling the audience that his family was forced to leave Ireland "because of what the Brits had been doing" (Bennett, 2021). And in one of his first official engagements with the Irish Taoiseach Micheál Martin during St. Patrick's Day festivities in 2021, Biden reportedly told Martin, "I'm a phone call away." The RTE's Paul Cunningham described the remarks as a diplomatic win for Ireland because it indicated that Biden's Irish affections would be "beneficial for the 'old country'" in the new administration (Cunningham, 2021).

Biden also surrounded himself with staff members in key positions who had deep knowledge of Northern Ireland and the peace process. For example, Jake Sullivan, his National Security Advisor, has been quite public about his pride in his Irish American heritage. Through his work as Deputy Chief of Staff to the then Secretary of State Hillary Clinton and as National Policy Director for her campaign in 2008, Sullivan was also familiar with the peace process in Northern Ireland and opportunities for American engagement. In 2019, he signed on to one of the Ad Hoc Committee's first letters to Leo Varadkar and Theresa May. He has also long been a supporter of the Washington Ireland Program (WIP), a leadership training program in the US for youth and community leaders in Ireland and Northern Ireland focused on promoting peace and prosperity. He addressed incoming WIP participants annually for many years and even traveled to Ireland and Northern Ireland on behalf of WIP in 2017.

Other staffers had similar Irish American credentials. Biden's first Deputy Chief of Staff, Jennifer O'Malley Dillon, and his Domestic Policy Council Director, Carmel Martin, both served on the board of the WIP. Dr. Amanda Sloat, the head of the European desk on the National Security Council, did a postdoctoral program at Queen's University, Belfast, and was a member of the Ad Hoc Committee before her appointment. Likewise, Biden's appointee at the United States Agency for International Development, Samantha Power, was born in the UK to Irish parents and raised in Dublin. His Senior Advisor, Mike Donilon, was also Irish American, as was his first Secretary of Labor, Marty Walsh, his White House Cabinet Secretary, Evan Ryan, his Secretary of Veteran's Affairs, Denis McDonough, his Environmental Protection Agency chief, Gina McCarthy, and his Special Advisor for Political Engagement, John McCarthy. The Irish press took note. Suzanne Lynch from the *Irish Times* argued that the fact that there will be "several Irish Americans in president-elect's cabinet" meant that "Ireland's position is stronger [than when President Trump was in office]" (Lynch, 2021b).

## British engagement

Biden's inauguration in late January 2021 coincided with the launch on February 1 of a damning report on British diplomacy in the US produced by Policy Exchange, a London-based think tank. The report sparked a shift in British lobbying in Washington. Policy Exchange was influential in conservative circles and its staff was close to government officials in Boris Johnson's cabinet. Indeed, Michael Gove, then serving as Minister for the Cabinet Office, the third highest-ranking minister in the cabinet, had previously chaired the group.

The report began with a preface from Lord Powell, who distilled the argument, noting that the "British had lost influence with Washington institutions," especially Congress, because of its "declining influence with Europe as a result of Brexit" and its "clumsy presentation of Northern Ireland issues," among other problems (Judah, 2021). In the body of the report, the author, Ben Judah, warned that the British had "a narrative problem in America" (p 9) and pointed to the British failure to explain and defend "the government's view on Northern Ireland and the Brexit problem in Washington against accusations it was endangering the Good Friday Agreement, first over the so-called 'backstop' and then over the Internal Market Bill" (p 8). He implored the UK government to re-engage with Congress and US think tanks, arguing that: "The absence of a strong and proactive British voice on Northern Ireland in Washington recently had an adverse effect on prospects for a UK-US trade deal" (p 17). He also suggested that the British Embassy in DC could take a lesson from the Irish Embassy, which he argued "was highly proactive in engaging with the media, diaspora groups, think tanks and a small number of champions in Congress on the issue" (p 17).

Judah's report carried 20 recommendations, including increasing the staff in Washington to support the ambassador, specifically working on the trade deal, increasing funding (for conferences, policy debates, and international travel), getting cabinet ministers to travel to the US and engage with US media more frequently, and developing tactics that would reshape US perception of British policy on Brexit in particular.

The report hit London at what the *Sunday Times* called "a febrile moment for US-UK relations" (Glancy, 2021). Not only was the UK government seeking to establish itself with the new Biden Administration; it was also still stinging from a diplomatic embarrassment the previous September, when both Nancy Pelosi and Joe Biden tweeted criticisms about the Internal Market Bill while Dominic Raab was in Washington to persuade US policy makers on its merits. The report was studied by 10 Downing Street and the Foreign, Commonwealth and Development Office, and was debated in the British and Irish media (see Glancy, 2021; Sheahan, 2021).

The government issued no official response to the assessment that the British needed to do more to protect its interests in Washington, but signaled in March that it was sending a senior official to DC to communicate the British perspective on events (*Irish News*, 2021). It quickly followed this up with two important appointments. One was the secondment of a member of the Northern Ireland Office, Lyndon Hughes-Jennett, to the British Embassy in Washington in April 2021 as Political Attaché. This new appointment meant that the embassy would now have an attaché with staff working full-time to represent the interests of the British government in Northern Ireland in DC. The second appointment was the creation of a special envoy to the US in June 2021, filled by barrister and former rugby player from Northern Ireland Trevor Ringland. As the new envoy, his job was to promote "Northern Irish interests in Congress, the Biden Administration, and the Irish American community" ("UK Government Appoints Special Envoy to the US on Northern Ireland," 2021).

These appointments were interesting because the Northern Ireland Executive already has an office in DC to represent Northern Ireland interests: the Northern Ireland Bureau (NIB). And, unlike staff for the UK's other devolved governments (Scottish and Welsh), NIB staff are not housed within the British Embassy. The NIB's separate structure was established in response to Nationalist political parties' view that the power-sharing government's interests could not be appropriately represented *from within* the British Embassy.

Given Northern Ireland's existing representation in DC via the NIB, Ringland's appointment suggested two things. First, the position of special envoy was uniquely created to represent British positions on "Northern Irish interests," not Northern Irish interests per se. Second, the tasks of the new position seemed to parallel the shortcomings of British diplomacy identified in the Policy Exchange report, underscoring the extent to which the UK government valued the American perspective and sought to shape it. Indeed, in addition to Ringland's multiple visits, the UK stepped up its other efforts to lobby the US government in DC. Between January 2021 and March 2024, its two SOSNIs visited the US a collective seven times—three visits by Brandon Lewis and four by Chris Heaton-Harris.

## Implementing the Protocol

For many on both sides of the Atlantic, the adoption of the UK-EU trade deal at the end of 2020 was welcomed with a sense of achievement and relief that crisis had been averted. However, its implementation was proving to be enormously complex, and both sides had begun threatening unilateral action. Indeed, less than a month after the UK-EU trade deal was announced in December, the UK government began to publicly distance itself from the Protocol. And by the end of January, news broke that the EU intended to prevent COVID-19 vaccines made in the bloc from being sent to Northern Ireland in order to keep sufficient supply within the EU. This would trigger Article 16, a safeguard built into the Protocol that allows each side to take unilateral measures in violation of the Protocol if its application is likely to lead to "serious economic, societal or environmental difficulties." Although the EU quickly backtracked from the threat to breach the Protocol, the fact that it had even considered the measure fueled already-nascent campaigns in the UK, particularly among Unionists in Northern Ireland, to activate Article 16 and/or to rewrite the Protocol.

Relations deteriorated quickly from there. In early March, the SOSNI announced that the British government was unilaterally extending the grace periods for implementing the new customs checks for several months past the agreed-upon start date in April. The EU responded by triggering a formal infringement process under the Withdrawal Agreement. Thus, the first round of St. Patrick's Day celebrations of the Biden Administration unfolded amid increasing tensions and intense Irish American activism.

*March Madness*

St. Patrick's Day is always a lively time in DC, with numerous events—some informal, some black tie—and plentiful politicians from Ireland, Northern Ireland, and Britain. In 2022 Pat Leahy and Martin Wall described DC's St. Patrick's celebrations in the *Irish Times* as a one-day holiday that has stretched into a week of events:

> It's the best week of the year to be Irish in Washington, an annual flexing of the diplomatic and political muscle the country enjoys in the world capital of politics. This is true even when the president is less conspicuously Irish American; with the most Irish president ever in the Oval Office, the Irish clout is off the charts. (Leahy and Wall, 2022b)

As Leahy observed, "St Patrick's Day offers an unbuyable opportunity to project Irish soft power and influence" (Leahy, 2022).

The first St. Patrick's holiday of President Biden's Administration was especially eventful, even if most of the regularly held affairs were canceled and the others occurred online due to COVID-19. On Capitol Hill, the Irish Minister for Foreign Affairs Simon Coveney and the European Commission's Vice President Maroš Šefčovič briefed the Congressional Friends of Ireland Caucus on the tensions over Brexit the week before St. Patrick's. Then, on March 16, Senators Susan Collins (R-ME) and Robert Menendez (D-NJ), in a strong showing of bipartisanship, introduced a resolution with 13 co-sponsors, reaffirming the US government's support for the Belfast/Good Friday Agreement and asserting that the Protocol was necessary to "protect the peace forged" by it. The resolution explicitly stated that the reintroduction of "barriers, checkpoints or personnel on the island of Ireland," as a consequence of Brexit, "including through the invocation of Article 16 of the Northern Ireland Protocol, would threaten the successes of the Good Friday Agreement."

The resolution also referred to other, as of yet unmet, obligations in the Belfast/Good Friday Agreement and subsequent agreements, such as the 2014 Stormont House Agreement, which called for new mechanisms for addressing the legacy of the Troubles. And as it did in 2020, Irish Americans in Congress tied protection of the agreement, now widened to include legacy issues, to a trade deal, noting that the Senate "will take into account, as relevant, conditions requiring that obligations under the Good Friday Agreement be met as the United States seeks to negotiate a mutually advantageous and comprehensive trade agreement between the United States and the United Kingdom" (US Senate, 2021). It passed the Senate in May as Senate Resolution 117 by unanimous consent with 16 co-sponsors.

The Biden White House began its first "March madness" with White House press secretary Jen Psaki commenting on the ongoing dispute about the Protocol by asserting that President Biden "is 'unequivocal' in his support for the Good Friday Agreement" (*Irish News*, 2021).[2] Though his joint statement with the Taoiseach on March 17 did not mention the Protocol specifically, instead calling for "the good faith implementation of international agreements designed to address the unique circumstances on the island of Ireland," his staff made his position clear, and the message was received in Belfast. Indeed, Sam McBride noted in the *Belfast News Letter* that Unionists viewed Biden's comments as counter to their interests:[3]

> Just hours before Mr Biden met virtually with the Taoiseach for St Patrick's Day, one of the President's senior officials told the *News Letter* that the new occupant of the Oval Office supports the Northern Ireland Protocol which creates the new GB-NI trade frontier. That highly unusual and significant statement places the US on the same side of the debate as Sinn Féin, the SDLP, Alliance, the Green Party, the Irish government,

---

[2] Nationalists and Unionists have different interpretations of the Protocol. Nationalists believe that it kept the Belfast/Good Friday Agreement intact, while Unionists argue that it contravened the agreement and needed revision.

[3] When the reporter asked the Biden official to explain why he was "picking sides," the official replied: "The US administration is not looking to take sides in this agreement; the Northern Ireland Protocol is something that was legally binding, that was agreed to by both sides and there was support for it here as a way to manage the practical challenges around the EU single market while preventing a return of a hard border" (McBride, 2021).

the EU and Boris Johnson's government – but directly opposing the position of all the unionist parties, who are campaigning to remove the protocol. (McBride, 2021)

President Biden also conveyed support for the Protocol directly when he met with First Minister Arlene Foster and deputy First Minister Michelle O'Neill on March 17 (The White House, 2021).

## Back at home

As the differing views about the Protocol among Nationalists and Unionists detailed earlier suggest, Unionist leaders' opposition to the Protocol grew stronger in 2021 as it was being implemented. The DUP and other unionists, principal among them David Trimble, who had won the Nobel Peace Prize jointly with John Hume for their work on the Belfast/Good Friday Agreement, challenged the legality of the Protocol in two separate cases. The DUP released a five-step plan to thwart the implementation of the Protocol and attempted to force a parliamentary debate on the topic by garnering 100,000 signatures on a petition in February 2021. The DUP's Brexit spokesperson also pledged in February to use "guerrilla warfare" against the Protocol (Hutton, 2024). Then the DUP minister in charge of creating the infrastructure for the new border checks ordered staff to stop work and ceased hiring for new positions, further escalating tensions between the Unionists and the UK government.

On the ground, Loyalists also protested the Protocol, using posters, graffiti, and social media to express their anger. Then, in April, a brief but intense period of street violence erupted in Loyalist neighborhoods, a situation *The Guardian* described as "the most dangerous for years" (O'Carroll and Walker, 2021). Shortly thereafter, the Loyalist Communities Council, an umbrella group representing Loyalist paramilitary groups, sent a letter to Prime Minister Johnson, saying that they were withdrawing their support for the Belfast/Good Friday Agreement.[4]

---

[4] This was a significant move. Both the political parties connected to the Ulster Volunteer Force and the Ulster Defence Association were signatories of the agreement.

Fortunately, community leaders succeeded in calming the immediate situation. The Northern Ireland Executive issued a statement condemning the violence, as did the UK and Irish governments in a joint statement. In May the two governments announced they would hold the first meeting in two years of the British-Irish Intergovernmental Conference, a creation of the Belfast/Good Friday Agreement that had been suspended during the Brexit negotiations. However, periodic episodes of violence continued through the summer and fall, as did Loyalist protests, with regular, weekly rallies beginning in September 2021. The DUP continued its pressure campaign as well, suspending participation of their ministers in North-South Ministerial Council in May and eventually withdrawing from the Northern Ireland Executive entirely in February 2022, triggering the collapse of the Northern Ireland Assembly for the next two years.

## *Mr. Biden goes to Britain*

The violence in Northern Ireland in April 2021 shocked many on both sides of the Atlantic. It prompted a meeting of the Friends of Ireland Caucus and statements from various members of Congress condemning the violence and pointing to the need for economic development. The White House and State Departments also expressed concern.

In the face of Unionist and Loyalist retrenchment, Irish America responded with additional pressure. In May the House Foreign Affairs Subcommittee on Europe, Energy, the Environment and Cyber, under the Chairmanship of Bill Keating (D-MA) hosted a hearing entitled at "Reaffirming the Good Friday Agreement." The same week, the AOH wrote to Congressman Keating calling for a signal that the US is committed to the full implementation of the Belfast/Good Friday Agreement and asking that the committee request President Biden appoint a special envoy for Northern Ireland.[5]

---

[5] The envoy role was not filled until December 2022. News reports suggest the administration decided to delay the appointment until after both the new Irish and British ambassadors were in place (IrishCentral Staff, 2022). In the interim, Irish America continued to press President Biden on the envoy (*Irish Echo* Staff, 2022).

Congressman Keating then initiated a letter to President Biden with 25 co-signatories.[6]

In June 2021, Biden traveled to the UK for the G7 summit and held a bilateral meeting with Prime Minister Johnson. It was another opportunity for Irish America to press the UK government on the Protocol. The meeting came at a particularly low point in UK-EU relations as both governments were expressing frustration with each other over issues related to the implementation of the Protocol, and commentators were speculating that the two seemed to be headed toward "a full-scale trade war" (Crisp and Yorke, 2021). Pat Leahy, Political Editor for the *Irish Times*, explained the fault line this way: "The EU is accusing the UK of reneging on an agreement, and warns that it will take legal steps to seek redress. The UK's position is that the EU has adopted a more legalistic and nitpicking approach than the UK thought it would when it agreed the protocol" (Leahy, 2021b).

Considerable speculation and energy surrounded the trip as various Irish American groups called on Biden to communicate a strong position on the Protocol to Prime Minister Johnson. The Ad Hoc Committee in particular urged Biden "to stand up for the Good Friday Agreement and assert American leadership" (O'Donovan, 2021). Citing anonymous sources, *The Times* reported that the President would "explicitly express America's support for the Northern Ireland protocol" and warn Johnson "not to renege on the Northern Ireland Brexit deal," which the US saw as "as an integral part of maintaining long-term peace in Northern Ireland and in particular the Good Friday Agreement." It was also reported that he would "warn that the prospects of the US trade deal with the UK will be damaged if the situation remains unresolved" (Wright and Charter, 2021). Jake Sullivan, the National Security Advisor, went on to tell the BBC that "Biden has 'deep' concerns that a UK-EU trade row could endanger peace in Northern Ireland," insisting that in the context of the US/UK trade deal, "he was not trying to 'negotiate in public' or issue a 'warning' to Boris Johnson's

---

[6] In an address to Irish Americans in New York City, the Irish Foreign Minister, Simon Coveney, indicated his government's support for the appointment (see Lynch, 2021b).

government, but merely stating 'how the president feels about this issue'" (BBC, 2021b).

Despite Sullivan's cautious language in the BBC interview, as Biden arrived in London, *The Times* reported that US Chargé d'Affaires Yael Lempert had issued Lord Frost, the UK's Brexit Minister, with a *démarche* (a formal diplomatic reprimand) in advance of Biden's visit (Maguire and Wright, 2021). *The Times* reported that Lempert told Frost the issue was "commanding the attention" of her boss and urged "the UK to come to a 'negotiated settlement' with the EU, even if that meant making 'unpopular compromises.'" Lempert was also said to have told Frost that "the [UK] government was 'inflaming' tensions in Ireland and Europe with its opposition to checks at ports in the province" (Maguire and Wright, 2021).

The Biden Administration denied that it had sent a formal *démarche*, instead describing Lempert's letter as simply "laying out of long-standing US concerns" that Brexit not undermine the Northern Ireland's peace agreement or "the two decades of progress stabilizing the border" (Bennett, 2021). White House officials said that Biden just wanted to deliver the message that "he believes very, very deeply about peace in Northern Ireland" (Bennett, 2021). After Biden's meeting with Johnson, Jake Sullivan told the press that Biden shared his thoughts with "deep sincerity" and "may have delivered his message with some feeling" (Cordon, 2021). Conservative media outlets responded with anger. *The Telegraph* went with the following headline: "Joe Biden Should Keep His Sneering Anti-British, Anti-Brexit Views to Himself" (Gardiner, 2021).

In June 2021, US Trade Representative Katherine Tai also met with Lord Frost and further signaled that securing a trade deal was contingent on accepting the Protocol. The *Irish Times* characterized the situation as "Having applied a wrecking ball to the UK-Ireland and the UK-EU relationship," noting that "Brexit is now taking its toll on the 'special relationship'" (Leahy, 2021b).

## *Tensions build: July–December*

Brexit continued to take a toll on the "special relationship" throughout the remainder of 2021. Despite the drama surrounding Biden's visit (Abbas, Bradley, and Symington, 2021; Leebody, 2021), it appeared that American pressure was having little effect. Indeed, the situation between the UK and the EU continued to deteriorate, and the UK government moved even further away from commitments it had made previously.

By mid-summer, commentators such as Denis Staunton in the *Irish Times* argued that pressure from the US was not translating into changes to policy so much as changes to communication. The new goal was to shift blame:

> British officials are more dismissive than before of the role of Irish American politicians in influencing the Biden administration's approach to the protocol. They are confident that, if they avoid unilateral actions that are in clear breach of international law, they can persuade the US that European intransigence rather than British backsliding is responsible for the impasse. (Staunton, 2021)

Within days of Staunton's prescient assessment, the UK government issued two command papers that directly contrasted with American positions: one on the legacy issue (which we will discuss in more detail in Chapter 8) and one on rewriting the Protocol. In the latter, "Northern Ireland Protocol: The Way Forward," the UK government demanded a renegotiation of the Protocol, asserting that border checks on goods from Great Britain to Northern Ireland "had proved unsustainable." Specifically, they were "harming business and were damaging the 'fabric' of the UK" (BBC, 2021a). The command paper demanded the end of all customs checks on goods moving from Great Britain to Northern Ireland and the end of EU court jurisdiction over disputes over the Protocol (Secretary of State for Northern Ireland, 2021).

When he introduced the command paper to the House of Lords, Lord Frost went further, arguing that the conditions had been met for the UK to trigger Article 16, but that it was "not the right moment to do so" (BBC, 2021a). The EU responded later that day with a series of proposals, working within the framework of the Protocol, but they fell on deaf ears. In a speech to the British-Irish Association in September, for example, Lord Frost declared that partial "solutions which involve 'flexibilities' within the current rules won't work" for the UK government ("Lord Frost Speech at

British-Irish Association: 4 September 2021," 2021). Prime Minister Johnson followed this up in late September, saying that the Protocol must be either "fixed or ditched" (*Irish Times*, 2021).

The US response to the British command paper on the Protocol came in September with high level US-UK meetings in London, New York, and Washington. First, Speaker of the House Nancy Pelosi traveled to the UK, where she had meetings with numerous officials, including Prime Minister Johnson. In her meeting with Johnson, she delivered a stark message: walking out of talks on the Northern Ireland protocol would prove "problematic" for striking a trade deal (Zeffman, 2021).

Days later, Johnson and Liz Truss, who was at that time the new Foreign Secretary, flew to the US for the opening of the UN General Assembly and, afterwards, met with President Biden in DC. The press described the meeting as a "charm offensive" (Stewart, 2021b) designed to repair the "frayed" relationship and reverse what some Conservative MPs had called a "disastrous deterioration in transatlantic relations" (Stewart, 2021a; Stewart and Sabbagh, 2021). The two leaders spoke of cooperation on climate change and other matters, but Biden warned Johnson "not to abandon the Northern Ireland protocol" (Zeffman, Charter and Wright, 2021). Although he did not expressly link a trade deal to UK government policy, Biden also didn't dispel the notion that the trade deal wasn't a top priority for the US at the time. In other meetings that week, the UK government team was "understood to have urged Biden's team to re-energise trade talks between the two countries," pointing out that the UK's recently signed trade deals with Canada and Mexico meant it had closer trading relations with those two countries, despite the special relationship (Stewart, 2021a). However, Biden would not be drawn on this in public and would only comment that they would discuss "trade 'a little bit', adding: 'We're going to have to work that through'" (Zeffman, Charter, and Wright, 2021).

In October, when Lord Frost set a deadline of November for a solution to the disagreement with the EU over the Protocol, National Security Advisor Jake Sullivan told the BBC that the US had "significant concern" about the British approach:

> [T]he two sides should work together in a constructive way to find a deal and a way forward ... Without

something like the Northern Ireland Protocol and with the possibility of the return of a hard border between NI and the Republic of Ireland, we will have a serious risk to stability and to the sanctity of the Good Friday Agreement. (Wilcock, 2021)

In November, Biden met with European Commission President Ursula von der Leyen in DC. After the meeting, she reaffirmed for the press that "the EU's position on Northern Ireland has the support of the US president." Later that afternoon, the White House issued a statement saying that both leaders "expressed their continued support for political and economic stability in Northern Ireland" (Boffey and Walker, 2021). However, concerns that the UK government was preparing to introduce Article 16 remained high (Leahy, 2021a).

Later in November, the Ad Hoc Committee issued a statement on the British threats. Senators Chris Murphy and Pat Toomey also wrote a letter to Boris Johnson expressing the "strong interest in Congress" to see a negotiated solution on the Protocol that would protect the Belfast/Good Friday Agreement and would preserve "peace and stability in Northern Ireland" (Murphy, 2021). Four members of the House of Representatives, all chairs of important committees/subcommittees (Gregory W. Meeks, William R. Keating, Earl Blumenauer, and Brendan Boyle), issued a statement calling on the UK government "to commit to implementing the Northern Ireland Protocol in full" (Carr, 2021). The statement referred specifically to recent British threats to walk away from the Protocol: "In threatening to invoke Article 16 of the Northern Ireland Protocol, the United Kingdom threatens to not only destabilize trade relations, but also that hard-earned peace." The Ad Hoc Committee then quickly issued a follow-up statement in support of the one released by Meeks and his colleagues (O'Shea, 2021a).

Amid this increasing drumbeat of statements, the US made its boldest and most direct move. In early December the *Financial Times* reported that the US Commerce Department had sent a letter to the UK government suspending talks to remove Trump-era steel and aluminum tariffs, which the US had lifted on EU trade in October but had left in place for the UK: "In a communication seen by *The Financial Times*, a US commerce department official stated that talks with the UK on easing metals tariffs could not move ahead. The official cited US concerns about UK threats to trigger Article 16" (Williams and Bound, 2021).

The *Financial Times* also reported that: "Three people familiar with the matter also said that talks were stuck after pressure from Congress over the UK's threats to trigger the clause," although the National Security Council denied any link between the talks and the UK's position on the Protocol (see Williams and Bound, 2021).

*Politico* also covered the issue and quoted trade expert Sam Lowe of Flint Global on the state of play: "While it's not the only reason the U.K. is finding it difficult to agree a deal with the U.S. to remove steel and aluminum tariffs, as the EU has done, the ongoing standoff over Northern Ireland is certainly making it more difficult" (Casalicchio, 2021).

*Politico* also reported that an insider in the Department for International Trade said that even though the Brexit dustup had nothing to do with the Protocol, it was acting as "political blocks" to an agreement between Washington and London" (Casalicchio, 2021). In *The Hill*, Woodrow Wilson Center fellow Diana Villiers Negroponte offered a blunter assessment, describing the cancellation of talks as "a slap in UK Prime Minister Boris Johnson's face" (Villiers, 2021).

Moreover, though International Trade Secretary Anne-Marie Trevelyan, traveled to Washington, and Junior Trade Minister Penny Mordaunt toured Western states in December, the US declined to restart talks into January 2022 (Casalicchio, 2022). The UK government thus ended 2021 without the bilateral trade deal it coveted.

In fact, in an ironic turn of fate, the UK could not even secure the same tariff relief on trade in steel and aluminum that it would have enjoyed had it had stayed in the EU. Though 2021 saw the signing of a new defense and security treaty between Australia, the UK, and the US (AUKUS), the relationship between the Johnson government and the Biden Administration was strained. As Leslie Vinjamuri observed in *Foreign Affairs* at the beginning of 2022:

> [U]nresolved questions about the future of Northern Ireland have fueled instability in British relations not just with Europe but also with the United States. Johnson's inability to resolve the uncertainty over the Irish border

> ... has contributed to an atmosphere of mistrust between him and an Irish Catholic U.S. president who is deeply committed to the 1998 Good Friday Agreement. (Vinjamuri, 2022)

As 2021 concluded, tensions remained high and Irish America remained highly active. Indeed, it had been a busy year. Over the course of 2021, the Ad Hoc Committee held 25 meetings with high-level British, Irish, and American officials, most of them requested by the officials themselves. The AOH had also "made the defense of the Good Friday Agreement its number one priority" (FitzGerald, 2021), ramping up its letter-writing campaigns and other means of lobbying Congress. Irish America also founded at least two new organizations—the American Irish State Legislators Caucus (AISLC) and the Young Friends of Ireland Group—in intentional efforts to grow interest and engagement in Irish affairs in the US, with the AISLC specifically committing itself to protecting "the peace process as a cornerstone of our ongoing mission" in its founding documents ("American Ireland State Legislators Caucus: About," no date). Both of these organizations were designed to build up a next generation of Irish Americans, the first by creating a pipeline of state legislators who could eventually run for Congress (see Moore, 2021), and the second by creating a civil society organization of youth.

Members of the Congressional Friends of Ireland Caucus and other Members of Congress also wrote directly to Prime Minister Johnson on multiple occasions, and the Senate passed a resolution urging a change in tack from the UK government on the Protocol. Members also held hearings, sent open letters to the US Secretary of State, traveled to the UK, and planned a Congressional delegation (CODEL) to Ireland/Northern Ireland for 2022.

The White House also played an active role in communicating its concerns about British policy on the Protocol, and it did so in frank terms, both publicly (in the press) and behind closed doors (in Lempert's *démarche*). And, though British officials asserted that they would not be swayed by American pressure, they also increased their lobbying efforts in the US. The addition of a NIO political attaché inside the embassy and a new special envoy clearly signaled British concerns about how they were perceived in Washington and their desire to change American views on the Protocol.

## 2022: a war on Europe's border brings focus

*Russia invades Ukraine*

The year 2022 began with a familiar pattern: Irish America (in and outside of government) pressing the British government to change course through formal statements and interviews with the press. However, in February, the Russian invasion of Ukraine shifted the calculus for all four main actors—the US, Ireland, the UK, and the EU. In particular, the invasion clarified the threat Russia posed to the West and to Europe. It spurred a Western response that was quick and surprisingly unified. And almost overnight, as the stakes were raised, the room for disagreement between the US, UK and EU governments shrank. As one Biden Administration official told the *Irish Times*: "Transatlantic unity and UK/EU unity is so critical to achieving our shared objectives in Ukraine" (Wall, 2022c).

Despite calls for unity, the conflict over the Protocol intensified in the first half of 2022, with the British introducing new legislation to override the Protocol midway through the year and the EU threating to retaliate. While the US continued to press the UK to find common ground with the EU in implementing the Protocol, it also began to frame the issue in terms of the need for Western unity.[7] In May, the *New York Times* reported that Derek Chollet, Counselor of the US Department of State, told the UK government that forcing a trade clash with the EU "could weaken the West's solidarity in helping Ukraine turn back the Russian onslaught" (Landler, 2022). *Politico* quoted an EU official saying that "Biden is taking an even keener interest in the row [between the EU and the UK] to avoid splits in Western unity amid the war in Ukraine. 'They don't want any wrong messages going to President Putin'" (Casalicchio, Lanktree, and Whale, 2022).

---

[7] The Russian invasion of Ukraine also complicated the US relationship with Ireland. Specifically, the Irish government's longstanding commitment to neutrality, which it declared at the outbreak of the Second World War and has maintained ever since, caused tensions between the two countries at a moment when they were both laser-focused on protecting the Protocol (see Boulter, 2023; Everett, 2023).

Some commentators speculated that the war might, in the end, bring the two countries back together and put Ireland back in its historic place as a "secondary" player. During the 2022 St. Patrick's Week, Martin Wall observed in the *Irish Times* that:

> Some figures who are very familiar with Capitol Hill expressed fears privately during the week that the Ukraine war could reawaken cold war-style sentiments that the strategic interests of the US may be best served by closer alignment to the UK given the traditional military and security links ….Shortly afterwards former Trump national security adviser John Bolton popped up with an article essentially arguing that Ireland had nothing to offer from a security perspective and Washington needed a politically strong UK to lead NATO. (Wall, 2022d)

As the war progressed into the spring, the US and the UK both leaned into the common effort to help Ukraine defend itself, and the relationship appeared to warm up again as a result. The *New York Times*, for example, commented that: "The close collaboration has given new purpose to a 'special relationship' that, by many accounts, had drifted since Brexit" (Landler, 2022). *Politico* also reported on the warming, quoting a UK government official saying that the war had improved the US-UK relationship, noting "[the US has] been less aggressive about it [UK policy on the Protocol] and the bilateral working on Ukraine has helped. We definitely seem to be running scared less than we used to when it comes to Washington" (Casalicchio, Lanktree, and Whale, 2022). More evidence of the *détente* emerged in March, when the Biden Administration lifted the steel and aluminum tariffs on imports from the UK and began a "series of 'dialogues'" with the British on ways to improve bilateral trade (see Morales, 2022).

However, this thawing of the relationship was primarily felt in interactions with the Executive Branch. In fact, British officials were quoted in the *New York Times* in May 2022 as saying that "the subject [of Brexit's implications for the peace process in Northern Ireland] comes up far less in conversations with the White House than on Capitol Hill" (Landler, 2022). Despite the *détente* at the executive level, pressure on the British continued to build in Congress throughout 2022. On January 28, Congressman Bill Keating (D-MA) and 35 co-sponsors introduced a House resolution calling for justice for the Bloody Sunday victims, along with the full implementation of the Belfast/Good Friday Agreement and the Protocol. The final text of the resolution stated that "the avoidance of a hard border on the island of Ireland is essential for maintaining the peace" (US House, 2022). The resolution also called on all parties to act "in good faith" in their dealings on Brexit, a not-so-subtle jab at the British threat to withdraw from the Protocol. HR 888 passed by unanimous consent on March 17, with 50 co-sponsors (US House, 2021). The Ad Hoc Committee and the AOH were instrumental in garnering support for the resolution (Wall, 2022a). In gratitude, the AOH took out a full-page ad in the *Irish Echo* thanking members of Congress for their support the next day. The British were watching. The *Irish Times* reported that the UK government had lobbied Congress to alter language in the resolution: "It is understood that the British embassy in Washington contacted the staff of politicians on Capitol Hill with their concerns about the proposal. Sources said the British side had raised 'technical legal issues' about the text. But these were largely rebuffed" (Leahy and Wall, 2022a).

HR 888 was also rushed through the typical processes so that its passage would coincide with the upcoming St. Patrick's March madness, which in President Biden's second year in office was mostly held in-person. During that week, among other activities, the Taoiseach met with the President, where he described the West's defense of Europe as a common struggle between "autocracies and democracies," and added that it was a fight on which Ireland was anything but neutral (Leahy, 2022). He also met with Congressman Richie Neal.

At the American Ireland Funds gala dinner on March 16, Neal and Speaker Pelosi both told the marquee crowd that there would be no US-UK trade deal if the British moved to undermine the Belfast/Good Friday Agreement, a point that President Biden made repeatedly as well and that Congressman Neal reiterated in an interview with *The Guardian* (see O'Carroll, 2022). Senators Dick Durbin (D-IL) and Pat Toomey (R-PA) also introduced legislation to create 5,000 more visas for Irish citizens. Senator Robert Menendez (R-NJ) issued a statement encouraging the full implementation of the Belfast/Good Friday Agreement and expressing concern about the UK government's threats to trigger Article 16 and its plans to introduce amnesty legislation for Troubles-era crimes (Targeted News Service, 2022).

## The Northern Ireland Protocol Bill

As has been alluded to earlier, the situation intensified in May when the UK announced its intention to introduce legislation to override the Protocol through domestic legislation (the Northern Ireland Protocol Bill) and unveiled the Northern Ireland Troubles Legacy and Reconciliation Bill, which we will discuss in Chapter 8. The plans for the Protocol Bill, as sketched out by Foreign Secretary Liz Truss to Parliament in mid-May, would have allowed:

> ministers unilaterally to reduce customs checks and food-safety controls on goods moving from Great Britain to Northern Ireland that are not bound for Ireland or the rest of the EU single market; to let Northern Ireland benefit from value added tax (VAT) policies applied to the rest of the UK; and to allow Northern Irish firms to produce goods according to British standards. (Gallardo, 2022a)

The legislation would also give the UK the power to determine how disputes would be settled, re-introducing the idea of removing the European Court of Justice from any role in conflict resolution. While the proposed bill fit the agenda of the more strident Brexiteers in the Tory Party, it was also widely recognized as a gesture to appease Unionists in Northern Ireland, making it possible for them to return to Stormont, which they had left in February, triggering the collapse of the institutions and new elections.

Not surprisingly, from the moment that these plans were first leaked in mid-May, they were denounced by multiple American policy makers. Speaker of the House Nancy Pelosi immediately issued a statement on Twitter condemning British threats to override the Protocol, again connecting them to the potential trade deal (Landler, 2022; McGrath, 2022). She warned: "As I have stated in my conversations with the prime minister, the foreign secretary and members of the House of Commons, if the United Kingdom chooses to undermine the Good Friday Accords, the Congress cannot and will not support a bilateral free trade agreement with the United Kingdom" (McGrath, 2022). The position was reiterated by Congressman Bill Keating (D-MA), a member of the Foreign Affairs Committee and Chair of its subcommittee on Europe, who spoke of "a step backwards in terms of trade relations" (see Casalicchio et al, 2022). Trump's former Special Envoy to Northern Ireland, Mick Mulvaney, also repeated the warning he gave to Brandon Lewis about the Internal Market Bill in 2020: "if folks start unilaterally changing an agreement, it makes it difficult to move forward on future deals" (Goodall, 2022). Derek Chollet, Senior Advisor to US Secretary of State Antony Blinken, also cautioned both sides to "refrain from unilateral acts" (Savage, 2022) and urged them to "lower the temperature" (Landler, 2022).

When the legislation was formally announced in mid-June, the Congressional Friends of Ireland issued a statement, with Senator Robert Menendez calling the move "irresponsible" and saying it "threatened" the peace. The Biden Administration agreed, condemning the move and urging the UK to "resolve its issues with the EU" (Bond, 2022). Senate Majority Leader Chuck Schumer likewise "warned that 'rash, unilateral actions' that threatened international agreements would undermine support in Congress for any bilateral trade proposal" (Wall, 2022c). Secretary of State Antony Blinken also raised the proposal with Foreign Secretary Liz Truss (Wall, 2022c), while the United States Trade Representative (USTR) Katherine Tai raised it with British International Trade Secretary Anne-Marie Trevelyan on the sidelines of the WTO ministerial conference in Geneva (Stacey, 2022). The Ad Hoc Committee also strongly criticized the British move in a public statement (Whelan, 2022), going so far as to accuse the British of acting in "bad faith" and urging President Biden "to suspend any talks on trade until the protocol legislation was rescinded" (Wall, 2022d).

The timing of the news about the Protocol legislation could not have been worse from a diplomatic perspective. First, as we noted earlier, the US and the UK had begun a series of conversations on bilateral trade (albeit not a restoration of the official trade negotiations that had occurred in 2020), and the UK's International Trade Secretary Anne-Marie Trevelyan had even begun suggesting that a full bilateral trade agreement would be possible by the end of 2022 (see Milligan, 2022b). Many observers noted that the legislation would likely produce a backlash on trade. "Just cutting off these nascent trade dialogues doesn't really seem to move the needle," said Garrett Workman, a senior director of European affairs at the US-UK Business Council. "So there might be pressure to do more than that" (Casalicchio, Lanktree, and Whale, 2022). Others argued that the Biden Administration would be "passive-aggressive": "The response will be very subtle and it will be hard to decipher," explained Alexander Bobroske, an expert on relations between the UK, the US, and the EU at the Global Counsel advisory firm. " 'I don't think it would be anything explicitly said,' he noted—but brace for 'foot-dragging' on trade ties into the summer as Biden's team waits to see how the spat unfolds" (Casalicchio, Lanktree, and Whale, 2022).

When the legislation was finally introduced in June, senior Biden Administration officials told *The Guardian* that while "it is true that there is no formal linkage between the protocol and a free trade agreement ... the current situation does not create a conducive environment" for negotiating a trade deal (O'Carroll and Borger, 2022), a message reiterated in September by the President Biden's Press Secretary Karine Jeanne-Pierre (BBC, 2022).

Second, the timing was unfavorable for the British because it coincided with a long-planned CODEL from the House Ways and Means Committee to continental Europe, the UK, and Ireland in May. Before arriving in London, as part of the EU-US Inter-Parliamentary Meeting's Transatlantic Parliamentary Dialogue, the delegation signed a joint statement with the EU calling on "the government of the United Kingdom to implement fully the Northern Ireland Protocol, which avoids a hard border on the Island of Ireland, preserves the integrity of the EU Internal Market and protects the Good Friday Agreement in all its parts." The statement went on to assert that "renegotiating the Protocol is not an option" and "Only joint solutions will work" (EU-US IPM, 2022). The delegation then traveled to the UK and Ireland, where Congressman Neal gave a strong speech to the Oireachtas in which he said that the delegation's message was "firm, clear and unambiguous": "the number one priority for the US on this island is to ensure that the hard-won peace in Northern Ireland is preserved and reinforced" (*RTÉ News*, 2022). Later, in an interview with the *Irish Times*, Neal also pointed to Britain's growing credibility problem in the international sphere:

"I don't think that there ought to be an arbitrary decision to abandon the protocol without negotiation. I think abrogating an international treaty is not only bad faith but it sends ... the wrong message ... that expediency takes place over all" (Carswell, 2022).

From Dublin, the nine-member CODEL traveled to Northern Ireland, where they met with the leaders of all of the parties. The group's meeting with the DUP was reported to be tense, given the delegation's statements. The DUP was also smarting over Chairman Neal's indelicate comments in Dublin that the conflict over the Protocol had been "manufactured" and that if the problems really were about trade, they could be "ironed out quickly" (Carroll, 2022; *RTÉ News*, 2022). Past, present, and future DUP leaders and the leader of the UUP, Doug Beattie, all made public denunciations of the CODEL (PA Reporter, 2022; Preston, 2022). DUP MLA Diane Dodds even filed a formal complaint with the House Ways and Means Committee about Congressman Neal's comments (Leebody, 2022).

Third, the timing ended up highlighting the failure of the UK's heightened diplomacy stateside. In May, for example, Prime Minister Johnson appointed Conor Burns as his Special Representative to the US on the Northern Ireland Protocol and dispatched him to Boston and Washington. Burns' mission was to "bend ears over the UK predicament" and to convince "a skeptical White House that the protocol needed to change" (Elgot, 2022). Burns met with Members of Congress, the administration and Irish American groups, including the Ad Hoc Committee. Though he "told reporters he believed Britain's message was getting through" (Landler, 2022), when asked about his trip on ITV in June, he couldn't name a single American supporter of the legislation (Hickey, 2022).

The poor results were unsurprising. While Burns was in the US in May, the plans to introduce the Protocol legislation were leaked. *The Guardian* reported that "US diplomats and key lawmakers fumed at being blind-sided," no doubt, undermining Burns' credibility and that of the government he served (Elgot, 2022). However, even before the leak, *The Times* reported that Burns had "struggled to persuade the Biden administration of Britain's case" and that he and his team adjusted their tact and tone "after Washington warned him against 'theatre' over the issue" (Smyth, Waterfield, and Charter, 2022).

Burns, for his part, took a firm line, asserting that the UK government would never cave in to US pressure and denying any connection between the bilateral trade deal his government sought and the Northern Ireland Protocol (Gutteridge and Crisp, 2022). Yet, he made multiple trips to the US over the next few months in the hope of persuading Americans of the Johnson government's position.

Despite Burns' comments to the contrary, the extent to which the British felt pressure from the Americans on the proposed legislation was commonly cited in the news coverage. *Politico* noted that Brussels was "confident that it has Biden on its side in the row" and as one EU official said, "the threat of retaliation from Washington acts as a 'game changer'" (Casalicchio, Lanktree, and Whale, 2022). In the immediate aftermath of the leaks about the Protocol plans, commentators in *The Times* observed that there appeared to be a row *within* the Johnson government about how to proceed—evidence that the US pressure campaign was working (Smyth, Waterfield, and Charter, 2022). After the leak, *Politico* also reported that the UK government "may have cooled its jets amid fears of a US backlash" (Casalicchio, Lanktree, and Whale, 2022). Similarly, the *Irish News* ran commentary discussing the role of American pressure in postponing the legislation (Manley, 2022).

Despite the pressure campaign, the Johnson government would go on to introduce the Northern Ireland Protocol legislation in the House of Commons in June. However, many reporters refused to take the move too seriously, instead seeing the bill as part of the familiar, hardball negotiating strategy by the Johnson government. *The Guardian*, for example, suggested as much even before the legislation had been released:

> Those with even medium-term memories will remember a similar tactic on the internal markets bill and its plans to break international law "in a limited and specific way." The bill was a transparent negotiating tactic and was dropped as soon as it became expedient to do so. (Elgot, 2022)

Likewise, *The Times* contended that "after Washington warned him against 'theatre' over the issue," instead of using the legislation as an alternative to continued negotiations, Prime Minister Johnson stressed his government's willingness to "'keep the door wide open' for further talks" (Smyth, Waterfield, and Charter, 2022). Others, like

John Manley in the *Irish News*, noted that even if the legislation never came into effect, it would still allow the Johnson government to assert that it was addressing the Unionists' concerns about the Protocol and get them to go back into government. In short, the bill gave Johnson room to maneuver in a context where pressure was building on both sides (that is, from the Americans and the Europeans on the one side, and the arch-Brexiteers and the Unionists on the other):

> While ostensibly this week's congressional committee visit lessens the likelihood of the legislation happening, it's very possible the US will reluctantly tolerate the moving of the bill if it leads to a restoration of the Stormont institutions. After all, the UK government is expected to re-engage in negotiations with the EU any day now, making the new legislation nothing more than a paper exercise. Some kind of retaliatory action from the EU and latterly from the US is only likely if the British actually decide to go on a substantive solo run. (Manley, 2022)

## *Headspin: three prime ministers in two months*

It is impossible to know what might have happened to the legislation or the negotiations with the EU had Johnson remained in power. Though he hung on to power longer than many expected, he was finally brought down in July by a series of scandals, most notably "Partygate." Indeed, while ordinary Britons missed the funerals of loved ones to comply with the government's pandemic lockdown orders,[8] Johnson and his staff held parties at Number 10. And when investigators began asking questions, Johnson repeatedly misled them about what had happened. When the official report emerged, the public outcry was intense. After 50 members of the government resigned in July 2022, Johnson tendered his resignation from the leadership of the Conservative Party, though he remained as Prime Minister until the Conservative Party leadership contest was resolved in August with the selection of Liz Truss.

---

[8] Even the Queen buried her husband of 73 years, sitting alone in a pew in the chapel at Windsor Castle.

There was initial skepticism about Truss' premiership, given her hardline stance on the Protocol as Foreign Minister and her reference to the relationship between the US and UK as "special but not exclusive" (Madhani and Superville, 2022). However, Truss' government appeared willing to improve relations with the EU (Gallardo, 2022b). While she was in office, for example, arch-Brexiteer Steve Baker, Minister for Northern Ireland, apologized at the Conservative Party Conference for having not "shown respect to the 'legitimate interests' of Ireland or the EU during the campaign to leave the bloc" (O'Carroll, 2022). The comments were warmly received in Ireland and the EU more generally. And in October, SOSNI Chris Heaton-Harris and Baker met with Simon Coveney at the British Irish Intergovernmental Conference. At the end of the meeting, the pair offered conciliatory comments to the press. In particular, Coveney praised UK ministers for making a "real effort to reach out" (Gallardo, 2022b).

For his part, President Biden kept the heat up, raising the importance of protecting the Belfast/Good Friday Agreement and of reaching a negotiated agreement with the EU on the Protocol with Prime Minister Truss on their first phone call (The White House, 2022) and again at their first meeting in New York City (Webber, 2022). The pressure campaign from the Americans at the UN meeting to get the Protocol issue resolved was apparently so intense that the UK Ambassador called White House Chief of Staff Ron Klain to complain about Jake Sullivan's and Amanda Sloat's hardline tactics. However, even before she arrived, Truss told journalists on the plane to the US that there was little chance of achieving a bilateral trade deal and that negotiations were not even likely in the short or medium term (Crerar, 2022a). Weeks later, when US State Department Counselor Derek Chollet visited London, he kept up the pressure on the UK to find resolution with the EU over the Protocol with the "unusually blunt" statement that "[t]he last thing we need is flare-ups" over Northern Ireland (Wintour and O'Carroll, 2022).

However, Truss' tenure as Prime Minister was brief and overshadowed by the death of Queen Elizabeth II, which thrust the UK into a 10-day period of mourning that ate up 20 percent of Truss' time in office. Truss also lost support of her party colleagues after a disastrous tax and borrowing proposal and was replaced by

Rishi Sunak as head of the party and Prime Minister in late October, kicking off a new phase in US-UK-EU relations.

After the economic turmoil created by Truss' government and worries of a looming recession, there was little public appetite for continued conflict or further economic disruption. Sunak's government, installed in late October, moved quickly to calm the waters. Unlike Truss, he was viewed as a pragmatist (Honeycombe-Foster, 2022) who would stabilize the economy and "be reluctant to exacerbate conflict with the EU over Northern Ireland" (Leahy, 2024).

In one of his first diplomatic forays after his election, Sunak attended the British-Irish Council in November, which had, in recent years, been attended by lower-level British officials. Sunak's participation was broadly interpreted as signaling a recommitment by the UK government to the bilateral approach of the Belfast/Good Friday Agreement (Pogatchnik, 2022). Sunak himself affirmed the Irish government's expectations at the Council meeting: "What I want to do is find a negotiated solution preferably. I'm pleased with the progress that we're making in these early days in this job. My focus is to try and find a resolution [and] get the institutions back up and running" (Pogatchnik, 2022). Taoiseach Martin walked away from that encounter with a positive impression: "I'm very clear after the meeting that the UK government and the prime minister is very, very keen on getting a negotiated settlement" (Pogatchnik, 2022). Sunak also met with Ursula von der Leyen, President of the European Commission, at the COP27 conference in Egypt in November, which was seen as part of a campaign to rebuild relationships. Sunak communicated a similar message about the desire to resolve the difficulties around the Protocol to President Biden on the sidelines of the G20 conference in Bali later that November, where he said that he shared Biden's desire to see "a negotiated settlement that protects the Good Friday Agreement" and promised to deliver one by April, the 25th anniversary of the Agreement (Elgot and Adu, 2022). In December, Sunak also signaled that his government would not bring the Protocol Bill back up in the House of Lords before the end of the year in order to "give room to the negotiations" with the EU (Wheeler, Shipman, and Wheeler, 2022).[9]

---

[9] By this point, the bill had racked up more than 90 amendments in the House of Lords.

Getting a deal in place between the UK and the EU by April 2023 had begun to figure prominently in the discussion around the Protocol. Even before Sunak took over as Prime Minister in October, British officials indicated that the 25th anniversary of the agreement would be a "key decision point" on protocol negotiations (Webber, 2022). They also suggested that Biden was likely to travel to the UK to mark the occasion, so it would be good to have things sorted before then (Crerar, 2022b). The US also became more overt about this deadline in the fall of 2022. On his trip to Belfast in October, for example, Derek Chollet commented that: "Next year's anniversary of the Belfast/Good Friday Agreement offers a potential platform to showcase Northern Ireland's excellent proposition as a place in which to invest and do business" (US Mission to the United Kingdom, 2022). To incentivize the UK to strike a deal (and Unionists to go back into government) before the commemoration, Chollet also suggested the US government would be interested in supporting investment opportunities in Northern Ireland if the matter was put to rest.

### *The special envoy*

The American desire to focus on potential investment opportunities in a post-Brexit Northern Ireland, which sits uniquely in both the UK and the EU common markets, was finally realized in December 2022 with the long-awaited appointment of Joe Kennedy III as US Special Envoy for Economic Development. Irish American groups and members of Congress had been lobbying for this appointment since Biden's arrival in the White House. When Kennedy was finally appointed almost two years later, Irish America warmly received him. Indeed, he had been a member of the Ad Hoc Committee before he was appointed, and as the grandson of Robert F. Kennedy, many expected he would bring the Kennedy magic to the position.

Although Kennedy's title—US Special Envoy for Economic Development[10]—implied that he would focus on economic issues, he faced political issues almost immediately. Indeed, separating political

---

[10] This title drew attention because it seemed to limit the special envoy's purview to solely economic matters, but it should be noted that Senator George Mitchell's special envoy title also included reference to economic affairs.

and economic issues was almost impossible at the time, given that Northern Ireland's economic prospects were still tied up in the fate of the Protocol. As Dan Mulhall, then the Irish Ambassador, told the BBC's Jane McCormick:

> While I would not expect a special envoy to want to get involved in the nitty-gritty surrounding the Northern Ireland Protocol, I do think that somebody coming over to Britain and Ireland with a mandate from the US president does have a certain ability to change the mood and convey some of those general messages from the US that have been, in the past, very effective. (BBC, 2022)

Ultimately, Kennedy's role vis-à-vis Protocol negotiations was muddled from the start—for example, the State Department said that the appointment was focused on economic issues, but the press varied in its explanations. An early BBC story on the appointment said that Kennedy would "focus on economic development and closer ties and not political issues such as Brexit or the Northern Ireland Protocol" (Glynn, 2022). However, *Bloomberg* suggested that US officials were "keen" to have Kennedy play a role in getting a deal on the Protocol (Wickham and Donaldson, 2022). The *Bloomberg* piece also reported that the UK was enthusiastic about his role because: "They hope the US will encourage the EU to agree to make changes to the text of the protocol" (Wickham and Donaldson, 2022). Kennedy himself joked later that the distinction between focusing on economics versus politics would not last beyond "one conversation" (Landler, 2023).

The confusion about the Biden Administration's motives was cleared up later when *The Times* reported that Biden and his aides had decided that Kennedy should "back off" discussing the Protocol at the urging of the UK government. As someone involved in the discussions told the paper: "It is not helpful for anyone on either side to make it look like there has been a deal because the Americans told us to do it" (as quoted in Shipman, 2023). *The Times* also reported that British officials were complaining about the Americans' involvement: "'The Americans like to think of themselves as honest brokers,' said one senior source, 'but they are not'" (Shipman, 2023).

Given this landscape and the sensitivity of the moment, the Biden Administration clipped Kennedy's wings almost as soon as he was appointed, preventing him from traveling to Northern Ireland while the EU and the UK negotiated the Protocol, a situation that reportedly rankled with Kennedy (Landler, 2023). Kennedy would not make his first trip until four months into the job, when Biden visited to celebrate the 25th anniversary of the Belfast/Good Friday Agreement.

## *Getting to Windsor*

Given the posture of the Sunak government, 2023 began with a great deal of optimism on the issue of the Protocol. The press commented extensively on the shift. Indeed, the term "mood music" was used widely from late 2022 on to capture the intangible sense that a new form of cooperation was in the air. The term appeared in a speech by the Irish Foreign Minister, Simon Coveney, at the Carnegie Endowment for Peace in DC (Wall, 2022b), in statements by Congressman Bill Keating (*Irish Echo* Staff, 2024), and in various newspapers, including *The Guardian* (Bismarck, 2022), *Bloomberg* (Wickham and Donaldson, 2022), the *Irish Times* (McDonagh, 2022), and *Politico* (Gallardo and Webber, 2023).

Even journalists who did not use the term "mood music" used similar wording to capture the shift. In mid-January, for example, Mick Fealty, writing for *Slugger O'Toole*, spoke of a new "seriousness" in the EU/UK talks (Fealty, 2024). *The Times* referred to a new "entente-cordiale" and also noted that "Both sides would like to secure a new deal before the middle of next month" in anticipation of a "possible state visit by Biden to the UK and Ireland" to commemorate the 25th anniversary of the Belfast/Good Friday Agreement (Shipman, 2023).

And so, very quickly in 2023, concrete progress occurred. After having tested the system for a couple of months (Milligan, 2022a), on January 9, the EU and the UK announced an agreement to give the EU full access to a new British database of real-time information on the movement of goods from Great Britain to Northern Ireland (O'Carroll and Rankin, 2023). Then, on January 13, the two announced a second mini-deal on tariff rate quotas, which had, in 2022, "prevented Northern Ireland benefiting from reduced U.K. import tariffs on products such as steel … after EU quotas for global imports ran out" (Gallardo and Webber, 2023). Speculation was mounting that the UK and the EU were working on low-hanging fruit in preparation for more intensive, behind-closed-doors negotiations before the end of January (Gallardo and Webber, 2023; Shipman, 2023). In mid-January, the SOSNI, Chris Heaton-Harris, also declined to call new elections (a decision expected under previous legislation to be made by January 19) in order "to give Brexit talks a chance" (O'Carroll, 2023).

While speculation about a deal swirled for weeks, the UK and the EU did not announce that they had concluded their negotiations until the end of February. The deal, which became known as the Windsor Framework, was expected to smooth trade between Great Britain and Northern Ireland primarily by creating different systems for goods that were expected to remain in Northern Ireland and those that were expected to move into the EU through the open border between Northern Ireland and the Republic. The agreement also established that members of the Northern Ireland Assembly would have an opportunity to temporarily stop the implementation of changes to EU regulations in Northern Ireland, pending a review by the UK government. Its passage through Parliament in March 2023 halted the Northern Ireland Protocol Bill, but preserved an open border on the island of Ireland.

Though passed by an overwhelming majority in the House of Commons (515 to 29), the Framework was not enough to get the DUP to return to government or permit the Assembly to function in Northern Ireland. Instead, the DUP argued the deal failed to meet its seven criteria for returning to government. The party would dig its heels in, only coming back into government in January 2024 after negotiating a new deal with the Sunak government to address concerns about the constitutional status of Northern Ireland and the movement of goods across the Irish Sea into Northern Ireland (Lawless, 2024).

In the months leading up to Windsor, the Biden Administration was relatively quiet in public, but behind the scenes, it continued to meet with relevant actors. In January, for example, the SOSNI, Chris Heaton-Harris, traveled to the US for five days and met with Amanda Sloat of the NSC, US Special Envoy Joe Kennedy, and the Ad Hoc Committee, among others. Micheál Martin, at that point Irish Foreign Minister, also traveled to DC the same month and met with NSA Jake Sullivan, State Department Counselor Derek

Chollet, and the Congressional Friends of Ireland. And in February, *The Guardian* reported that the Prime Minister was considering a multi-day trip to DC to speak about the deal being negotiated (the bill was then in the House of Lords, where it was expected to pass) (Stacey et al, 2023).

For its part, Congress continued to apply pressure consistent with its stance in the last two years: in mid-January, members of the House of Representatives, including members of the Congressional Friends of Ireland Caucus *and* the Congressional UK Caucus, introduced a bipartisan resolution calling for the full implementation of the Belfast/Good Friday Agreement with 18 co-sponsors (US House, 2023).

Once the Windsor Framework was announced, the President welcomed the news in an official White House statement (The White House, 2023), as did many other American figures. Within days, news began circulating of plans for President Biden's long-anticipated trip to Ireland and Northern Ireland to celebrate the 25th anniversary of the Agreement. Congress also proposed swift action. On March 2, Senators Chris Coons (D-DE) and John Thune (R-SD) introduced legislation to grant President Biden authority to negotiate a free trade deal with the UK, with one Congressional aide saying: "The resolution of the special status of Northern Ireland post Brexit was a necessary precondition to the negotiation … now that is done, we think the time is right for FTA negotiations between the US and UK" (Fedor and Politi, 2023). As Brendan Boyle (D-PA) said: "There is no question that a major irritant in the bilateral US UK relationship has been taken off the table." Congressman Bill Keating agreed (D-MA), commenting: "I think hopefully with this behind us, in short order there will be [trade] discussions" (Fedor and Politi, 2023).[11] In addition, Senators Robert Menendez (D-NJ) and Susan Collins (R-ME) introduced a Senate Resolution heralding the 25th anniversary and the Windsor Framework and calling for the full implementation of both agreements in late March.[12]

---

[11] HR 3653 was introduced in May 2023 by Congressman Adrian Smith (R-NE) and James Himes (D-CT) directing President Biden to initiate negotiations with the UK on an FTA. S4450 with a similar purpose was introduced in June 2022 by Senators Coons and Rob Portman (R-OH).

[12] SR Resolution 157 passed the Senate in May with 14 co-sponsors.

## Assessing Irish America's impact

There were many factors that worked together to explain the successful conclusion of negotiations over the Protocol after more than two years of discord. Principal among the external factors was Russia's invasion of Ukraine. Russia's hostile actions posed a threat to the West at large, and incentivized the UK and the EU to get back to the negotiating table. And American pressure helped move things along, especially on the British side, where Johnson's intransigence and Truss' chaos had backed the UK into a proverbial corner. In short, European and Western security united the European and British actors around a common project (Wickham, 2023). As a British diplomat explained in *Politico*:

> Suddenly we realized that the 2 percent of the EU border we'd been arguing about was nothing compared to the massive border on the other side of the EU, which Putin was threatening ... there wasn't any electoral benefit to keeping this row over Brexit going—either for us or for governments across the EU. (Gallardo, Webber, and Kijewski, 2023)

The change in leadership in the UK was also a huge part of the formula that produced the Windsor Framework. In contrast to his predecessors, Rishi Sunak is known for caution, pragmatism, and attention to detail rather than grandstanding. As a result, he and his team built trust relatively quickly with his counterparts in the EU, who were also eager for progress and more willing to grant concessions after two years of difficult negotiations. Sunak had many motives in working to resolve the issues of the Protocol, including the need to protect financial markets and stabilize the political and economic system of the UK, amid a broad popular consensus among Britons that Brexit was not working.[13]

By the time Sunak arrived in 10 Downing Street, it had also become apparent to the Brexiteers that the EU would not budge

---

[13] YouGov polls in Jan 2023 showed that more Britons thought the government was handling Brexit poorly than at any time since before the Protocol was negotiated (Alfaro and Viser, 2022).

on some of the key issues of Brexit, including their need to protect the single market from products made in the UK. The seriousness of the EU's stance seemed to have taken time to dawn on British negotiators. And whereas many Brexiteers had anticipated the EU would splinter and eventually give in to their intransigence, by this point, it had become clear that some of the Brexiteers' demands were simply impossible from an EU perspective. In short, Sunak arrived at a time when the British were in the process of coming to terms with the limitations of their options.

Yet, Sunak was also motivated by American pressure, which was a fourth major part of the equation. The Irish American lobby persuaded members of Congress, the State Department, and other parts of the Biden Administration to make strong statements in opposition to British policy, urging the British to find a negotiated solution to its problems with the EU and warning about the risks to the future bilateral trade deal. At all levels, American foreign policy actors responded with one voice, continuously raising the issue and making it clear to three successive UK governments that one of the main prizes of Brexit—the ability to negotiate a free trade deal with the US—hinged on the UK's ability to resolve the problems with the Protocol in ways that prevented a hard border, by decision or by default. It is also worth noting the involvement of groups like the Ad Hoc Committee that first helped define what America's interests were as the UK negotiated a withdrawal deal with the EU, and continued their efforts to pressure the British when they sought to renege on it.

The importance of this relationship to the British was also a leverage point for Irish America. As the Policy Exchange Report noted in stark terms, the UK government had taken the "special relationship" for granted, and in the process had been outmaneuvered by the Irish government and, of relevance here, Irish America. Indeed, Irish America's activism (in and out of government) created pressure that the British government could not ignore. We can see this clearly in how the UK government responded to the Policy Exchange Report: it stepped up its game in Washington to try to control American perception of its conduct on Brexit. The most obvious example was the Northern Ireland Office's decision to add one of its staff to the embassy detail in Washington, but the appointments of a Special Envoy (Trevor Ringland) and a Special Representative (Conor Burns) to the US are also clear evidence of a shift in UK engagement with the US. Though these offices were not always successful in getting the British message across, the very fact that the UK government believed that it needed to deliver a message at all indicated that it felt Irish America's political heat. It is also notable that the UK government sent the SOSNI or the Minister of State for Northern Ireland to DC a collective five times in 2021 alone.

Even Boris Johnson grudgingly acknowledged the importance of working with the Americans, which in this case meant Irish America specifically. In his departing speech to the House of Commons, for example, one of his primary pieces of advice for all future governments was to "Stay close to the Americans"! He did this even though he also clearly resented the American role, which he saw as constraining British choices. Indeed, at one point during heated discussions with colleagues in the Commons chamber during debate about the Windsor Framework, Johnson was reported to have said "'F★★★ the Americans!'" (as quoted in Shipman and Wheeler, 2023).

Sunak saw Johnson's folly and responded differently. As McDonagh notes, he understood "that playing 'silly buggers' on the protocol is incompatible with deepening the UK's relationship with the Biden administration" (McDonagh, 2022). And the Americans used the looming 25th anniversary of the Belfast/Good Friday Agreement and the potential of a state visit by Biden to focus minds and increase the pressure on the British to strike a deal.

In short, this chapter demonstrates that Irish America was effective in using its leverage to pressure the UK government to implement Brexit in a way that would prevent a hard border in Ireland. Though its activism was not the only causal factor in play—Russia's invasion of Ukraine created a welcoming opportunity structure and the Irish and EU were pulling in the same direction as the US—it was important because it constrained the space in which the British could act.

Irish Americans were able to do this because they exploited the unique features of their ethnic community in the US—their coherent political culture and sense of identity, their dense political networks, their bipartisanship (no small feat in today's political climate), and the quirky institutional opportunities afforded by the St. Patrick's Day week-long jamboree—to shape American foreign policy toward Brexit. They began by leveraging longstanding support for the Belfast/Good Friday Agreement, reminding law makers that the agreement was a signature US foreign policy achievement that both parties could celebrate. They then laid out the stakes of Brexit, arguing that it threatened a key dividend of the agreement—an open border between Northern Ireland and the Republic of Ireland. With the stakes defined, Irish America was well placed to encourage Irish Americans in Congress and the White House to beseech, cajole, and ultimately demand that the UK protect those peace dividends and to use a bilateral trade deal—the Brexiteers' golden egg—as leverage.

# 8

# Legacy and the Limits of Irish American Influence

This chapter provides a look at the limits of Irish American activism regarding how best to grapple with the legacy of the Troubles in Northern Ireland. Irish America was a forceful opponent of the UK government's so-called "legacy legislation," which halts most ongoing investigations into Troubles-related crimes, but its lobbying to stop the legislation did not help prevent its passage in 2023. Irish America's inability to move the needle is all the more notable, given that it had a larger set of partners than it did during debates about revising the Protocol. Opponents of the legislation included the Irish government, victims and human rights groups in the UK, Ireland and the EU, the Labour Party in the UK, and all the political parties in Northern Ireland.

The key features that allowed Irish America to function successfully as a lobby in all the same ways it had defended against a hard border were still in force when the legacy legislation passed. Irish America was unified in its opposition to the legislation and it still occupied key positions of power in Congress and the White House. And even though Nancy Pelosi was no longer Speaker of the House when the legislation was introduced, Irish Americans in Congress were united across party lines in their opposition to the legislation, and President Biden offered to assist Ireland after it lodged a case in the European Court of Human Rights (ECtHR) against the UK government ("New British Government Should Keep Its Manifesto Promise and Immediately Repeal Northern Ireland Legacy Act," 2024). The Americans were also willing to share those views with Members of

Parliament and the UK government. The main difference in this case was that the opportunity structure for Irish America to have influence was different in both the US and the UK.

In the US, two factors thwarted Irish America's activism. The first was that the border and trade were seen as naturally connected in a way that legacy and trade were not. Indeed, Brexit raised questions about the border and highlighted the need for new terms of trade. Legacy, by contrast, was not connected in any obvious way to trade. Timing was also important. The hard border was a more imminent threat than the legacy legislation, so it made sense for Irish America to use the trade deal to address the more immediate threat—the potential reimposition of a hard border. And once the British took the threat of a hard border off the table, the US needed to make good on its promise to talk trade.

In the UK, Irish America's activism ran up against domestic considerations, most notably from the Conservative Party, which wanted to keep private potentially embarrassing details about the UK government's management of the Troubles. The Conservative Party also worried that investigations would embarrass key institutions, including the former RUC, the Special Branch unit inside the RUC, and British military units that served in Northern Ireland. There was also the risk that investigations would expose high-level government officials involved in covering up military misdeeds.

In the remainder of this chapter, we begin by laying out the basic outlines of the legislation and the process through which it became law. We then discuss Irish American activism relating to stopping the legislation. Because the activism did not ultimately stop Parliament from approving the bill, we do not provide a full review of Irish America's efforts; instead, we provide highlights that demonstrate that it followed the same patterns as Irish American activism against a hard border. In other words, it involved high-level, bipartisan pressure from Irish Americans in Congress and the White House, and was steady throughout the period in which the proposal and later the bill were under discussion. The purpose of these highlights, then, is to demonstrate that differing levels of activism or distinct features of ethnic lobbying on this issue in contrast to the Brexit issues cannot explain the differential outcomes regarding the border and legacy. Rather, as we note in the third section, Irish America faced a different opportunity structure relating to the legacy issue—one that was less welcoming and ultimately insurmountable. As we will demonstrate, our interview subjects pointed to two contextual issues that limited Irish American influence. The first was that Irish America lacked leverage it could use against the UK government. In particular, the trade deal was taken off the table once the Windsor Framework was signed and there was no other, equally compelling source of pressure to replace it. Second, Tory elites wanted to put a stop to embarrassing details of collusion between the security forces and paramilitaries on both sides of the conflict. Irish American lobbying was clearly effective at shaping US policy on the legacy legislation, but taken together, these two variables proved more powerful than Irish American activism in shaping British policy on legacy. We conclude by discussing future steps Irish America may take to undo the legislation after the July 4 general election in 2024, in which the Labour Party ousted the Conservatives from 10 Downing Street.

## The legacy legislation in a nutshell

### Background

The Belfast/Good Friday Agreement is a consociational peace agreement. Writ large, the term "consociationalism" refers to democratic power sharing in states that have sharp ethnic, religious, or other social cleavages. In the context of peace agreements, it often means developing power-sharing arrangements that guarantee each ethnic or religious group a proportional place at the political table. A variety of contemporary peace agreements have adopted consociational principles, including South Africa, Bosnia-Herzegovina, and North Macedonia. Northern Ireland, however, is often held up as the quintessential example of a successful consociational peace agreement (Lundy and McGovern, 2007).

Although consociational agreements tend to emphasize political solutions, most of them also have processes for establishing a factual record of the conflict (total death tolls, responsibility for death by combatant groups, and so on), and mechanisms for justice, especially for civilians. Justice mechanisms can vary substantially, from conditional amnesty to criminal trials, but they are seen as important for helping a society move away from violence by affording victims some level of closure, and in doing so paving the way toward wider societal reconciliation.

The Belfast/Good Friday Agreement took a minimalist and forward-looking approach to truth and justice. The agreement, for example, recognized that addressing victims' suffering was "a necessary element of reconciliation," but only gave a general nod to how that would happen, noting that "support will need to be channelled through both statutory and community-based voluntary organisations facilitating locally-based self-help and support networks." Most notably, calls for a truth and reconciliation commission or other justice-oriented commissions were absent from the agreement. Instead, the agreement laid out provisions for repairing areas where injustices had historically occurred, most notably in policing and prisons.

Perhaps unsurprisingly, scholars have described the agreement's approach to legacy in negative terms, as "piecemeal" (Bell, 2003: 1097) and "bespoke" (McEvoy, 2006: 28). Lundy and McGovern (2007: 323) even argue that "avoiding talk of the past, rather than addressing it, was the defining leitmotif of the Irish Peace Process in the 1990s." Others point out that the Belfast/Good Friday Agreement dedicated far more discussion to the perpetrators of the violence than its victims. Victims of the Troubles tend to agree that legacy issues have largely been ignored since 1998. Indeed, many victims feel like the Police Service of Northern Ireland (PSNI) has dragged its feet on investigations, hoping victims will "die off" and it can move on to other things (McMahon-IM, 2014).

Scholars and those directly involved in the negotiations point to three interrelated reasons why truth and justice measures were left out of the agreement. The first is that neither the Republican nor Loyalist paramilitaries wanted it to be included. During the negotiations, prisoner release was the paramount issue for paramilitaries on both sides of the conflict. Taylor (1999) argues that it was the make-or-break factor in ensuring that Loyalists signed on to the agreement. Establishing a truth and reconciliation commission ran counter to these sentiments by drawing the public's attention back to the very actions that had put Republican and Loyalist combatants in prison in the first place. Speaking at an event marking the 25th anniversary of the agreement in Dublin, for example, Bertie Ahern, who was involved in the negotiations as Ireland's Taoiseach, said that he raised the issue of a truth commission with paramilitary groups party to the negotiations after speaking to Nelson Mandela and F.W. de Klerk on how the process worked in South Africa. He was met with stiff resistance: "to say that they ran out the window is an understatement" (Ahern, 2023).

Second, the security forces were also loath to participate. As has become clearer in the 25 years since the agreement was signed, the special branch of the RUC and the British military extensively colluded with Loyalist (O'Loan, 2007) and Republican paramilitaries (Boutcher, 2024). Many political observers believe the UK government would be deeply embarrassed by the extent to which its agents engaged with the very groups they were said to be fighting. It is also important to note that many in the security forces viewed their work as honorable—protecting civilians and the British crown from groups they deemed to be domestic terrorists. The idea that the security forces had something to make amends for was insulting to many frontline members.

It is also important to recognize that all of Northern Ireland's armed actors (paramilitaries and security forces) saw their respective fights as political rather than criminal and thus as legitimate. Indeed, the IRA hunger strike in 1981 was a protest against Margaret Thatcher's commitment to eliminate paramilitary prisoners' "special category status," which McEvoy (2001) notes was akin to prisoner-of-war status. They believed Thatcher's decision to recategorize paramilitary prisoners as "ordinary decent criminals" was a blatant attempt to dismiss the political nature of their struggle. Although Loyalist paramilitaries did not go on a hunger strike, they did participate in the earlier blanket protests (at the same time as Republican paramilitaries did) to protest wearing prison uniforms, which they also saw as counter to their status as political prisoners.

Security forces likewise saw their work as legitimate, even when it involved collusion. As McGovern (2015) explains, collusion was not only "premised on a 'doctrine of necessity,'" but also a continuation of Britain's longstanding counterinsurgency policy. Thus, while many ordinary people might have been repulsed by collusion if they had known what it entailed, constables and military brass treated it as ordinary operating procedure.

The final reason the agreement contained no provisions for truth or justice was because negotiators themselves worried that forcing the issue would impede the ability to get an agreement done. Speaking at the same 25th anniversary forum mentioned earlier, Jonathan Powell, Tony Blair's chief of staff during the final year of negotiations, explained the omission this way:

> Most peace processes have a truth and reconciliation part to them. We did not put that into the Good Friday Agreement. We did not put that into the nine years of negotiations on the implementation, because we didn't want to make it [the negotiations] even more difficult than it had been. (Powell, 2023)

*Early efforts to address legacy*

Early efforts to address legacy emerged slowly in Northern Ireland. They included independent[1] and institutional efforts. Most of them encountered problems that limited their scope and ultimate success. The result is that most victims are still waiting for acknowledgment of the crimes they or their families faced. In the interests of space, we will only review some of the most notable efforts to address legacy here.

One of the first independent efforts was the Independent Commission for the Location of Victims' Remains (ICLVR). The commission was established in 1999 through a treaty between the UK and Irish governments and was tasked with finding 16 persons who were missing and presumed murdered during the Troubles. The total number was later increased to 17. All of the people on the initial list of disappeared were Catholic and are believed to have been killed by Republican paramilitaries ("The Disappeared," no date). The disappeared were targeted because they were believed (often incorrectly) to have been working with the security services.

The goal of the commission was to find the bodies of the disappeared so that families could bury their loved ones. The commission could obtain information directly (for example, from paramilitaries) or indirectly (from RUC files) and would share it

---

[1] In this case, "independent" means not situated within an existing institution focused on justice.

with the family members of the disappeared, including the location of bodies and details about the cause or circumstances of the death. However, in exchange, families had to agree that the information could not be used in future prosecutions. The ICLVR is widely regarded as having been successful. During its period of operation, 11 of the 15 verified bodies were recovered.[2] The primary problem with the ICLVR was that its scope was so limited relative to the total number of people victimized.

There were also a number of parliamentary inquiries into high-profile murders or mass killings during the Troubles. These were conducted under two Acts of Parliament—the Tribunals of Inquiry (Evidence) Act of 1921 and the Inquiries Act of 2005. The most notable of these was the Bloody Sunday Inquiry, also known as the Saville Inquiry, which was organized under the 1921 Act. The Saville Inquiry took more than a decade to complete. Once the 2005 Act replaced the 1921 Act, many families refused to participate, given rules they saw as protecting the UK government. For example, the family of Pat Finucane, a solicitor killed in his home by Loyalist gunmen, boycotted the proceedings ("Pat Finucane and the Inquiries Act – Amnesty International Calls for Boycott," 2005).[3]

Another important independent effort to address legacy happened in 2007, when the UK government formed the Consultative Group on the Past. This was co-chaired by Robin Eames, a primate in the Church of Ireland, and Denis Bradley, a former priest who went on to serve as the Vice-Chair of the Northern Ireland Policing Board. Although the group would produce 31 recommendations in its final report, a leak about one proposal would scupper the entire set of findings. That recommendation—that the closest living relative of anyone killed in the Troubles would receive a one-time payment of £12,000—received immediate and vociferous pushback. Like much else in Northern Ireland, many people viewed the report through the prism of their community background. Nationalists, for example, were suspicious of the group because it was organized by the UK

---

[2] The exact number of people disappeared in this period is disputed. Many believe the number is higher.

[3] Hilary Benn, SOSNI in the new Labour government of Keir Starmer, announced an inquest into the Finucane case in 2024.

government. For their part, Unionists complained the commission was "appeasing terrorists" (Hancock, 2012). A sense that victims are not created equal also underlined the opposition. In particular, many people opposed treating family members of paramilitaries killed or wounded during the Troubles as victims, even when they were from the same community, because those loved ones had been perpetrators. In short, for some survivors in Northern Ireland, there is an implicit hierarchy of victims, and paramilitary members and their families are at the bottom of the list, or not even on it (Lawther, 2010). Despite broad agreement on many of the group's other recommendations, the report's findings were overshadowed by the furor and were quickly put to one side.

One of the first institutional steps to creating a truth and justice mechanism, albeit indirectly, was the creation of a Police Ombudsman of Northern Ireland (PONI), which was established as part of broader police reform under the Police Acts of 1998 and 2000. The office's mandate was to investigate two streams of complaints relating to police misconduct. The first were current cases investigated on an annual basis, while the second stream was smaller and focused on historical abuses. Specifically, the Chief Constable could decide to investigate an historical crime if the behavior was especially egregious (for example, an officer was involved in a murder). Most of these cases happened during the Troubles and were related to the conflict.

In 2007, for example, the first Ombudsman, Nuala O'Loan, published an investigation into Special Branch collusion with the commander of an Ulster Volunteer Force (UVF) unit in North Belfast. In 1997 the commander, who was eventually unmasked as Mark Haddock, had ordered the murder of Raymond McCord Jr., who was arrested while moving a drug shipment for Haddock (O'Loan, 2007). McCord's father, Raymond McCord Sr., believed Haddock ordered his son's murder because he did not want the UVF leadership, based on the Shankill Road, to know that he was selling drugs. After trying to get the PSNI to investigate his suspicions, McCord Sr. alleged that Haddock was being protected from prosecution because he was an informant. O'Loan verified many of the elder McCord's suspicions, including that Haddock was an informant and there were important failings in the investigation, which "significantly reduced the possibility of anyone being prosecuted for the murder" (O'Loan, 2007: 9). Though it took ten years, O'Loan's investigation of Raymond McCord Jr.'s murder was the first verified case of collusion between the Special Branch and paid informants in paramilitaries. Others would follow.

A second, more targeted institutional effort on legacy began in 2006, when the PSNI established an in-house Historical Enquiries Team (HET). The unit was set up in response to the ECtHR's rulings on the so-called McKerr cases, a collection of lawsuits filed in the early 2000s by families whose relatives were killed by security forces during the Troubles (Connolly, 2007). The ECtHR used the same legal principle to adjudicate all of them, ruling that the UK courts had failed to guarantee the European Convention for the Protection of Human Rights and Fundamental Freedoms (ECHR) "right to life" clause by refusing to investigate the state's use of lethal force in several Troubles-related cases.

Although the HET oversaw a number of important cases, a 2013 review by the Inspector General of Constabulary identified several critical problems with the HET's operations (HMIC, 2013). In particular, it faulted the HET for having unclear systems and processes, and a poorly defined process for complaints. The report also found that the HET had adopted an official policy that allowed it to treat cases involving state involvement (that is, security forces) differently from those involving paramilitaries. According to the report, this approach was legally "wrong" and made it difficult to assess and ultimately hold state actors accountable. Most damningly, the Inspector General found that the HET's work on cases involving violence by security forces was not in compliance with the ECHR. That is, the team designed to bring the UK into compliance with the ECHR was working in such a matter as to prevent that compliance.

The next effort to deal with legacy issues was the 2014 Stormont House Agreement (SHA). The Act was the result of negotiations between the Irish and UK governments and all but one of the major parties of the Northern Ireland Executive (the Ulster Unionist Party or UUP). Its reach extended beyond legacy to include broader identity issues, such as parades, the Irish language, welfare reform, and government finances. In light of criticisms of the HET's operations detailed earlier, the SHA called for the establishment of a new Historical Investigations Unit (HIU), which would carry forward the HET's open cases and other legacy-related work by the PONI. The HIU would also be overseen by the Northern Ireland

Policing Board rather than the PSNI itself. Other then-ongoing legacy inquests would continue separately.

The SHA also called for an Independent Commission on Information Retrieval (ICIR). This commission was designed to build on the successes of the ICLVR, which we described earlier. Indeed, the ICLVR was seen as very successful, buts its impact was small because of its focus on a small subset of victims.

The SHA envisioned legacy investigations proceeding differently from many earlier inquiries. Most notably, the HIU would follow the legal requirements of the ECHR's Article 2. It would also adopt a victim-centered approach. It was to have support staff for the families from the start of any investigation. The SHA also established that families could bring cases already heard by the HET to the new HIU if there was new evidence. HET cases flagged for re-investigation could also be re-examined by the HIU. Families could also request criminal prosecutions, though the final decision to charge and prosecute continued to lay with the Director of Public Prosecutions.

While the SHA had broad support, it needed implementing legislation to go into effect. That legislation was never passed. Indeed, over the next eight years, the UK government moved from fully supporting the SHA to calling for changes, and from there to introducing new legislation altogether.

The first step in the new legislation was a public consultation, which occurred in the late spring/early summer of 2018 (Boutcher, 2024). A year later, in July 2019, the NIO released the findings of the consultation, indicating that it was still committed to the agreement, but laying out no clear next steps. Later that same month, the House of Commons Defence Committee issued a report calling for a statute of limitations to protect veterans in any such probes. The Conservative Party Manifesto, also released in 2019, had a similar statement calling for the protection of veterans (Boutcher, 2024).

The following March, the then new Secretary of State for Northern Ireland, Brandon Lewis, issued a statement through the NIO announcing new legislation to protect veterans. The statement also offered the first hint that the SHA was on shaky ground, declaring that "significant changes will be needed to obtain consensus for implementation of any legislation" ("Addressing Northern Ireland Legacy Issues," 2020).

More than a year later, in July 2021, the NIO released a so-called Command Paper, which laid out the government's new approach to legacy. The paper landed poorly with victims' families because it proposed introducing a statute of limitations on investigations of Troubles-related events (Boutcher, 2024). On March 17, 2022, the government published the Northern Ireland Troubles (Legacy and Reconciliation) Bill (that is, the "Legacy Act"). As Jon Boutcher, Chief Constable of the PSNI, notes, the bill's approach to legacy represents a remarkable departure from earlier attempts at justice because it "moved the focus away from police investigations and court cases and towards measures intended to lead to information recovery and reconciliation" (Boutcher, 2024: 76). One of the most controversial elements of the bill is that it closes all ongoing investigations on legacy cases between 1966 and 1998, and prevents new criminal cases from being opened. For many victims' families, this amounted to a slap in the face. Indeed, in 2018 there were 1,186 ongoing Troubles-related death investigations (Winters, 2018). One of those cases was for Raymond McCord Jr.'s death. Although O'Loan's report verified that a key suspect in McCord's murder was a paramilitary informant with the Special Branch, the case was never reopened and solved by the PSNI (Erwin, 2024).

Another controversial measure is that the bill provides conditional amnesty to those involved in Troubles-related crimes. Although it is not uncommon for peace agreements to have amnesty provisions, Troubles victims and their families opposed the way in which amnesty was structured in the Legacy Act on two grounds. First, participation in information recovery is voluntary, and there were few incentives to encourage participation. In fact, many families worried that taking criminal prosecution completely off the table would weaken rather than strengthen incentives to share the truth. A second complaint is that the threshold for granting immunity is low. People applying for immunity do not have to provide new information and there is an unclear process for assessing the credibility of the information provided. The Committee on the Administration of Justice, a human rights organization in Northern Ireland, argues that the lack of checks is likely "indicative of disagreements within the UK Government as to how best to compel non-state actors to cooperate with the ICIR whilst providing broad immunity to veterans (*The Road to the Northern Ireland Troubles (Reconciliation and Legacy) Act 2023. A Narrative Compendium of CAJ Submissions*, 2023: 93).

The Legacy Act came into full effect on September 18, 2023 after it received the royal assent. It immediately faced legal challenges. Following its passage, more than 20 cases against the legislation were brought to the Northern Ireland High Court ("Northern Ireland Human Rights Commission Responds to Legacy Judgment," 2024). The Irish government also filed an interstate case against the UK in the ECtHR, a process that is quite rare (Dooley and Fernandez-Powell, 2024). The case alleges that the Legacy Act violates Articles 2 and 3 of the ECHR. Article 2—the right to life—was the same statute cited in the McKerr cases in the early 2000s. Article 3 provides a right to be free of inhumane and degrading treatment and torture. Both statutes guarantee that victims whose rights have been abridged have a right to take their cases to court for prosecution.

## Irish America's dim view of the Legacy Act

Many people in the Irish American lobby are invested in legacy issues because their activism during the Troubles put them into direct contact with victims and their families. And from that exposure, they learned about British collusion and other human rights abuses. For them, the Legacy Act is personal, not something abstract or distant. Mitchell Reiss, for example, pointed specifically to the victims' families he had met while working in Northern Ireland, telling us: "Not knowing what happened to their loved ones is tragic for the families. I've talked with many of them. I've helped some of them find bodies of their loved ones. But, right now, you can get information but not justice."

William Tranghese, Richie Neal's former chief of staff, also had interactions with victims of the Troubles. When we asked him for an example, he pointed to Bloody Sunday:

> The one that comes to mind is David Cameron issuing an apology to the Bloody Sunday families. And, when we did delegations and trips over [to Northern Ireland], we met with those families. The fact that the British government conducted the inquiry and issued the apology, that was influenced by Irish America continuing to raise the issue. Congressman Neal was on the phone with those families when that happened.

Others had followed particular cases and were disgusted with how slowly they had proceeded. Several people we spoke to, for example, pointed to the Ballymurphy inquest, which investigated the death of ten civilians killed during a British Parachute Regiment operation to round up suspected IRA men in the Ballymurphy housing estate. When we spoke to Martin Galvin, for example, he noted just how long it had taken to get a measure of justice:

> The Ballymurphy inquest, involving the murders of a Catholic priest, a grandmother and eight others finally exonerated the innocent victims nearly 50 years after their murders. NI's Chief Judge Siobhan Keegan said the inadequacy of the original investigation was "shocking"—there was no justification for shooting any of the deceased.

Many Irish Americans also recognized that addressing the crimes of the past were important for moving forward. John Connorton pointed to the difficulties of normalizing policing in Northern Ireland, telling us: "Former Chief Constable Hugh Orde told me that every time he seemed to be making good progress on police reforms someone would reach into the past and drag a legacy issue into the present." American Brexit Committee member Michael Cummings told us he has pushed Irish Americans in Congress to study the issue:

> It was something we had been asking for—to hold hearings on the progress of the GFA, its achievements and so on. It's hard to say it didn't have a measure of peace associated with it. Obviously, it did. The arms were made silent. But some of the justice issues have been burning over the last years.

Irish Americans were also, by and large, suspicious of the UK government's motivations for introducing the Legacy Act. Indeed, many saw the act as a chance to expunge the record of British involvement in the Troubles. In this way, Irish America complicated the narrative in Britain that the UK government's primary concern was about protecting ailing military veterans who had served in

Northern Ireland. Though Irish Americans agreed this was part of the equation, they thought it was only part of the rationale. Mick Mulvaney laid out the argument succinctly—"Brits and Unionists are worried about opening all these cases up and having them spiral out of control." Another interviewee who asked to go off the record elaborated: "It's about hiding serious misdeeds, criminality and murder, state sponsored murder by the UK government and its agents." Peter Kissel was even more direct. When we asked him what he thought about UK government claims that it was too late to collect actionable evidence, he replied:

> I respond with anger. That is the playbook of every totalitarian regime. You bury the past, destroy evidence. The British game has always been delay, deny, till death. The Ballymurphy families have compiled an incredible amount of evidence. But, if you keep putting it off, sure, more folks are going to die. And then the truth won't come out.

Michael Cummings even went so far as to say that he thought the Conservatives' motivation for Brexit was as much about legacy as distrust of Brussels:

> I believe there is evidence to show, none probably well-documented, but evidence that the Brexit idea for the Tories is as much about the angst about Northern Ireland as about dealing with Brussels bureaucrats. Because more and more of the cases that are being brought in Northern Ireland are coming to the attention of the ECtHR, more and more of the cases are being exposed because of the work of the ombudsman, so they see this gradual unraveling that is going on legally as a threat to their image. Brexit is a way of getting around Brussels, to the extent that there was any justification to do so.[4]

---

[4] It is important to note that the ECHR and the ECtHR are not part of the EU, but the Council of Europe. The ECtHR is not even based in Brussels, although the EU and the Council of Europe are commonly conflated.

Irish Americans were also disturbed that the UK government had abandoned its prior commitment to deal with legacy. Peter Kissel reminded us, for example, that the Belfast/Good Friday Agreement was not the final word on peace; rather, the process was being continually updated with new agreements on specific postconflict reforms. The Stormont House Agreement was one of those: "Every one of those has reaffirmed the UK's commitment to fund legacy investigations. And, every one of those, they've broken in terms of legacy inquiries. The Stormont House Agreement? The UK Government has shredded that … And the amnesty bill is the next step in shredding the agreement."

Only one person we interviewed—Mitchell Reiss—had anything positive to say about the idea of amnesty. We spoke to him before the bill was published, so his comments were not about the specific legislation. Yet, even he described amnesty with reservations:

> Amnesty is very problematic. It doesn't make you feel warm and fuzzy except for the alternative. If you want to look for the silver lining, you say, will this help some of the Protestant paramilitaries transition? Will this help some of them turn in their weapons if they don't have to worry that they will be tested forensically for some crime? Will this help move the peace process forward? I think that is to be determined, but it is certainly possible.

## Irish American activism on legacy

Irish American activism on legacy proceeded in tandem with its efforts to prevent the UK government from scrapping the 2020 Withdrawal Agreement. However, two things about this dual-track process are worth noting. First, saving the agreement and preventing a hard border took precedence over legacy. Temporally but also practically, the border was seen as a more immediate threat to the Belfast/Good Friday Agreement. For much of this period, the Withdrawal Agreement was already a law—it came into effect on February 1, 2020—and Irish America was focused on defending it. The Legacy Bill was introduced in 2022 and received the royal assent in September of 2023, so it occupied a much smaller amount of Irish American time and focus in the period we are analyzing.

Second, despite this informal ordering, activism on legacy followed a similar path to activism on preventing a hard border. In other words, it involved pressure campaigns by key groups, including the AOH and the Ad Hoc Committee. It also involved Congressional resolutions, high-level warnings from Congressional committees, and pressure from the Oval Office, and it was often coordinated in tandem with other actors in Northern Ireland and Ireland. Irish Americans spoke about the issue as consistently and as steadily as they did the Withdrawal Agreement. Indeed, between March 2020 and the Windsor Framework, most Irish American statements opposing efforts to scupper the agreement included references to amnesty, and there were standalone statements as well, suggesting that while legacy may have taken second billing, it was sufficiently important to receive the single-minded attention of Irish Americans. Moreover, until the Windsor Framework was signed, the threat of a trade deal was often included in statements about legacy.

Given the fact that these efforts ultimately did not stop the bill's passage, we don't provide a forensic accounting of Irish American activism on the legacy issue and the results thereof, as we did in Chapters 4 through 7. Rather, we provide highlights to demonstrate that the activism was on a par with efforts to prevent a hard border, with highlights from Irish American civil society groups, Irish American Congressional actions (focused on the US and UK governments), and the US Executive Branch. This will allow us to rule out weaker activism as an explanation for why Irish America was unable to levy sufficient pressure to prevent the bill from coming into force. Indeed, as we will demonstrate in the next section, the loss of leverage helps explain the limits of Irish American activism on the issue and domestic pressures in the UK.

## Civil society group pressure campaigns

As we noted earlier, Irish American lobbying began almost immediately after Brandon Lewis announced the new legislation on legacy issues, with the AOH taking a lead role. Less than a week after Lewis's announcement, and just over two weeks after Mulvaney's appointment as special envoy, the AOH sent a formal letter to Mulvaney asking him to "express opposition" to the planned legacy legislation (Cosgrove, 2020). It also suggested leverage Mulvaney might use in his communications with Lewis:

> We ask you, Mr. Mulvaney, to contact Secretary of State for Northern Ireland Brandon Lewis asking for an explanation of these actions which violate the US brokered Good Friday Agreement. The Hibernians also request that you communicate to Secretary Lewis that the United States has stated it shall take a dim view of any British actions that jeopardize the Good Friday Agreement; such action may have consequences for future post-Brexit US-UK trade negotiations.

The AOH kept up its activism. In one example, it organized a Legacy Justice Webinar in late January 2021 to cap off a week of activism in Ireland and Northern Ireland with victims' families ("Hibernians Webinar – Legacy Justice Appeal," 2021).

The Ad Hoc Committee also pressured high-level officials. In September 2021, shortly after the House of Commons Committee on Defence released its report, the Ad Hoc Committee sent a lengthy letter to the then Prime Minister Boris Johnson urging him to withdraw the proposal for new legacy legislation. Although the committee chairs who signed the letter—Jim Walsh and Bruce Morrison—noted that the agreement "does not impose specific obligations with respect to legacy," they also reminded Johnson that the agreement "does mandate that both state parties observe and implement the European Convention on Human Rights." The letter also hinted that moving forward with a Legacy Bill could cause problems in the US, though unlike the AOH, it did not specifically mention the trade deal:

> We have strong reason to believe that this proposal will not be met with approval in Washington by either Congress or the Biden Administration. It will be a further source of disagreement with US political leaders who have already raised serious concerns about your government's recent approach to implementation of the Northern Ireland Protocol.

Though there is no indication the Ad Hoc Committee received a reply, the group's letter was covered in the press (BBC 2021c; O'Shea, 2021) and by human rights organizations ("Ad-Hoc Committee to Protect the Good Friday Agreement to Boris Johnson," 2021).

Nine months later, the Ad Hoc Committee wrote another letter, this one addressed to Joe Biden's Secretary of State, Antony Blinken. In that letter, the committee pointed to its September letter to Prime Minister Johnson and subsequent meetings it had with Brandon Lewis, Conor Burns, the Prime Minister's Special Representative to the US on the Northern Ireland Protocol, and Lord Jonathan Caine, the Parliamentary Undersecretary for Northern Ireland. The Ad Hoc Committee expressed its frustration that the UK government had made no progress on meeting its promises:

> On each and every occasion when we have met with our British counterparts, we were assured that a revised legacy proposal would be compliant with both the spirit and core tenets of the GFA and incorporate human rights standards as well as reflect the concerns of victims and survivors. The pending Bill does none of these things. (As quoted in O'Hanlon, 2022)

With that track record in mind, the Ad Hoc Committee requested that Blinken "use all possible diplomatic channels necessary to oppose this potential violation of the GFA without delay" (as quoted in O'Hanlon, 2022).

The committee continued its pressure on the Sunak government, sending Sunak a letter in late August 2023 (just prior to the bill's arrival in the House of Commons) expressing its "deep dismay" at the proposal. And unlike its earlier letter, this one indicated the legislation's passage could imperil a trade deal: "This legislation will also harm your concerted efforts to develop a new trade relationship with the United States, given the clear bipartisan opposition in the US Congress to the current legacy proposal." Not surprisingly, the Ad Hoc Committee's letter once again received media attention. In the US alone, two groups posted the letter in full on their websites—the Irish American Unity Conference (IAUC, 2023) and the Friends of Sinn Féin (O'Loughlin, 2023).

## Congressional pressure on the Executive Branch

Irish Americans in Congress also lobbied the Biden Administration to come out forcefully against the UK government's plans to put forward its controversial plan on legacy. In mid-November 2021, for example, Tom Suozzi, a member of the House of Representatives from New York, wrote a letter to Secretary of State Antony Blinken urging the Biden Administration to publicly condemn the bill's proposed approach (*Irish Legal News*, 2021). The bipartisan letter had 20 co-signatories and was supported by Amnesty International. Grainne Teggart, the manager of Amnesty UK's Northern Ireland campaign, said in a statement that "we strongly welcome this intervention from members of Congress" (as cited in *Irish Legal News*, 2021).

## Congressional pressure on the UK government

In addition to lobbying the Executive Branch around the Legacy Bill, Irish Americans in Congress also used their official perch to put pressure on the UK government. On July 15, 2022, for example, William Keating, then Chairman of the Foreign Affairs Committee's Europe Subcommittee,[5] held a public forum where committee members spoke to groups in Northern Ireland who work with victims' families, including most notably Wave Trauma Center (for a video of the hearing, see "Public Briefing on Truth and Accountability for Victims of the Troubles in Northern Ireland," 2022). It is difficult to overstate how uncommon such a hearing is. Indeed, though US Congressional committees regularly hold hearings about state abuses in authoritarian regimes, it is exceedingly rare to speak to victims of state abuses when the state is not only an ally but also party to a "special relationship" with the US.[6] It would have been similar to the House of Commons hosting a hearing

---

[5] The full name of the subcommittee is the Subcommittee on Europe, Energy, the Environment and Cyber.

[6] According to the Sutton Index of Deaths (Sutton, no date), British security forces were responsible for 10 percent of the total Troubles-related deaths.

with victims of police violence in the US—something that most Americans would find unthinkable behavior from an ally.

Three weeks after the briefing, Keating and Brian Fitzpatrick, the subcommittee's ranking member, wrote a letter addressed to the Speaker of the UK House of Lords, John McFall, expressing their strong opposition to the Legacy Act. The letter, which was co-signed by a bipartisan group of 30 members of Congress, was sent to every member of the House of Lords, where the bill was receiving its second reading (O'Shea, 2022).

Two CODELs were also scheduled in 2022—one in May and the second in November. Although the first one was focused on preventing a hard Brexit (and thus a hard border), the second one also included discussions of legacy. In the second CODEL, Keating tweeted a picture of himself with Sinn Féin's Mary Lou McDonald. The picture's caption touted a "fruitful discussion" on legacy issues (Keating, 2022).

### *Executive Branch weigh-in*

The Executive Branch of the US government, most notably the State Department, also weighed in at key points against the Legacy Bill. In June 2022, for example, then Secretary Blinken wrote a letter to the UK government on behalf of the Ad Hoc Committee. In it, he warned Boris Johnson, then in his last days as Prime Minister, that the bill appeared to "violate" not only the 1998 peace accord but also international law. He also argued that the bill "undermines" the peace process and as structured would invite numerous legal challenges: "Litigation over these deficiencies is certain to lead to years of further delay in addressing Northern Ireland legacy issues" (as cited in Hyland, 2022). The Biden Administration even continued to publicly oppose the bill after it received the royal assent in September 2023. When Biden met with Taoiseach Leo Varadkar in New York just after the bill's finalization, for example, he offered US support should Varadkar choose to file a legal challenge against the law in the ECtHR (Crisp, 2023).

## **Assessing Irish America's impact: a question of leverage**

As the preceding short review makes clear, Irish America's activism on the legacy legislation stayed true to form—that is, its activism on legacy mirrored its activism on preventing a hard border. It involved high-level pressure from Congress, in the form of letters, resolutions, and CODELs, as well as backup from the President and other key Executive Branch figures. It was also steady, though in both cases activity tended to increase and cluster around impending deadlines or after actions considered particularly egregious. Just as it had after Boris Johnson threatened to trigger Article 16, Irish America stepped up its public pressure in the wake of the release of the UK government's July 2021 Command Paper.

However, to test our sense that the two campaigns proceeded on a similar footing, we asked William Tranghese for his opinion. As Congressman Neal's chief of staff for much of the period and principal staffer for the Congressional Friends of Ireland Caucus, he was in a good position to know: "I think that it's a certainty, our voice was heard in the legacy process and continues to be heard in that process. Whether the British government will take heed to the Friends of Ireland Caucus on this, I don't know, but every opportunity we had to raise the issue, it was done."

Given the near-identical level and type of lobbying, we asked several of our interviewees why they thought the outcome of Irish American activism was different in the legacy case. People gave multiple reasons. The first was that Irish America lacked the kind of leverage it had held during discussions about a hard border. Many of our interview subjects told us, for example, that the ability of Congressman Neal and Speaker Pelosi to threaten to withhold a trade deal was a crucial part of the pressure on the UK up to the Windsor Agreement, but by the time the Legacy Bill was in its final stages in 2023, Republicans had taken control of the House of Representatives. Richie Neal was no longer the Chairman of the Ways and Means Committee and Pelosi had stepped down as Speaker of the House. Though Irish America's bipartisan ethos meant that it could still wield influence, no two Irish American figures were as well placed moving forward.

Relatedly, our interview subjects explained that Brexit created both the problem of a hard border and the need for a new trade deal—that is, the two issues were intrinsically linked and were as such easy to connect. By contrast, it wasn't as easy to see an automatic connection between the legacy issue and trade. Though the Irish Americans had made the link in their statements and resolutions, there was a sense that some members of Congress would have difficulty seeing the connection. As one of our interviewees who asked not be quoted put it: "This [the legacy legislation] is not a reflection on Irish America. As you said, all the major parties opposed it, EU human rights groups, global human rights organizations, all of the parties in the US. But, I do think it's different from Brexit: Brexit was tied to trade."

Another explanation was that the US tacitly took the trade deal off the table as a stick after Windsor. Indeed, the trade deal was not just a stick; it was also a carrot, and the American government needed to be able to deliver that carrot for a promise kept. As an interviewee who asked to speak anonymously about this topic told us: "Our position was that if the GFA were protected, we would make an effort to ensure that Northern Ireland benefited from any US/UK trade deal." Irish Americans made this point in the press as well. For example, Congressman Bill Keating (D-MA) told the *Financial Times*: "I think hopefully with this [the Windsor Framework] behind us, in short order there will be [trade] discussions" (Fedor and Politi, 2023). And, as we discussed in Chapter 7, after the Windsor deal was signed, members of Congress introduced bipartisan legislation in both chambers immediately to grant President Biden fast-track authority to negotiate a US-UK trade deal.

Once the trade deal was taken off the table, there was nothing of equal power to replace it. As another interviewee, who also requested anonymity to talk freely, explained: "The problem with the legacy legislation is that the sanctions available to the US on that issue were limited. What could they do in the event of the UK bringing in that legislation?" This person also noted that the Irish government was now better situated than the Americans to address the bill, noting: "There are options for the Irish government through the European courts to challenge that, which is the route they're going down at the moment."

Our interview subjects also pointed to Britain's domestic context to explain the differential outcomes in the two lobbying campaigns. For its part, the Conservative Party has often pointed to the spectacle of elderly veterans facing trial as a reason to scrap ongoing inquests. While many Irish Americans believe the party does not want those optics, they also believe the issue goes deeper. They think the UK government is also trying to cover up the extent of its security services' collusion with paramilitaries. As Martin Galvin succinctly put it to us: "They [the UK government] don't want to show collusion, so their position is to bury the truth."

Professor Katy Hayward offered a similar analysis when we asked her why Irish American pressure had failed to have an impact, telling us:

> Nothing appears to move them on the legacy point ... The Legacy Bill comes from two things. One is the pressure from media about veterans and soldiers. There are votes to be lost from veterans and soldiers, electoral pressure. And, then there are the internal things they want to hide. They don't want to be exposed.

When we asked Hayward why the UK government was acting now, given that the government's collusion during the Troubles has been fairly well exposed, she said "I think there's a sense of fatigue on this they want to exploit," adding ruefully, "Northern Ireland can take the brunt to save the British government."

Another interviewee, who requested anonymity, also believed there was little the Americans could do to stop the Legacy Bill. He also told us that the push to stop inquests was specific to the Conservatives: "Legacy is a Tory party domestic agenda. So, the leverage was lesser. And the worst part of collusion happened under Tory governments, so that far outweighed other things. I do think Irish America gave pressure and forced them to explain themselves."

Only one of the people we interviewed thought the UK government's motives were at least partly well intentioned. This official was not involved in UK decision making, although they followed current conversations closely. They told us: "There's a general message that this [legacy] is the British government looking after old geezers, but I think it's not that." This official pointed to two other reasons. The first was keeping stability in Northern Ireland: "It could be convenient for the British government for people to think it's just Britain protecting themselves. But they want Northern Ireland to work, and some of this stuff could blow it all up again. It's a long game being played out." They elaborated by pointing to the 2024 Kenova report authored by Chief Constable Jon Boutcher about the management of a British Army agent inside the IRA codenamed Stakeknife, telling us that many people feared the report would "contaminate the current Sinn Féin leadership." Indeed, even though Michelle O'Neill and her leadership team had nothing to do with Stakeknife, the report could discredit the party as a whole, making it "hard to have power sharing." The second reason this official cited underscored the importance of Irish American activism on Northern Ireland, albeit in unintended ways. They explained that each investigative report provided fodder for critics of the UK's handling of the Troubles, especially Irish Americans. Stopping investigations would mean less public outcry in the US: "It's much, much better politically for the UK government if you can keep the Irish Americans at bay on this issue." Thus, because the legacy legislation would cut off investigations in five years, it was better to pass it now and avoid antagonizing Irish America in the future.

Despite Irish America's persistence and its successful track record on helping to prevent a hard border, the opportunity structure on legacy was not in its favor. Specifically, Irish Americans may have been able to convince Tory elites to substantially modify the Legacy Act if it had been able to wield a meaningful carrot or stick as leverage. However, the lack of leverage, post-Windsor, when paired with fear of unearthed secrets, was insurmountable even for the savviest of lobbies.

## Room for future activism?

Although Irish America was not able, in conjunction with a host of important partners, to prevent the Legacy Act from coming into law, its high-powered activism on legacy issues seems unlikely to be over. Indeed, the Americans continue to press the British government to address legacy in a way that is consistent with the wishes of the people of Northern Ireland and international law. Irish Americans point out that Prime Minister Keir Starmer campaigned on a promise to overturn the Legacy Act, but his government has only moved to modify the prior legislation rather than remove it. This discrepancy is likely to continue to drive Irish American engagement on the issue. The legacy legislation is also subject to numerous legal challenges. Irish America here too is well placed to encourage the British government to ensure its legal approach is in compliance with the ECHR.

9

# The Elephant in the Room: Irish Unity after Brexit

Irish unity is the ultimate goal for many people in the Irish American lobby. And since the Good Friday/Belfast Agreement provides a mechanism for calling a referendum on a united Ireland, defending the agreement is paramount for those who want unification. Former Congressman Joseph (Joe) Crowley (D-NY) distilled this view in our interview in 2020 when he explained why he had continued to keep tabs on the agreement long after others had moved on: "the possibility of a united Ireland." Crowley made similar comments at an event sponsored by Friends of Sinn Féin USA in 2020: "it is still "important for Irish-Americans to not only stay engaged, but re-engage' on the issue of unifying Ireland" (Crothers, 2020).

Irish America worked to protect the agreement between 2018 and 2023, however it did not focus on the question of Irish unity. The primary reason for this was that Brexiteers never threatened the agreement's referendum guarantee. Rather, the more immediate threat was a no-deal Brexit, which would have reimposed a hard border on the island of Ireland, disrupted the all-island economy, unsettled the delicate balance of Northern Ireland identities, and possibly provoked violence.

While the question of Irish unity was not activated by Brexit, it could be in the near future. There is a growing consensus in academic and policy circles that Brexit makes a referendum for a united Ireland more likely to happen and to pass (Pogatchnik, 2023; Dugan and Doyle, 2024; Walsh, 2024). One reason for this is that a majority of Northern Ireland's voters supported remaining in the EU—including a third of Unionists—so reunification would be a way to remain part of the EU despite Brexit. Another reason, which we discussed in Chapter 4, is that the Protocol keeps Northern Ireland's ties to the Republic of Ireland intact. As the rest of the UK goes its own way, Northern Ireland may come in time to see its interests as more aligned with the EU (and thus Ireland) than its fellow compatriots.

None of this means that reunification is imminent. The 2022 Life and Times Survey (Hayward and Rosher, 2023) found that "a plurality of respondents (48%) continue to believe that the long-term policy should be for Northern Ireland to remain part of the UK." However, the same survey also reported that support for Irish unity had more than doubled since Brexit, from 14% in 2015 to 31% in 2022. Given this context and Irish America's role in helping foster the 1998 peace accord and its related support for a united Ireland, this chapter looks at the latent politics of Irish unity within Irish America.

We begin by noting the obvious. The overwhelming majority of Irish America is "green" and, as such, supports Irish unity. Yet, as we will note in the second section, Irish Americans have disagreements over the timing and feasibility of unification. Moreover, as we will demonstrate in the third section, they are also divided on how, or even if, they should work to reassure Unionists and Loyalists that reunification would not be a threat to their identity or political rights. With this context in mind, the fourth section examines what Irish America is doing to encourage/support/prepare for potential Irish reunification. As we will demonstrate, this question divides the ranks.

## A sea of green

Irish America is widely viewed on both sides of the Atlantic as "green," which is a shorthand way of saying that it favors the Catholic Nationalist cause over the Protestant Unionist one. The structure of Irish migration to the US explains why. As we noted in Chapter 2, Irish migration to the US happened in two distinct waves—the first in the mid- to late 1700s and the second in the mid-1800s as a consequence of the Great Famine that began in the 1840s. The first wave came to the US in the 1700s. They were mostly Protestant and settled across the then colonies. By the time the second wave came, after the Great Famine, this generation was largely consolidated. The second wave, by contrast, were poor, traumatized, and clustered in enclaves within fast-industrializing cities like Boston, New York, Philadelphia, Baltimore, and Chicago. While migrants from both waves tended to support some variant of Irish independence, the second wave had a closer, visceral connection to the issue. That shared experience, and their need to organize collectively for survival in their new home, fostered a distinct political culture. The part of Irish America that is politically active today *as Irish Americans* traces its ancestral and political lineage from this second wave.

This context was relevant backdrop for many of the key figures we interviewed for this book and explains why most see themselves as "green" and support Irish unity. Some grew up in households with family members who hailed from Ireland/Northern Ireland or were one generation removed from it. Others grew up in Irish neighborhoods surrounded by Irish politics even if they were not Irish. Given this demographic context, news about the Troubles was not only at the top of people's minds, but was also a motivating factor in Irish American support for unification.

Pointing to this history, Ted Smyth, President of the Advisory Board of Glucksman Ireland House at New York University, told us: "I think Irish America emotionally would be in favor of unification but without a clear idea of what that might mean in a diverse and modern Ireland." Peter Kissel, President of the Irish American Unity Conference, agreed. While he emphasized that Irish Americans were not "monolithic on their view of the North," he told us that most supported Irish unity. When we asked why, he described the support as an almost received position, one that had been handed down: "They support unity. It's a very strong emotional connection." Another interview subject, who requested anonymity to speak freely on this particular topic, also suggested support for Irish unity was built in, even ingrained: "Irish America will reflexively say we want a border poll and a united Ireland."

Other interview subjects pointed to geography to explain their "green" leanings. When we asked William Tranghese, Congressman Neal's long-time chief of staff, what Irish America meant for him, he pointed to where he grew up:

> Well, it means an awful lot coming from western Massachusetts and the city of Springfield. There's a large Irish American population there who come from Kerry.

And people from the Blasket Islands. It would not be uncommon to have friends whose parents/grandparents came from there and read the *Kerryman* newspaper.

In Tranghese's case, geography even trumped ancestry:

> My father was Italian American and my mother was a Polish American, but you get this incredible exposure. I grew up going to Irish American social events, Cathedral School. That's where I met Congressman Neal. He was my teacher. He came from an Irish American area called Hungry Hill. From an early age I got exposed to the culture, history, and politics of Irish America, even though I'm not Irish.

Tranghese also told us that he thinks most Irish Americans are primed to support reunification efforts, telling us: "You have an army of Irish Americans ready to be ignited. It will take just a modicum of prodding."

Christopher Carey, who helped co-found the Young Friends of Ireland, had a similar origin story. Like Tranghese, Carey's ancestral roots are not in Ireland—"I'm Colombian," he told us—but he was adopted by an Irish family and was steeped in its culture and politics while growing up. As he explained: "A big part of my Irish American identity was informed by being civically active. My family has always been active. It was the Irish American political culture I grew up in." Carey's story was similar to that of Tranghese in another way. "I grew up in Massachusetts," he laughed, "in the first Congressional district that Richie Neal represents."

Other Irish Americans pointed to the history of the Troubles to explain their political leanings vis-à-vis Northern Ireland's politics. Brian O'Dwyer, who was the national chairman of Irish Americans for Clinton-Gore in 1992 and 1996 and for Irish Americans for Gore in 2000, told us: "Those of us who lived through it, who were there during the Troubles, every Irish American has a border story." His story involved having a gun pointed at him:

> I was going through the border in Donegal and had this very scared 18-year-old from Scotland point his

gun right at me while he was interrogating me. He was more frightened than I was and could pull the trigger at any minute. It invokes a visceral reaction. So, for Irish America, the main thing is the preservation of the Good Friday Agreement. And, concomitant with that is that the border is removed.

## Timing and feasibility

Given Irish America's green bonafides and the presumed momentum for unification post-Brexit, we asked our interview subjects whether they thought a successful referendum was more likely now than before Brexit, and if so, what the timing for reunification would likely be. We found that the majority of the Irish Americans we interviewed think that a united Ireland is much more likely in the wake of Brexit. However, most added caveats regarding feasibility.

Brian O'Dwyer described reunification as "inevitable." As he explained, "eventually it will happen, but when, I don't know. But, I don't think anyone who looks at this rightfully, or thoughtfully sees it any other way." He also argued that Brexit had brought the question back to the forefront of public conversation: "Brexit has economically opened this up. It's silly to have two markets on an island as small as this, with one smaller than the other. The EU took away that distinction, but now it's back in full force."

Lobbyist Erik Huey also used the term "inevitable" to describe the likelihood of a united Ireland. And he argued that Brexit shifted the terms of the debate in important ways:

> The grand irony is that the British people have sped the timeline considerably, by virtue of leaving the EU. Because in the olden days, with the question, "would you rather be a UK citizen or an Irish citizen?", people would say, we're going to miss the National Health Service. But now the question becomes would you rather become an EU citizen or a UK citizen? And that puts a new wrinkle into the question. And it cuts across demographics more. It's less about Protestant versus Catholics and more about EU money powering the economic renaissance over several decades. And the EU

put a lot of investment into NI. The northern people are going to miss that money.

Jim Walsh, former Congressman and Co-Chair of the Ad Hoc Committee to Protect the Good Friday Agreement, also agreed that Brexit had pushed reunification to the forefront in a powerful way: "It forced a thought process on the idea of a united Ireland. I know it drove the Unionists crazy. This issue has really solidified the momentum for a unified country. There will be no physical border."

Michael Cummings, Secretary of the American Brexit Committee, also thought unification was much more likely now, telling us in July 2020: "The stars are aligned. Academics, economists, a taskforce in Ireland, are all studying this, trying to establish what the ground rules might be." He also told us Brexit inspired him to try to make it happen: "I heard Richard Haass, President of the Foreign Relations Council, describe Brexit as 'the end of the United Kingdom.' I was relatively inspired by that. What led me to get involved was thinking, 'We could help make this happen.'"

Although many Irish Americans argued that Brexit had made a united Ireland more likely, former Ambassador Barbara Stephenson, who served as US Consul General in Belfast, argued that it was the push to prevent a hard border that had really started the ball rolling. As she explained, preventing a land border had produced the Protocol, which in turn pushes unification along:

> I think the idea of maximum regulatory convergence [between Northern Ireland and the Republic] is one of those wonderfully Latinate multisyllabic ways of saying it's not the same as united Ireland but we know where it's headed, where it's leading, right? A united Ireland is a flashpoint that causes people to get out Molotov cocktails and other things that do more damage than them, but maximum regulatory convergence kind of lulls people into it. It knits together an economy on that island.

However, many of the people we interviewed expressed reservations that it would be an easy or necessarily quick process. For example, Michael Cummings told us he thought the Conservatives would prevent a referendum from happening:

I don't think this government will ever let a referendum be held. The Secretary of State for Northern Ireland doesn't have that power. They could spend a year or two to figure out how to do it, then pass it to the Attorney General, who could also slow-walk it, then Parliament, who could go through all the readings. I'm not sure this party could allow it.

Kevin Sullivan, Project Director for the Ad Hoc Committee to Protect the Good Friday Agreement, had a similar take, telling us in 2020: "You aren't going to have a united Ireland without a Labour government." Sullivan also offered a cautionary note about reunification:

> The strategic work has not been done for a united Ireland. There will be polls and studies around the centennial[1]—100 years, what to make of it? Especially after Brexit, possibly a new strategic landscape. The non-aligned are the ones to watch, the Good Friday Agreement generation in their late twenties and thirties. And the Irish have to develop a commitment to pay for unification.

Ted Smyth also thought that a united Ireland was not likely to happen in the near future, and dismissed those arguing it should happen soon: "People who've worked to support reconciliation believe that has to be the priority before options for a united Ireland can be considered." Former Congressman and Co-Chair of the Ad Hoc Committee Bruce Morrison offered a similarly cautious note in the summer of 2020: "Objectively, this [Brexit] has created a much stronger case for a united Ireland, but the cultural case is weaker. Brexit has widened the divisions between Nationalists and Unionists. They see Brexit completely differently."

---

[1] Northern Ireland was created on December 6, 1921 as part of the Anglo-Irish Treaty, which ended the Irish War of Independence (though a civil war would continue through to May 1923).

Only a small number of the Irish Americans we spoke to thought a united Ireland remained a distant possibility. Susan Davis, former head of Irish American Republicans and current board director of the Ireland Funds, told us: "I'm skeptical there will be a united Ireland in my lifetime."

Numerous people we spoke to also warned against holding a referendum if opinion polls or other data suggested it would only pass by a narrow margin. In the same interview quoted earlier, Morrison told us:

> One has to think of this in terms of what happens the day after. In the US, we've seen four years of the consequences of an election in which the minority won. Think what that would be like in Northern Ireland if it [the referendum] passes by a one percent margin. I think the border poll could happen quite soon, but the result will be narrow. There's no one with a plan of "we're all in this together."

Ted Smyth also worried about a narrow referendum win, telling us:

> [Former Deputy First Minister of Northern Ireland and leader of the SDLP] Seamus Mallon pointed out the danger of majoritarianism. Fifty percent +1 can become "my way or the highway." We saw the disastrous outcome of such a vote in Brexit. In many ways, options for a united Ireland should emerge from the shared island process. To avoid the mistakes of the Brexit referendum, people north and south must know what they are voting on before the two referenda are held.

Former US Special Envoy to Northern Ireland Mick Mulvaney made the same point about narrow wins and the costs that come with them. He nodded not only to Brexit but also to several divisive policies in the US:

> Please, take a lesson from Brexit, Obamacare, Trump tax cuts. All the major things that have happened in major democracies with 51 percent have caused more problems

than they solved. You don't win in the 51/49 percent range. You want the folks who lose to accept it without violence. Wait until victory seems inevitable.

The majoritarianism that Smyth and Mulvaney point to is particularly relevant in a postconflict context. Twenty-five years on from the peace process, Unionists and Loyalists feel like they won the war but lost the peace. As former Special Envoy Mitchell Reiss, who is currently a member of the Independent Reporting Commission (IRC),[2] put it:

> The Loyalists argue that they haven't seen any peace dividend. They claim that the schools aren't better. Jobs aren't more plentiful. Communities aren't more livable than they were before. They also see a narrative that Sinn Féin has adopted—"we're winning!" One of Gerry Adams' great attributes was that he was relentlessly positive, confident that he and Sinn Féin were going to own the future. There is a feeling, maybe it's the dour Presbyterianism of Ian Paisley, Sr., but the future is bleak. Today is bad but tomorrow is going to be even worse. They do think that they are losing. That's absolutely a widely shared perception. And, the everyday experience for many Loyalists seems to confirm that. You could argue that life is slightly better for them, they're not in the middle of the Troubles. That is certainly significant. But again, it's all against expectations. It's captured in the phrase, "what about them-ism?" Forget about how I'm doing, they're doing better. Then you pile on Brexit and it's acted as an accelerant.

Susan Davis also emphasized the fact that Unionists and Loyalists were not on board to even discuss the issue: "The Irish government has

---

[2] The Independent Reporting Commission was established in 2017 by the joint authority of the UK and Irish governments. Its mission is to track ongoing paramilitary activity and develop mechanisms for ending it.

formed a special unit to look at how it [reunification] would look and work. There isn't a similar unit in Northern Ireland. It's really hard to get the parties to work together. I wonder if the Unionists would even work on it. I'm skeptical."

Perhaps most importantly, many in the Irish American lobby realized that the decision was not theirs to make. This was the case even for those who want reunification. As one senior staff member in the Senate put it:

> I think when dealing with issues of such import that impact everybody, I think you need more than a slim majority. So, I would lean more in the direction, although I'm also loath to, to be a little reluctant to push the issue. The people in Northern Ireland get to make that determination.

## The Loyalist question

While romanticism swirls around the idea of a united Ireland, Unionist and Loyalist opposition to unification presents a significant obstacle to its occurrence and, if it occurs, its success. In many ways, this sort of disjuncture is familiar territory for Irish America. As we discussed in Chapter 2, one of Irish America's major contributions to ending the Troubles was to make Nationalist views legible (and acceptable) to American leaders and, eventually, to the UK government. This work in turn gave American leaders the credibility to nudge the IRA toward peace in the 1990s. President Reagan, under pressure from Irish America, asked Margaret Thatcher to accept the Anglo-Irish Agreement, pushing the British to deal with Nationalists differently than they had before. President Clinton, under similar pressure from Irish America, gave Gerry Adams a visa to travel to the US. This move simultaneously pressured both the British and the Irish Republicans. As Clinton would later say in a documentary about the Troubles, the visa was designed to show Republicans what kinds of opportunities would be available to them if they were to announce a ceasefire, while also calling their bluff if they didn't (*Endgame in Ireland*, 2021).

This history prompted us to ask key Irish American leaders what they thought might assuage Unionist/Loyalist fears about post-Brexit Northern Ireland. Given the timing of our interviews, this meant talking about how Unionists and Loyalists responded to the Backstop, the Protocol, and the Windsor Framework. Our goal was to understand how Irish America *interprets* Unionism and Loyalism, and, from this, what roles they could fruitfully play if a referendum were to be called.

We begin by returning to something Mitchell Reiss told us in his 2021 interview (and that we first quoted in Chapter 4) about the changing nature of the conflict post-Brexit:

> The nature of the challenge has changed and that is the conundrum. It's not about getting the IRA to decommission its weapons and having Sinn Féin pledge to purely peaceful means and support justice and politics. That's where they [Irish Americans] had huge leverage and were able to use it effectively. Now, you want to restore confidence in the DUP? Well, good luck with that. That's not really what they [Irish America] are built for.

Reiss' comments distill the disconnect between Irish America and Unionism/Loyalism. And Reiss wasn't our only interview subject to point to the gulf between them. Niall O'Dowd, founder of *IrishCentral*, made the same point, telling us: "They [Unionists] don't believe us and they don't want us. Our influence historically, traditionally, is with Sinn Féin." Former Consul General in Belfast Susan Elliott offered a similar assessment:

> When I was in Northern Ireland, I felt like I represented all people in Northern Ireland, not just one party. But now that I've retired from the US government, I've realized how green Irish America is. They supported the Good Friday Agreement, but in general, I'm surprised about how little they know about Loyalists, or even the Alliance Party. They saw the IRA as freedom fighters, and Loyalists as criminal thugs.

As we discuss later on, how Irish Americans view the source and the nature of this disconnect varies across the lobby.

## Sources of disconnection

A primary reason for the disconnect is that Irish America's contacts with Unionists and Loyalists are not as deep as they are with Nationalists and Republicans. The shallowness of the relationship stems from many factors. One is religious difference. Mick Mulvaney told us, for example, that his first goal after becoming Special Envoy to Northern Ireland was "to establish credibility" with the Protestant community:

> I'm Irish Catholic, and I'm a devout Irish Catholic. So, I was worried. I was close to lots of members of the Irish government. I was worried how Unionists would view me. So, I was careful to reaffirm our nation's role as an honest broker. And my personal role. Just because I attended a meeting of the [Ancient Order of the] Hibernians, that I wasn't there to stick it to the Unionists.

Though Mulvaney, by all counts, made good on his promise, he was starting from zero (or close to it) in establishing relationships on the Unionist/Loyalist side. Indeed, as he indicated, he could not draw on dozens of contacts from his own "rolodex." This is common for Irish America. As Mitchell Reiss told us: "For many Irish Americans it's been more difficult for them to connect with the Unionists and the Loyalists than it has been to connect with the other side of the table. Historically, that's been true." When we asked key leaders in Irish America who they had met with on the Unionist side, for example, interviewees usually mentioned the same handful of people. For example, the leader of the DUP for some portion of this period, Jeffrey Donaldson, was frequently cited, but very few of the people we interviewed named younger politicians or civil society actors within Unionism/Loyalism. The only young person who did receive multiple mentions was Jamie Bryson, but he was not seen as a potential interlocutor. Instead, for many Irish Americans, he was, as Kevin Sullivan described him, someone "you have to worry about." Deep and continuing connections—and their transfer to rising members—can take years to establish. The relationship between Irish Americans and Republican leaders like Gerry Adams and Martin

McGuinness, for example, developed over more than a decade before the march to peace began in the mid-1990s.

A second factor in the disconnect is the flipside of the coin. In other words, several interview subjects told us that Unionists and Loyalists were not particularly interested in engaging with Irish America. One interview respondent, who asked to go "off the record" to discuss Irish America's relationship with Unionists and Loyalists, told us that Arlene Foster, then leader of the DUP,

> doesn't like the United States. She thinks everyone is green, despite sincere efforts to reach out to her. For example, a meeting was put together and hosted by some of the key American women in DC, women who had worked on the peace process for over 20 years to reach out to the First Minister but nothing came of it. She was pleasant, but she doesn't see any merit in talking to Irish America to my knowledge.

When we asked AOH President Danny O'Connell if his group had ever met with Loyalists, he replied "yes." When we asked what they had told him, he laughed and said, "They think we should mind our own business." In a similar vein, another interview subject who asked to go off record for this comment explained efforts to reach out to Unionists as unsuccessful. When we asked why, the person noted that "we've tried, but they've pulled back." Jim Walsh agreed, pointing to the difficulties former Director of the Northern Ireland Bureau Norman Houston had in bringing Irish America and Unionists together: "Norman Houston really worked hard to put Northern Ireland in front of the US business community. But, it was a tough sell to get Robinson, Paisley, and Foster to agree. Unionists haven't cultivated relationship with spokespeople, business connections for investment opportunities, etc."

A third factor our interview respondents pointed to as an obstacle to working together was the intransigence and miscalculations of DUP hardliners, who entered into a confidence-and-supply agreement with Prime Minister Theresa May in 2017 in the hopes of winning influence over the UK government, only to see Boris Johnson cave in and adopt a deal that implemented an Irish Sea border. From the perspective of many Irish Americans, Unionists and Loyalists had refused to see the obvious, instead grasping on to false promises that Brexit could happen without consequences to the border, trade, and so on. In the same interview, O'Connell told us: "The DUP, they knew this day was going to come. The Unionist population is shrinking and the Catholic side is growing. Instead of hardlining everything, instead of saying no, no, no, they could have said this is what we're going for."

Hilary Beirne, founder and chair of the New York City St. Patrick's Day Foundation, agreed, noting that Boris Johnson had made fanciful promises to Unionists and Loyalists, and they were now paying the price for taking him seriously: "The impression for Unionists that's been created is that they've been isolated from Westminster. Boris Johnson did that in many ways by selling them a bill of goods." Mitchell Reiss made a similar assessment, pointing to the DUP's confidence-and-supply agreement with Prime Minister May's government: "They had the greatest amount of power they ever had when they had the ten seats that were the difference for Theresa May, and they absolutely squandered that opportunity. They've been on the backfoot ever since."

Although many people we interviewed were pessimistic about whether and how Unionists and Loyalists could move on after their sense of betrayal by the Conservatives generally and Boris Johnson more specifically, others thought it was an important wake-up call. Niall O'Dowd argued, for example, that some Unionists were already primed to "rethink things," and Johnson's behavior would reinforce those instincts:

> Unionists supporting remaining was not in line with normal sectarian vote. Over half voted against Brexit. That's a very critical 5–10 percent of people whose minds are open to a different constitutional structure. I think the other thing they must have seen in this Boris Johnson hodgepodge of PMs coming and going is that he completely betrayed the Unionists. What he said he would do and then didn't do. It would be wrong to watch what Boris Johnson did and not see that he doesn't give a fig about them.

A further factor is that some people in Irish America, though certainly a small minority of them, have an almost hostile view of

Unionism and Loyalism. This was especially the case for Loyalism. Many of our interview respondents don't think Loyalists even have political positions. As a result, they don't take their political views on Brexit, the Backstop, the Protocol, or the Windsor Framework seriously. When we asked Peter Kissel, for example, what steps Brexit negotiators could take to reassure Unionists and Loyalists that their interests/identity would be preserved once the Withdrawal Agreement was signed, he told us:

> I'm going to speak here only of the Unionists, not the Loyalists. I'm not going to try to assuage the paramilitary thugs and criminals. They will never, ever change their view. They're criminals. That's how they make their living. But let's talk about Unionists. There's a large swath of Unionists who aren't bigoted. But they're comfortable being brought up British. We need to explain how unification would be beneficial to them. It's a challenge to their culture, and that's difficult to get over. But they could come to understand that Great Britain doesn't want anything to do with them.

At times, the contempt was aimed at Unionists in general. Michael Cummings told us, for example: "If Boris Johnson builds that bridge [between Northern Ireland and Scotland], I hope they [the Unionists] all cross over to Scotland."

A final factor is a sense of paternalism that pervades how Irish America treats Unionist and Loyalist fears about a united Ireland. Some believe that Unionists and Loyalists will change their views if they learn about the benefits a united Ireland could bring them. One argument that was put forward by several people is that Unionists would be able to play the role of kingmaker in the Dail, the Irish Parliament. Kevin Sullivan told us, for example, that "Unionists would have more power as a power bloc with 20 percent of the vote in Leinster House than in Stormont. It might actually be attractive [to them]." Niall O'Dowd voiced a similar view, telling us: "In a united Ireland, Unionists would have a very powerful voice, and would be very good coalition partners for Fianna Fail or Fine Gael." At times, Irish Americans' paternalism switched carrot for stick. For example, even though O'Dowd thought that some Unionists could be won over through the benefits of coalition politics, he also suggested holdouts would learn the hard way that a united Ireland was the best course: "My grand theory of this is that ultimately Unionists will be faced with a choice to be deeply disliked and dishonored, orphaned son of the UK, or join a united Ireland under EU rules."

While there may be benefits for Unionists in Irish politics, many Unionists and Loyalists would likely see these arguments and observations as tone deaf or even arrogant. For Unionists and Loyalists, putting the border in the Irish Sea is as much an emotional issue as it is a technical one. For many of them, Brexit puts their very identity at stake. Though some of our interview subjects acknowledged these fears, every person we interviewed insisted that a sea border was necessary to avoid a hard border. They all saw the Protocol as something the Unionists would just have to learn to accept.

Although many of the comments in this section bring the depth and sometimes enmity of the disconnect between Irish America and Unionism/Loyalism into sharp relief, it is also true that Irish American broadly recognizes that its relationship with Unionism/Loyalism needs repairing. Many also hope that Irish America could play its traditional role as broker between the parties in the unification process. Niall O'Dowd, for example, was, as we noted earlier, blunt in his assessment of Unionists' place in the UK—"disliked and dishonored"— but he also argued that Irish America had worked with Loyalists in the past, and to good effect:

> William Flynn, Chairman of Mutual America, since deceased, was very important for getting the Loyalist ceasefire. He provided a foreign policy forum and used to bring over Unionist leaders all the time. It was very important involvement. That's where I could see a footprint being set up for Irish America.

Susan Elliott pointed to the State Department as a vehicle for building a better relationship with Unionists. She told us that during her time as Consul General, she focused on promoting positive connections with *both* communities. Katy Hayward, Professor of Political Sociology at Queen's University Belfast, also thought the State Department could play a productive role. In particular, she pointed to Paul Narain's efforts as Consul General in Belfast during Brexit negotiations:

> Paul really played an active part in trying to ensure a deep understanding of the concerns on all sides ... he was great at building relationships ... Paul was somebody who had the confidence of all the political parties and a wide range of stakeholders from all different backgrounds that he would talk to. And then he was also able to communicate with the EU, with various Member States, as well as with the British and the Irish.

## Push or proceed with caution?

Although most of Irish America is resolutely green, how they approach unification varies. Here, we look at two approaches to unification. These two approaches replicate the traditional pattern of divisions within Irish Nationalism—the constitutional Nationalist approach of the SDLP, and the Republican approach spearheaded by the IRA and its political wing Sinn Féin.

The first approach is akin to a push. Some Irish Americans, working alongside Sinn Féin, are openly advocating for a united Ireland and are working to bring about a referendum on unity in the near future. The second approach to Irish unification in the post-Brexit moment is to proceed with caution and only at the behest of the people of Northern Ireland themselves. Irish Americans in this camp want to help people in Ireland and Northern Ireland sort out the big and small questions that would need to be addressed before a referendum is called. This approach mirrors, to some degree, what parts of Irish America did in the 1990s—convening the relevant parties in safe spaces where difficult conversations could be had and publicly applauding positive steps toward reconciliation, especially when those making them would face fierce blowback at home.

### *The push camp*

The campaign for Irish unification in the US is led by the Friends of Sinn Féin. The group, which is registered with the US Department of Justice (DOJ) as an agent of Sinn Féin under the

Foreign Agents Registration Act, was established in 1995 and is tasked with mobilizing American supporters. American donations also provide a "key source of funds" for the party back in Ireland (McGee, 2008). In fact, the Friends of Sinn Féin raised more than $2 million between 2018 and 2023, according to filings the group made to the DOJ (Wall, 2023). In recent years these donations have been used to pay for ads in major US newspapers like the *New York Times* and the *Washington Post* around St. Patrick's Day calling on the US government to urge the UK government to hold a referendum on Irish unity. The donations have also helped cover expenses for "senior party figures who visit Washington and other parts of the United States for meetings with key political and other figures on several occasions each year" (Wall, 2023).

Several interviewees told us that Sinn Féin actively courts American involvement, and even expects it. In our 2020 interview with Niall O'Dowd, for example, he recounted: "The Border poll will galvanize them [Irish America] within the next five years. It's what Sinn Féin is trying to do now." As evidence, he pointed to a virtual event the Friends of Sinn Féin USA hosted between Gerry Adams and Joe Crowley during the pandemic called "Irish Unity and the Role of Irish America" (O'Loughlin, 2020). During the webinar, Adams called on Irish America to lobby on behalf of the referendum. "Gerry Adams is trying to encourage Joe Crowley," O'Dowd told us, adding that "Gerry Adams is very much in favor [of our involvement]." Kevin Sullivan also told us that Sinn Féin wanted American help: "Sinn Féin wants support from Irish America to persuade Congress to support them. They were successful in getting Congress and President Clinton to support the Belfast/Good Friday Agreement and they hope to do the same in the long term when it comes to the issue of Irish unity." In 2024, for example, the Friends of Sinn Féin's St. Patrick's Day ads called on the diaspora to "join the debate and plan for Irish unity" (Finn, 2024).

Other Irish American groups and individuals, working alongside Sinn Féin, are actively pushing for a referendum on unification. The AOH is a case in point. In many ways, this is not surprising. The AOH is more unmitigatedly green than other groups like the Congressional Friends of Ireland Caucus or the Ad Hoc Committee to Protect the Good Friday Agreement. The group's history explains why. Unlike the

Caucus and the Ad Hoc Committee, which are the *outcome* of Irish American activism, the AOH was the *progenitor* of such activism. As we discussed in Chapter 2, the group was created in the US in 1836. It helped spur Irish machine politics and created a strong base for Irish Nationalism in the US before Irish independence. In 1919, for example, the AOH hosted Eamon de Valera at its annual convention in San Francisco, giving him a platform to argue for Irish independence and gather Irish American support for it.

The AOH's green credentials are also tied to its embrace of Catholicism. While the group is now most often viewed as a cultural organization, it still wades into politics, and its Catholic roots frame which issues it speaks on and how it speaks about them. In the US, for example, the AOH embraces a pro-life position and engages in "news, education, and advocacy for life from conception until natural death according to the teachings of the Catholic Church and the Holy Bible" (AOH, 2025b).

The AOH also staked out political positions during the Troubles that affirmed the Nationalist position on the conflict and at times highlighted its ties to Republican groups. And, as we discussed in Chapter 8, since the peace agreement was signed, the group has become one of the most prominent Irish American organizations advocating for restitution and justice for a variety of attacks aimed at Catholic civilians during the Troubles.

After the Protocol was adopted, the AOH began speaking more openly about Irish unity and pushing for the British government to call a referendum in the near future. Its emblem has appeared on each of the St. Patrick's Day ads produced by Sinn Féin that call for a referendum.[3] In February 2023, the AOH also hosted a webinar with Irish Senator Frances Black, who chairs a pro-unification group called Ireland's Future. During the webinar, Black petitioned Irish Americans to echo her group's push for a referendum.

The AOH's stance is significant because it is the largest Irish American membership organization in the US today. It has also been

---

[3] The other groups listed are the Brehon Law Society of New York, Suffolk and Nassau Counties, the Irish American Unity Conference, the James Connolly Irish-American Labor Coalition, and the Ladies AOH (Friends of Sinn Féin USA, 2023).

willing to go beyond what the Irish government has committed to so far (Fitzgerald, 2021). Although Sinn Féin in Ireland has long supported holding a referendum, Ireland's other main political parties have taken what Ger FitzGerald (2021) calls "a more incremental and consensual approach." By getting out in front of the Irish government on the issue, FitzGerald (2021) argues that the AOH may induce a "radical flank effect," effectively providing "some political cover for the Irish government by shifting the boundaries of discourse."

The AOH also supports the American Irish State Legislators Caucus (AISLC), which it sees as having multiple purposes, including promoting Irish American engagement in pushing for unification. As we discussed in Chapter 7, the group's formation in 2021 was spearheaded by Irish Senator and former chair of the Senate Mark Daly from Fianna Fail. Daly is a strong advocate of the Irish unity, albeit via a shared Ireland approach that acknowledges and aims to address the concerns of Unionists. The AISLC has, as one of its purposes, to "support the people of Ireland in their work towards a shared future for all people on the island of Ireland" ("American Irish State Legislators Caucus: About," no date). O'Connell explained to us that the strategy of the state level caucus was twofold. The first was to create a base of Irish American politicians who can "move up to the Congressional level." From there, it is implied, they could advance a variety of Irish American goals, including pushing for unification. The second part of the strategy was to create a cadre of state legislators who could push for unification at the state level. As he explained: "If you have 40 state legislatures saying they want a united Ireland, it puts pressure on the British government."

## *The proceed with caution camp*

In contrast to the push camp, those in the proceed with caution camp tend to follow the example set by groups like the Four Horsemen and the Congressional Friends of Ireland, who were more closely aligned with the SDLP and other groups advocating the constitutional Nationalist position. While they may champion Irish unity, they are cautious about campaigning for a united Ireland prematurely or without welcome. For example, former Irish diplomat and member of the Ad Hoc Committee Ted Smyth told us: "I think any responsible politician would not want to push the hard united Ireland option right now. Let's go back to the John Hume approach to agree on what we can agree on and base constitutional proposals on that."

Smyth also told us that he thought the Biden Administration agreed with him: "I believe that any diplomat or policy person in the Biden Administration would say we can't force a united Ireland now but we will help you with your shared island plans as part of the Good Friday peace process." Bruce Morrison, Co-Chair of the Ad Hoc Committee, took a similar tack. Though he told us that Brexit "created a much stronger case for a united Ireland," he also reminded us: "There's no evidence that people want it right now ... I'm much less sure that a border poll would lead to a united Ireland." Mitchell Reiss agreed:

> In Belfast, the polls that I've seen, it's not just Protestants who want to remain part of the Union, there is a significant percentage of Catholics who also want to remain part of the UK. So again, this idea that there is going to be unification and champagne corks popping, I think it's premature to be premature. It's unrealistic. I think talking about it is a feel-good distraction for some instead of rolling up your sleeves and getting involved in some of the hard-core problems that affect day to day life in NI.

Many Irish Americans we interviewed also recognized that reunification was premature because the pro-unity campaign was not having conversations with the very people they most needed to have conversations with—the Unionists and Loyalists who oppose reunification. Indeed, a referendum would likely not pass without some Unionist votes. And were a referendum to pass with only negligible Unionist support, Loyalists could still spoil the result on the back end by engaging in violence. Martin Galvin, the former Director of NORAID and the current Chairman of AOH's National Freedom-for-All-Ireland group, is firmly in the "push" camp, but he raised several difficulties in our interview: "One of the things is to get the British and the Unionists to be serious. The thing that concerns me is that you have people on the Irish side offering concessions but the Unionists don't want to even address possible concessions or talk about reciprocal actions."

The wider momentum toward a potential referendum means, however, that many Irish Americans do not want to sit out the issue completely. Hence, some of the people we spoke with, who were largely cautious about pushing for unity, talked about preparing for potential reunification by making sure that the UK, Northern Ireland, and Irish governments have sorted out key technical issues before a referendum is called. As we noted earlier, a common point of reference for how *not* to run a referendum was Brexit. For example, Irish Americans in this camp strongly believe that citizens of Northern Ireland should know exactly what they would be voting for in a referendum, in contrast to the confusion about Brexit.

There are a variety of issues to be sorted out. Our interview subjects explained that reunification would require, among other adjustments, numerous constitutional and legal changes. The Act of the Union, which still governs Northern Ireland, would need to be replaced by new domestic legislation and a new treaty with Ireland. Reunification would also require new Irish treaties with the EU to replace those between the EU and the UK that govern the territory of Northern Ireland. Another important question is whether Stormont would be abolished, or Northern Ireland would have a devolved parliament within Ireland. How two such parliaments would interact would also need to be determined. Likewise, the Irish Constitution would need to be changed to cohere with the Good Friday/Belfast Agreement's constitutional protection for British identity.[4]

There are also a variety of economic issues to consider. Reunification would be costly, and it is not clear whether the Irish government could cover these costs on its own. The current subsidy from the UK to Northern Ireland is approximately £15 billion per year. One study suggests the price tag for unification could reach €8 billion (Fitzgerald and Morgenroth, 2024). Though Sinn Féin has rejected that amount as unrealistically high (Bolton, 2024), no one doubts that unification will be costly. Smaller-scale economic questions also abound, including when, how, and how much of Northern Ireland's pensioners' benefits would be transferred after reunification. Our interview subjects also raised

---

[4] For more on these challenges, see the Working Group on Unification Referendums (2021) and O'Leary (2022).

questions about health and education, given that citizens of the UK receive healthcare through the National Health Service, while those in the Republic purchase it through private insurers. They also mentioned that national symbols would likely need to be changed as they were in post-apartheid South Africa. Given the symbolic weight that flags and emblems have carried in Northern Ireland, what these new symbols might look like is no trivial matter.

Given all of these potential complications, some groups, like the Ad Hoc Committee, believe the most important thing they can do is to make sure that the rules of the Belfast/Good Friday Agreement as it pertains to the referendum are respected. This means ensuring that any decision in a border poll, if it occurs, is for the people of the island of Ireland alone, and that the British government does not interfere or advocate for one outcome or another in the process in any form.

Finally, words of caution from various Irish Americans we interviewed also included concern that holding a referendum too soon, before it had sufficient support to pass, would mean further delays to reunification. Indeed, the SOSNI cannot call another referendum for seven years after a poll has been conducted. Irish Americans also worried that if a poll was called, and failed, the Good Friday institutions in Northern Ireland (the Assembly and the Executive) might struggle to function with parties and voters laser-focused on winning or defeating the next referendum. In short, the campaign for unification could undermine ongoing peace building in the meantime.

## The rub: sorting out the role of the US

Not surprisingly, given the differing opinions on calling a border poll, Irish Americans are also divided on what role the US should play in the unification process more broadly. Some argue for a muscular, interventionist approach, while others think a support role in the background, encouraging fair play and best practices, is best. Irish American groups largely pulled in the same direction on Brexit, but this issue could fracture their common cause.

A person with close ties to Irish American groups, who requested anonymity to talk on this subject, explained the Irish Republican position as two-pronged—appealing for direct involvement and looking to the US to check the UK government:

> If you support the Good Friday Agreement, you support the right of people to determine the constitutional agreement. So, you can't say you support the agreement and oppose unity referendums. We'd be looking at the US to make sure that when we get to that point, that they make sure the British government doesn't do things it shouldn't. They don't have to take a position but have to support the process for a referendum. The US could oversee the process.

Irish Senator Mark Daly explained that even moderate Irish parties may seek a significant, hands-on role for Irish America vis-à-vis unification:

> It's a simple as this: George Mitchell transformed Northern Ireland. He was appointed by the US President with the agreement of two sovereign nations, including the UK. So that's the kind of intervention we're talking about. It's not like, "everybody, do your best, and please play nice." No, no, no. It's more like, we'll invest, and, the United States are not going to be a bystander to this issue. They are not going to be a spectator to this. This issue is not a spectator sport.

Other Irish Americans object to Daly's approach and his understanding of Mitchell's role in 1998. Daly's optimism aside, it is highly unlikely any American president would openly support reunification because it runs counter to the position Mitchell himself hammered out during negotiations—that only the people of Northern Ireland can answer the constitutional question. More cautious Irish Americans support George Mitchell-type engagement if and when the time comes. Kevin Sullivan explained what this would look like to us. After emphasizing the fact that "Irish unification is not a subject that we are working on ... the Committee's sole focus is to protect the GFA," he asserted that:

> Irish America can play a constructive role. We can ask a lot of questions, send groups over to talk to them,

foster conversation and cooperation. Instinctively, Irish America will be attracted to the idea of a united Ireland, something they have been supporting for over 175 years. That said, there is clear awareness of the complexity of getting this done and real drivers of change will be the young people who make up the GFA generation.

Given these differences, it is possible that the AOH and other Irish American groups could play the radical flank role within Irish America as well as in Ireland, pushing more mainline organizations to begin advocating for a referendum. What is not clear is how many of them would be willing to play this role if they feel the particulars are not worked out, the referendum call stood outside the agreement's parameters, the vote is likely to be close, and/or violence was likely.

Regardless of the timeline, the importance of the US to this process was acknowledged by almost all our interview subjects. It was summarized nicely by a senior Congressional staffer: "It's remarkable how many people we see who see the fulcrum of decision being in Washington. They really put a lot of emphasis on what members of Congress think … This is an unfortunate byproduct of the agreement, that people rely on us to play that role."

# 10

# Irish America: A Force to Be Reckoned with on Brexit

When we began this book, we struggled with a basic question: is Irish America an ethnic lobby? As we explain throughout this book, contemporary Irish America does not lobby in any traditional sense. There is no formal interest group or even a few select firms that lay out Irish America's interests in Senate and House offices or to the Executive Branch. There are virtually no Irish American PACs. And while individual Irish Americans make political donations, there is no evidence that Irish Americans act as a group to support particular candidates. Moreover, though Irish Americans were traditionally associated with the Democratic Party, today they are now like the rest of America—split between the two parties in near-equal proportions. In fact, there is no longer even a unified Irish American voting bloc to mobilize.

Despite this anomalous behavior, we ultimately decided to treat Irish America as an ethnic lobby. The main reason for this is because there is still a small group of Irish Americans who lobby US policy makers on issues specific to Northern Ireland. And in the past few years, they have lobbied the US foreign policy establishment very effectively, to the point of shaping US foreign policy on the issues surrounding Brexit.

The success of Irish America in setting the terms of US foreign policy toward Brexit reveals some of the limitations of the ethnic lobbies literature. One of our main arguments is that while Irish America has some of the factors that scholars contend make ethnic lobbies successful, they lack others. Like other strong ethnic lobbies, Irish America has a sizable ethnic cohort to speak for—over 30 million people claim some Irish heritage according to the US Census. Strong ethnic lobbies also tend to have reliable representation in Congress and Irish America is no exception. There are a considerable number of Irish Americans in Congress, and they tend to act in concert, primarily through the Congressional Friends of Ireland Caucus, on issues considered important to Irish America.

However, unlike many other successful ethnic lobbies, Irish America is now fully assimilated, meaning that many people with Irish American heritage no longer define their interests in terms of their ethnic identity. As a result, on the eve of the Brexit referendum, Irish America's civil society infrastructure was smaller than its numbers would suggest. Many older Irish American groups had closed their doors, and the ones that remained, like the AOH and even the Friends of Ireland Caucus, were dramatically smaller than they once were. Moreover, as we noted earlier, Irish American organizations do almost no political fundraising. Irish America's success in the face of these anomalies suggests there are other important variables that may explain ethnic lobby success.

We argue that Irish America's power as an ethnic lobby in the Brexit period lies in five key traits, many of which are unique to it. For one, Irish America has a coherent sense of political identity, despite most Irish Americans being more than three or four generations out from their first Irish relative's arrival in the US. Though assimilated, well educated, and relatively privileged compared to contemporary immigrants, Irish Americans maintain a culture of shared anti-British grievance and anti-elitism that carries forward from their families' experiences. This creates a "tribal" bond[1] and the potential for ethnic action, especially when British decisions threaten Irish interests, as happened with Brexit.

Second, Irish Americans as a group also possess unusual political skills. Many Irish immigrants in the 19th century arrived having already been mobilized. As Tom McGurk argues, contemporary Irish Americans are:

---

[1] In her book, Caitríona Perry (2019) calls Irish America "The Tribe."

the descendants of the famine Irish and the thousands who followed, who arrived in penury with only the clothes on their backs and – post Daniel O'Connell and the land-wars in Ireland – a talent for political organization. Out of their earliest ghettos they created a political constituency from which the original Democratic Party was shaped and many of the trade unions emerged. (McGurk, 2019)

And they have continued to practice these political skills. They are networked, politically savvy, and strategic. As Irish American Niall O'Dowd cheekily observed: "We do communications, politics; Italians cook" (*The Economist*, 2019). Or, as Irish American lobbyist and lawyer Erik Huey told us when we asked him why Irish America doesn't have a single peak organization or a lobbying wing, they are "effective in ways that obviate the need for a larger structure."

The political skills Irish Americans possessed and the dense networks they formed also paid dividends. They used them to survive, and then to climb the American political ladder. Thus, the third feature of Irish American influence is that today, Irish Americans are in the halls of power—in Congress, the Executive Branch, and sometimes in the White House. That Irish Americans were in key high-profile positions to shape policy, especially once President Biden was elected, is an extremely important part of their success in lobbying on Brexit. But the picture is bigger than simply having Irish Americans in prominent roles in the public eye—once they are in power, they use those roles to defend Irish America's interests. During Trump's first term, for example, when it was unclear whether the President shared Irish America's concerns, Mick Mulvaney played a central role in steering the Trump Administration away from stances that could have been damaging to the peace process in Ireland. And during the Biden years, though his support and close familiarity with the issues was critically important, Biden was also surrounded by Irish Americans who had extensive knowledge of the situation and would see to important details as they pertained to US policy on Brexit.

Fourth, Irish America enjoys a quirky opportunity to build its soft power in the week-long spectacle that is the celebration of St. Patrick's Day in Washington, DC. Although parties and receptions are a big part of the celebrations, the real action happens on the sidelines, where high-level politicos from the US, Ireland, Northern Ireland, and Great Britain socialize, strategize, and strike deals. Pat Leahy and Martin Wall describe how this unfolded in 2022: "In a town where diplomats, politicians, lobbyists and visiting dignitaries cajole and wheedle for a few minutes of presidential attention, Biden was giving over the guts of an entire day for St Patrick's Day events" (Leahy and Wall, 2022a). As a former senior US diplomat notes about these occasions: "The influence, the access that Ireland has in Washington, it's just incredible" (Leahy and Wall, 2022a).

Finally, we argue that Irish American lobbying on Brexit was especially successful in part because it was pushing on an open door. The Irish are popular in Washington; their soft power attracts and the "brand" sells. As John McCarthy, who was the Vice President of Irish American Democrats before serving on President Biden's White House staff, told Caitríona Perry, the Irish "brand ... conjures up an image that people want to be part of" (Perry, 2019: 75). This goodwill was buttressed by the fact that the Irish American lobby was asking US policy makers to protect an agreement that is widely seen as a seminal American foreign policy achievement. In today's otherwise highly divisive politics, the Belfast/Good Friday Agreement and the US contribution enjoys broad bipartisan support. Indeed, many still feel a sense of ownership over the process. It's not uncommon, for example, for members of Congress to refer to the US as a "guarantor" of the agreement. Though technically untrue, their view signals pride in having been involved in achieving peace in Northern Ireland.

Our research on Irish America's efforts in the Brexit period also shows the importance of variables borrowed from the study of collective action—most notably the role of opportunity structure—in explaining the success of ethnic lobbies. Irish America's considerable resources were not, by themselves, enough to carry the day in its fight to prevent a hard border and the passage of legacy legislation; they also needed a favorable environment where they could wield these resources. In the case of the border question, Irish Americans' considerable political skills and high-level contacts meant they could get the ear of the UK Prime Minister, which is no minor thing. Indeed, when the Ad Hoc Committee wrote a letter to Prime Minister Theresa May, it expected and received a response—something most lobbies from another country could not do. But it was the UK's interests in a trade deal with the US, and Irish American Congressional leaders' ability to wield access to such a deal as both a carrot and a stick, that ultimately allowed it to force the UK government's hand. In other words, Brexit provided Irish Americans with opportunities to pressure the British that they had never enjoyed before Brexit. Absent the trade deal, it is not evident that Irish America would have had much effect on British policy.

Furthermore, our research reveals that Irish America's success in this moment was also due to its ability to shape US policy makers' sense of their strategic interests regarding Brexit. As we noted in Chapter 3, much of the literature on ethnic lobbies predicts that lobbies are most effective at influencing US foreign policy when their interests overlap with other national strategic interests. However, after the Brexit referendum passed, there was no clear sense of what US interests were, in large part because no one expected the referendum to pass. There was, in effect, a vacuum in the policy space, and to the extent that the US tried to fill it, it often did so in contradictory ways. President Obama, for example, personally opposed Brexit, writing an op-ed in *The Guardian* in support of the remain position just before the vote, but when Trump was elected, he spoke favorably about Brexit, even backing Boris Johnson's efforts to thwart May's proposed withdrawal deal. However, the Trump Administration was disorganized and uninterested in staffing up the State Department, so it never formulated a clear stance on how it thought Brexit should unfold. As efforts to strike a withdrawal deal began to unravel, Irish America stepped up to the plate.

In particular, the newly re-formed lobby reminded American policy makers of the importance of the Belfast/Good Friday Agreement to American interests and persuaded them that a hard border would undermine the agreement and the peace dividend it brought to Northern Ireland. Over several years, the Irish American lobby argued that British actions that risked producing a hard border by direct action or by default (that is, through a hard Brexit) violated the spirit and provisions of the agreement. Irish Americans also helped US policy makers to see where British undertakings risked violating international law and its own prior commitments. Thus, the Irish American lobby helped shape the US sense of its own interests in this confused and challenging period.

Despite the importance of the US's special relationship with the UK, particularly once Russia invaded Ukraine, the US came down firmly on the side of EU and Irish interests in the controversies over Brexit and pressured the British to modify and scale back their goals regarding Brexit in order to minimize their impact in Northern Ireland. In short, though the literature tends to focus the discussion of the success of ethnic lobbies on the extent to which they overlap with US strategic interests, our research shows how an ethnic lobby can help define US strategic interests.

## Assessing impact

We make two main arguments about Irish American influence on how Brexit would affect Northern Ireland in this book: that Irish America influenced US foreign policy on Brexit and that US policy constrained what the UK government was able to do when withdrawing from the EU. The first claim is relatively easy to establish. Irish America, greatly energized by Brexit and the threats posed by the potential of a hard border, reorganized itself, crafting a clear message about the risks to the Belfast/Good Friday Agreement and getting key stakeholders in Congress and the Executive Branch to communicate that message to British policy makers. Irish American influence on US foreign policy can be evidenced in all the statements, letters, resolutions, press releases, and so on issued by members of Congress and the Executive Branch on Brexit detailed in the preceding chapters.

In 2022 alone, for example, Irish Americans within Congress responded to British policy with a unified message communicated on two CODELs to Ireland/Northern Ireland, in two resolutions introduced, including HR 888, which passed by unanimous consent, and in multiple committee hearings. In 2022, the Biden Administration was also actively engaged in its own efforts to pressure the UK government, with messages delivered on multiple occasions and at multiple levels, such as directly from President Biden to all three UK Prime Ministers, plus those from Secretary of State Antony Blinken, US Trade Representative Katherine Tai, State Department Counselor Derek Chollet, the US ambassadors to Ireland and the UK, diplomatic staff in the Consul General's office in Belfast, and even members of the National Security Council. President Biden capped the year by appointing a special envoy.

Our second claim—that the US was able to influence UK policy concerning Brexit—is more difficult to assess. One reason for this is that the US was not the only force pushing the British to keep the border open or adhere to its commitments in the Withdrawal Agreement and the Northern Ireland Protocol. Rather, the US mirrored the positions taken by the EU and the Irish government that British demands were incompatible with EU policy and risked disrupting core elements of the Belfast/Good Friday Agreement. As a consequence, it is difficult to attribute responsibility solely or in majority part to the US. The US was one of a cacophony of voices that helped to persuade the British to adjust their stances. But we also believe that our evidence demonstrates that US leverage was important to British calculations and, thus, important to the final result of all of that joint lobbying. For example, as we observed in Chapter 7, after the British think tank Policy Exchange issued a damning report arguing that the UK was losing influence in the US and was being outmaneuvered by Irish diplomats, the UK dispatched extra hands to Washington to better make its case on Brexit.

Another reason why it is difficult to prove that the UK adjusted its policy stances in response to US pressure is that the UK's actions may have had many explanations. Domestic political actors, even within the Conservative Party, limited what the Brexiteers could achieve. As we detailed in Chapter 7, Johnson and Liz Truss lost their premierships not because they lost support in a general election, but because they lost the confidence of party members in the House of Commons; indeed, their fall brought Rishi Sunak to power.

Finally, getting interview subjects to provide unvarnished assessments about their intentions is often difficult, if not impossible. Sometimes actors refuse to explain why they take particular actions. More frequently, they offer only partial explanations for their decision making. Sometimes leaders may even lie about their reasoning, offering up propaganda that covers up factors that would be embarrassing or politically inconvenient to expose.

In our case, none of the prime ministers involved in the Brexit withdrawal negotiations—May, Johnson, Truss, and Sunak—have offered specific comments about how Irish American lobbying weighed on their decision making. We only have oblique references to the influence of Irish America, such as Johnson's parting warning in his farewell speech in the House of Commons to "Stay close to the Americans," or anonymous chatter from news articles that described his anger at Irish American pressure. To be fair, the UK government's refusal to speak openly about the US role is not surprising. The UK and the US are allies, leading pillars of "The West," and fully sovereign. If the UK government were to acknowledge bowing to US pressure, this would call its independence of action and self-determination into question.

To make our argument that Irish America did have some degree of influence in preventing a hard border, we sought evidence by following the process from the ground up; that is, we spoke to Irish Americans about who they talked to, who they wrote to, and what their interactions with these people were like. We also asked them if they felt like their lobbying worked and, if so, to explain why. Though there is always room for error in asking people seeking to exert influence to also assess that influence, it is not an unimportant piece of data. The Irish Americans we spoke to were cautious about exaggerating their effects and did not always present a rosy picture of their efforts. In fact, when we began this project, as we noted in Chapter 4, Irish Americans were not optimistic that they could wield influence. They also understood the limits of their influence regarding the Legacy Act, which we reviewed in Chapter 8.

To cross-check Irish American views, we looked at how the media described the impact of Irish American efforts. As we detail in Chapters 5–7, media coverage of the pressure Irish American placed on the UK government was extensive and frequently couched in terms of power politics.

We also conducted interviews with people outside of Irish America, but involved in some form or fashion in discussions about the UK's withdrawal plans, to consider how these people saw the influence of Irish America. We also looked closely at British government behavior for indications that they were concerned about the positions the US was taking and sought out counterfactuals, including dispositive measures that would clearly demonstrate a lack of influence—that is, if the UK government instituted a policy shortly after Irish Americans had lobbied against that policy.

Finally, in assessing the nature of Irish American influence, we took note of the opportunity structure at key junctures in debates on the UK's withdrawal from the EU. In so doing, we discovered that Irish America's influence was necessary but not sufficient. Irish America's political skills and its ability to have its message heard at the top levels of the US, UK, and Irish governments was important and rare among ethnic groups. However, it was leverage in the form of the trade deal that allowed Irish Americans to employ their skills to constrain what the British could do on the border. In contrast, lack of leverage during the legacy discussions meant that their influence did not bear fruit.

## Irish America's self-assessment

One of the things Irish America thinks it did well was framing the issues. Most of the people we interviewed, for example, thought that Brexit was a foolhardy endeavor. However, when mobilizing in 2019, they narrowed in on the negative consequence of Brexit that they had standing to comment on—maintaining the integrity of the Belfast/Good Friday Agreement. It helps to remember that several of the people we interviewed were in Congress in the 1990s and helped lay the groundwork for negotiations. Congressman Bruce Morrison, for example, helped get the Gerry Adams visas over the line—a "put up or shut up" moment for the IRA that ultimately paid a peace dividend. Congressman Jim Walsh had also served as chair of both the Ad Hoc Congressional Committee for Irish Affairs and the Friends of Ireland Caucus during the peace process. And others, like former Special Envoy Mitchell Reiss and former Consul General Barbara Stephenson, went to Belfast to help support the Belfast/Good Friday Agreement's implementation.

When we interviewed Stephenson, for example, she pointed to the Ad Hoc Committee's name as a smart move: "I think that 'protecting the Good Friday Agreement' was a great slogan. It was easy to understand and it was successful in keeping a border from going across Ireland." She also pointed to the broad nature of the word "protect" in this case. As she explained:

> The minute you define it [protecting the agreement], it begins to lose its power … The title gives the idea that

there won't be any just rolling over the Good Friday Agreement, it's much broader in its meaning. What exactly it means now I don't know, but I think it's actually very effective undefined.

Irish Americans also prided themselves on their message discipline—that is, they kept their focus by hammering home the same message over and over. As Kevin Sullivan told us in the run-up to Boris Johnson's eventual withdrawal deal: "Constant, consistent American support at all political levels, from Irish America to Congress and the White House, created an insurmountable green wall that Boris Johnson couldn't break." William Tranghese also pointed to Irish America's message discipline:

> I go back to the [Friends of Ireland] Caucus. They were very clear that they were against attempts to undermine the GFA. From the President and the Speaker on down you had members of Congress speaking with one voice. And, you have Irish American groups from across the country speaking with one voice.

Irish Americans also offered anecdotes and small asides that demonstrated their relevance with key actors involved in Brexit negotiations. One of these observations was historically note-worthy in its own right. When we interviewed Bill Tranghese, for example, we asked him about the Irish American role in late 2020/early 2021 as the EU deadline for implementing Johnson's 2020 Withdrawal Agreement was fast approaching (February 1, 2021). As we detailed in Chapter 5, the Conservatives and some Unionists in Northern Ireland spent much of 2020 in acrimonious efforts trying to unwind it, and the US was losing patience. So, we asked Tranghese what he and his boss, Congressman Neal, were doing in that period:

> Both embassies were in touch with us on an almost daily basis. So, they weighed in with the committee, and the British Secretary of State [for Northern Ireland] would come over relatively frequently to weigh in. In fact, as a sidebar, on January 6 at 2 pm just before the Capitol was stormed, we were sitting in Congressman

Neal's office and he was doing a Zoom call with the British Secretary of State and we had to get off because people were trying to break in. The office is on the second floor facing the Supreme Court. Once the West side was breached, people on the East side were literally standing outside the windows. We had to barricade the window and we had four armed guards in there with us. We had to barricade the door as well. They were trying to come in from both ends. He told the Secretary, "I'm going to have to end this call; we've got a little trouble here."

Tranghese also told us that as he and his colleagues were barricaded in the office for an hour, Northern Ireland was in the picture: "During that period of time, I heard from so many people from both sides of Ireland expressing concerns about our safety. Even on a day that traumatic, Ireland was on our minds."

### Assessments by actors in Ireland and Northern Ireland

To "test" Irish America's self-assessment of their success, we asked people in Ireland and Northern Ireland how they saw the role of Irish America. Some of these actors worked with Irish America, while others observed them from the sidelines. They all told us that Irish America had been successful at its mission, though they pointed to different reasons for their success and offered a variety of examples to illustrate. Dan Mulhall, who was the Irish Ambassador to the US for much of the time we cover in this book, told us that Irish America was so influential with the British because they had the ear of their own government. They had influence over US policy and could frame the conversation as a matter of US national interests:

> The story of US involvement in support of peace and reconciliation in Northern Ireland is one in which the interests of a small country, Ireland, came, by dint of the skillful deployment of the soft power of its diaspora, to get an important hearing in the United States, even when those interests were at variance with the preferences of one of the US's prime allies, the UK.

Mulhall also gave a nod to the history that gave rise to Irish American influence, telling us: "That continuing US dimension with regard to Northern Ireland is a benign legacy of the emigrant Irish." Indeed, Mulhall described the Americans' role in Northern Ireland as built in, as something the British cannot ignore. When we interviewed Mulhall in 2022, for example, he pointed to an article he had just read that distilled this view: "I saw a report over the weekend that Prime Minister Sunak plans to call President Biden to brief him on the Northern Ireland Protocol, which suggests that he recognizes an inescapable US dimension to this issue." We also return here to Mulhall's comments, first quoted in Chapter 5, in which he described Speaker Nancy Pelosi meeting with the ERG during the 2019 CODEL as "a genuine game changer."

A government official in Northern Ireland, who asked to go off the record on this topic, argued that Irish America was influential in shaping the final outcome of the UK's withdrawal negotiations. Specifically, he credited Irish Americans with pre-emptively setting the parameters of debate the UK would have as it worked through various withdrawal plans:

> The American role, it's not visible, but it was undoubtedly a massive factor in the background. If you are looking at the boundaries within which the UK could negotiate, there's a line of "you must not lose the US"—one of the boundaries for the UK was keeping the Americans on board.

Another interviewee, who requested anonymity to speak on this topic, also affirmed the importance of Irish America's role in setting US policy and the US in turn shaping UK policy:

> Long story short, once they [the UK government] learned they weren't getting a trade deal—and Richie Neal, Nancy Pelosi, and the Friends of Ireland made that clear—Britain had to realize they had to negotiate with the EU because the US had pushed for it so hard. And, then when Biden comes in, it becomes even more clear. I think it was the June G7 meeting, where Biden puts down the marker directly with the British and the

Europeans. And that was that, the resolution had to be true to the GFA and there can be no hard border.

We also asked Stephen Kelly, the Chief Executive of Manufacturing NI, how he saw Irish America's impact. Kelly is not a politician, but his group opposed a hard border and engaged in lobbying to prevent it. Kelly's lobbying put him in a position to meet Irish Americans who traveled to Northern Ireland, including members of CODELs and other diplomats working with the US State Department in Belfast. He also attended numerous St. Patrick's Day celebrations in the US, where he talked with members of Congress, the Ad Hoc Committee, and the AOH, among others. When we asked Kelly if Irish America's lobbying had made a difference, he replied: "The US absolutely made a difference." He went on to explain that Irish Americans had helped reign in the UK government: "There were key moments of real jeopardy, where US involvement was critical to get the UK to step back from taking actions that would have caused the whole thing to collapse ... they brought logic and clarity so they [the UK government] didn't do something stupid."

Kelly also noted that his interlocutors in Irish America had a remarkable influence on American policy, including having the ear of the President. Indeed, he marveled at the depth of their influence, telling us: "Some of the things we said as a business community appeared in presidential briefings before G5 and G7 [meetings]."

Professor Katy Hayward of Queen's University Belfast, who has established herself as the premier academic working on the impact on Brexit in Northern Ireland, brought the first and second parts of our argument together, emphasizing the influence of Irish America in shaping both US and UK position taking. "The US played a critical role," she told us. "It acted as a co-guarantor. Not in legal terms but in moral terms. It really came into its own." Hayward told us that the ability of Irish America to wield influence was connected to its involvement in the peace process. As she put it:

> You realize you are standing on top of decades of relationship building. The thing that really strikes me is the depth of that commitment and continued concern by the Americans. And that's individuals who have this remarkable capacity to engage on the details, who

really understand, and know how it would affect the peace process. The thing that struck me was that these individuals stayed on top of what was happening here. Some are retired or semi-retired but they brought those skills, those incredible networks. That opens up into fairly influential places pretty quickly.

Hayward also singled out the Ad Hoc Committee as having particular influence. She noted, for example:

> Kevin [Sullivan] would say to me, we're meeting with Lord Caine, the Ambassador, etc. And, they were getting these meetings with people you, as a citizen in Northern Ireland, would never have a chance to talk to. And they would be speaking at government meetings. So, he'd say to me, "We're meeting with the Secretary of State. What messages should we convey?" Then, he'd come back and tell me what he'd been able to convey.

Hayward also noted the two-way nature of the Ad Hoc Committee's relationship with scholars in Ireland and Northern Ireland. Each side fed the other side important information that strengthened their hand. In a 2019 visit, for example, Hayward told us that she and others highlighted for the Ad Hoc Committee just how important a US-UK trade deal was to Brexiteers. This information allowed the Ad Hoc Committee to identify this key source of leverage that Irish Americans in Congress would ultimately use to pressure the UK government against a hard Brexit:

> At the time [2019], the golden egg at the end of all of it was a trade deal with the US, so, we wanted folks in the US to know just how important the Brits saw the trade deal as their next step. We wanted to convey to the Americans that they could make a connection between getting a trade deal and avoiding a hard border.

Hayward also told us that the US internationalized Brexit, taking it out of a regional context and putting it under global klieg lights. She said American involvement meant that the UK government knew any moves it made would not go unnoticed stateside. And it wasn't happy about that: "Some of them were clearly irritated by it. They were irritated by Richie Neal's comments, by Nancy Pelosi's comments. Social media played a big part. So, you could see the effect of the US on the UK through the posts and comments on social media."

That said, Hayward also reminded us that the British were not likely to admit to feeling Irish American pressure: "They knew they were being watched. But, would they admit that necessarily? You'd probably have to wait for people to retire."

Another official who asked to speak off the record also highlighted the importance of Irish America's role. This person was careful to remind us that Unionists would take issue with the way Irish America defined protecting the Belfast/Good Friday Agreement. "Unionists believe the Protocol compromised the agreement," this person told us, adding: "An open border is not written into the peace agreement, for example." However, like the other anonymous interviewees quoted earlier, this person told us that Irish America successfully argued that the open border was a key dividend of the agreement, and that reinstating it would put the peace at risk. Then they kept "laying down markers" about the agreement that the UK government could not ignore:

> I think the place Irish America was most effective was when the UK government came to engage with the US. There was always a line dropped in at the end of the discussion to be careful to keep the Good Friday Agreement intact. So, a mission coming to talk about steel would have a mention to the Good Friday Agreement added in. It has a drip, drip, drip effect.

They also thought the markers had an effect, citing the British government's decision to send representatives to the US that we discussed earlier and in greater detail in Chapter 7: "The British Embassy realized their arguments weren't landing in the US. The Irish had gotten the upper hand and the Irish American lobby was crucial in that. Richie Neal was crucial in that. And [Bill] Keating was crucial, always working to have a CODEL to Ireland/Northern Ireland."

However, this official did caution that had other contextual factors been different, Irish America's success may have been more limited. In particular, they told us that Irish America's impact likely would have been weaker if Trump had been more focused on the issue: "If he'd been more organized on Brexit, he could have advantaged Britain over the EU, but he didn't get organized. And if Boris and Trump had aligned in power at the same time, it might have been different."

## Media assessments

The media also reported extensively on the pressure Irish America was putting on the UK government, reinforcing the notion that the British had to respond to it. An exhaustive review is beyond the scope of this chapter, but we noted numerous stories over the period covered in this book that follow this pattern, with many openly suggesting that the US had the upper hand in the relationship. A *New York Times* headline in May 2022, for example, described the US as issuing a warning to the UK: "Washington Warns UK to Temper Its Spat with the EU." Another *Politico* headline that same month read: "Joe Biden Could Ghost Boris Johnson over Northern Ireland Brexit Row." The tenor of reporting on the US-UK relationship regarding Brexit was so one-sided that American intervention was eventually normalized. A 2023 *UnHerd* article (Lynch, 2023) on a letter the House of Representatives sent to Prime Minister Sunak, discussed in Chapter 7, opened this way: "Another British government bill, another opportunity for American intervention."

We also note that the press often covered internal Conservative machinations in a way that suggested they were under pressure not to cross the line in the sand Irish America had drawn and was vigorously defending. As we mentioned in Chapter 7, a 2023 *New York Times* story suggested that Boris Johnson was privately fuming at the Americans' role, even using a profanity to describe how he felt about it: "F★★★ the Americans!" (Shipman and Wheeler, 2023). There was no similar treatment of Irish America in the press, even in the tabloid broadsheets accustomed to taking potshots at those it disagrees with. This may have been because its lobbying was consistent and disciplined and there was little daylight between Irish Americans in the White House, Congress, and civil society that the tabloids could play up.

## Conclusion

This book recounts a fascinating story of an ethnic lobby whose heyday had seemingly occurred decades before. Indeed, two years after the Brexit referendum passed, academics, public commentators, and even a good number of Irish Americans were predicting the lobby's continued and inevitable decline. Against all these expectations, Irish America rallied. Capitalizing on its deep network and insider skills, the lobby would ultimately shape US foreign policy by defining what American interests were in the Brexit debacle that was then engulfing its most important ally. The lobby also exploited the surprising opportunities of the moment to help constrain the actions of its historic nemesis.

In telling the unusual story of Irish America in the post-Brexit period, the book documents how US policy on Brexit was developed as the UK debated the terms of its withdrawal from the EU. The book also makes contributions to the scholarly literature on ethnic lobbies, pointing out the limitations of that literature and offering new variables that may help explain their function and efficacy more effectively.

Despite Irish America's extraordinary success in this Brexit moment, we are not especially sanguine about the future of Irish America's power and influence. We think it is more likely than not that the cohesion of the Irish American community and the salience of its identity will dissipate with time.

That said, there is some room for optimism, at least in the short term. Some Irish Americans will, undoubtedly, continue to follow the events of Northern Ireland closely and work to keep the US engaged in the broader peace process. The Ad Hoc Committee to Protect the Good Friday Agreement has, for example, pivoted from Brexit-specific issues to a broader campaign to ensure that the US keeps putting pressure on the British government to implement the parts of the agreement it has not converted into law, such as the Civic Forum and the Bill of Rights. It is also using its contacts in Congress and the returning Trump Administration to continue to lobby the British government to address deficiencies in its legacy legislation. The Irish government will also continue to be active and intentional about finding links to US policy makers. The government's "Global Ireland" strategy, which is aimed at doubling the country's diplomatic footprint by 2025, includes the creation of "a new flagship "Ireland House"—a hub for diplomacy, trade, business, and cultural promotion—in Los Angeles and plans to expand Irish diplomatic presence elsewhere in the Americas.

In addition, Irish Americans have formed new organizations in recent years that aim to keep American interest in Ireland/Northern Ireland alive into the future, including the Young Friends of Ireland and the American Irish State Legislators Caucus (AISLC). The AISLC aims to cultivate interest in Ireland/Northern Ireland among state legislators with the understanding that states are important centers of policy making in the US and that state legislatures are pipelines for future members of Congress In 2023, the organization took 20 members of Congress and nearly 200 state legislators from 50 states to Ireland and Northern Ireland to celebrate the 25th anniversary of the Good Friday Agreement. And the issue of Irish unification will likely stir many Irish American hearts if a referendum is called.

Though they may mobilize again (and even open their wallets), particularly in relation to Irish unification, the unique opportunities available to Irish Americans to shape US policy and contribute to shaping British policy in such a profound way as around Brexit may never repeat themselves. However, our point remains: whatever its demographic and other challenges in the years ahead, Irish America has more than proved its relevance in the Brexit era.

# APPENDIX

# Interviews

| Name | Date of Interview |
|---|---|
| **Bruce Morrison**<br>Former Member, US House of Representatives (D-CT), Co-founder and member of the Ad Hoc Committee to Protect the Good Friday Agreement | July 7, 2020 |
| **Kevin Sullivan**<br>Project Director, Ad Hoc Committee to Protect the Good Friday Agreement | July 23, 2020 |
| **Niall O'Dowd**<br>Founder, *IrishCentral* | July 24, 2020 |
| **John Connorton**<br>Retired Partner at Hawkins Delafield and Wood LLP | July 24, 2020 |
| **Joseph (Joe) Crowley**<br>Former Member, US House of Representatives (D-NY) | July 29, 2020 |
| **Michael Cummings**<br>Secretary, American Brexit Committee | July 30, 2020 |
| **James (Jim) Walsh**<br>Former Member, US House of Representatives (R-NY), Co-founder and member of the Ad Hoc Committee to Protect the Good Friday Agreement | July 31, 2020 |

# INTERVIEWS

| Name | Date of Interview |
|---|---|
| **Trina Vargo** <br> Former aide to US Senator Edward (Ted) Kennedy, Founder US-Ireland Alliance | August 7, 2020 |
| **Anonymous** <br> Congressional staff official | August 12, 2020 |
| **Susan Davis** <br> Former head, Irish American Republicans, Board of Directors Ireland Funds | August 14, 2020 |
| **Mitchell Reiss** <br> Former Special Envoy to Northern Ireland, Member of the Independent Reporting Commission | August 11, 2021 |
| **Susan Elliot** <br> Former US Consul General, Belfast | August 12, 2021 |
| **Peter Kissel** <br> President, Irish American Unity Conference | August 12, 2021 |
| **Martin Galvin** <br> Former Director, NORAID | August 13, 2021 |
| **Barbara Stephenson** <br> Former US Consul General, Belfast | September 14, 2021 |
| **Brian O'Dwyer** <br> Former National Chairman of Irish Americans for Clinton-Gore (1992 and 1996), Former National Chairman of Irish Americans for Gore (2000) | February 24, 2022 |
| **Ted Smyth** <br> President of the Advisory Board of Glucksman Ireland House, New York University, Chair of the Clinton Institute for American Studies, University College Dublin | March 3, 2022 |
| **Dan Mulhall** <br> Former Irish Ambassador to the US | March 11, 2022 and July 28, 2023 |
| **Danny O'Connell** <br> President, Ancient Order of Hibernians | March 24, 2022 |

| Name | Date of Interview |
| --- | --- |
| **Hilary Beirne** <br> Founder and Chair of New York City St. Patrick's Day Foundation | April 22, 2022 |
| **Chris Carey** <br> Founder, Young Friends of Ireland | May 18, 2022 |
| **Andrew McCormick** <br> Former Northern Ireland Civil Service Permanent Secretary | June 28, 2023 |
| **Mick Mulvaney** <br> Former Chief of Staff, President Donald Trump, Former Special Envoy to Northern Ireland | June 30, 2023 |
| **Katy Hayward** <br> Professor, Queen's University Belfast | August 2, 2023 |
| **Lyndon Hughes-Jennett** <br> Northern Ireland Office, Representative to the US | September 23, 2023 |
| **Anonymous** <br> British Embassy Official | September 23, 2023 |
| **William Tranghese** <br> Former Chief of Staff for Congressman Richie Neal | January 23, 2024 |
| **Eric Huey** <br> Lobbyist, Platinum Advisors, LLC | January 23, 2024 |
| **Stephen Kelly** <br> Chief Executive, Manufacturing NI | April 16, 2024 |
| **Andrew Elliott** <br> (Now Former) Director, Northern Ireland Bureau | April 22, 2024 |
| **Mark Daly** <br> Member, Seanad Éireann | April 24, 2024 |
| **Ciarán Quinn** <br> Sinn Féin Representative to the US and Canada | April 26, 2024 |

# INTERVIEWS

| Name | Date of Interview |
|---|---|
| **Chris Heaton-Harris** <br> Former Secretary of State for Northern Ireland | August 2, 2024 |
| **Hilary Benn** <br> MP, Secretary of State for Northern Ireland | October 15, 2024 |
| **Cited interviews by author(s) done prior to this project** | |
| **Paul Quinn** <br> Board of Directors, Ireland Funds (previously the American Ireland Fund) | March 23, 2015 |

# References

Abbas, M., Bradley, M. and Symington, M. (2021) "Biden Becomes a Divisive Figure in N. Ireland as Post-Brexit Tensions Simmer," *NBC News*, July 18. Available from: https://www.nbcnews.com/news/world/biden-becomes-divisive-figure-northern-ireland-post-brexit-tensions-simmer-n1274308

"Addressing Northern Ireland Legacy Issues" (2020) Northern Ireland Office. Available from: https://www.gov.uk/government/news/addressing-northern-ireland-legacy-issues

"Ad-Hoc Committee to Protect the Good Friday Agreement to Boris Johnson" (2021) Available from: https://caj.org.uk/wp-content/uploads/2021/09/Ad-Hoc-Comm-letter-to-PM-on-Amnesty-Proposal-090821.pdf

Adityo, A., Harapan, A.A., and Marihandono, D. (2019) "Re-examining De Gaulle's Rejection of British Membership in the European Economic Community," *Eastern Journal of European Studies*, 10(2): 5–18.

Ahern, B. (2023) "Comments Delivered as Part of a Council on Foreign Relations Forum 'Lessons from History Series: The Good Friday Agreement Twenty-Five Years Later,'" March 27. Available from: https://www.cfr.org/event/lessons-history-series-good-friday-agreement-twenty-five-years-later

Ahrari, M. (1987a) "Conclusions," in M. Ahrari (ed) *Ethnic Groups and US Foreign Policy*. Westport, CT: Greenwood Press, pp 155–158.

Ahrari, M. (1987b) "Introduction," in M. Ahrari (ed) *Ethnic Groups and US Foreign Policy*. Westport, CT: Greenwood Press, pp xi–xxi.

Alfaro, M. and Viser, M. (2022) "Biden to Appoint Joe Kennedy III as Special Envoy to Northern Ireland," December 16. Available from: https://www.washingtonpost.com/politics/2022/12/16/joe-kennedy-northern-ireland/

Amaro, S. (2020) "Biden Says Trade Deal with Britain Hangs on Respect for Northern Irish Peace Agreement," *CNBC*, September 17. Available from: https://www.cnbc.com/2020/09/17/brexit-biden-says-trade-deal-with-britain-hangs-on-respect-for-gfa.html

# REFERENCES

Ambrosio, T. (2002a) "Entangling Alliances: The Turkish-Israeli Lobbying Partnership and Its Unintended Consequences," in T. Ambrosio (ed) *Ethnic Identity Groups and U.S. Foreign Policy*. Westport, CT: Greenwood Publishing Group, pp 143–167.

Ambrosio, T. (2002b) "Ethnic Identity Groups and US Foreign Policy," in T. Ambrosio (ed) *Ethnic Identity Groups and US Foreign Policy*. Westport, CT: Greenwood Publishing Group, pp 1–19

"American Irish State Legislators Caucus: About" (no date) Available from: https://aislc.org/about

AOH (Ancient Order of Hibernians) (2025a) "About the AOH." Available from: https://aoh.com/about-the-aoh/#

AOH (Ancient Order of Hibernians) (2025b) "Pro-Life." Available from: https://aoh.com/pro-life-2/#:~:text=Larry%20Squires%2C%20National%20Pro%2DLife,every%20innocent%20being%20to%20life.&text=Before%20I%20formed%20you%20in,were%20born%20I%20consecrated%20you

Arthur, P. (1994) "The Anglo-Irish Joint Declaration: Towards a Lasting Peace?" *Government and Opposition*, 29(2): 218–230.

Arthur, P. (1997) "American Intervention in the Anglo-Irish Peace Process: Incrementalism or Interference?" *Cambridge Review of International Affairs*, XI(1): 46–63.

Arthur, P. (2001) *Special Relationships: Britain, Ireland and the Northern Ireland Problem*. Belfast: Blackstaff Press.

Asmus, R. (2004) *Opening NATO's Door*. New York: Columbia University Press.

Baker, P. (2020) "Trump Names Mark Meadows Chief of Staff, Ousting Mick Mulvaney," *New York Times*, March 7. Available from: https://www.nytimes.com/2020/03/06/us/politics/trump-mark-meadows-mick-mulvaney.html

Bayliss, C. (2020) "What a Biden Presidency Means for a UK-US Trade Deal," *ITV News*, October 31. Available from: https://www.itv.com/news/2020-10-31/what-would-a-joe-biden-presidency-mean-for-a-uk-us-post-brexit-trade-deal

BBC (2019a) "Brexit: EU and UK Reach Deal but DUP Refuses Support," October 17. Available from: https://www.bbc.com/news/uk-politics-50079385

BBC (2019b) "Brexit: What is in Boris Johnson's New Deal with the EU?," October 21. Available from: https://www.bbc.com/news/uk-50083026

BBC (2021a) "Brexit: UK Wants to Redraw Northern Ireland Protocol," July 21. Available from: https://www.bbc.com/news/uk-politics-57911148

BBC (2021b) "G7 Summit: Don't Imperil NI Peace, Biden to Warn UK and EU," June 9. Available from: https://www.bbc.com/news/uk-politics-57411343

BBC (2021c) "US Group Writes to PM over Troubles Legacy Plan," September 9. Available from: https://www.bbc.co.uk/news/uk-northern-ireland-58501467

BBC (2022) "NI Protocol: White House Warns Again against Unilateral Action," September 7. Available from: https://www.bbc.com/news/uk-northern-ireland-62818906

Beard, S., Padilla, R. and Garrison, J. (2023) "'The Most Irish of All Presidents': Joe Biden's Roots and Family Tree," *USA Today*, April 12. Available from: https://eu.usatoday.com/story/graphics/2023/04/12/joe-biden-family-tree/11640997002/

Beattie, K. (2018) "Jewish American Foreign Policy Lobbies," in *Congress and Diaspora Politics*. Albany, NY: State University of New York Press, pp 65–89.

*Belfast Telegraph* (2019) "Trump's Pick for Irish Ambassador Pledges to Uphold Good Friday Agreement 'at All Costs,'" April 12. Available from: https://www.belfasttelegraph.co.uk/news/brexit/trumps-pick-for-irish-ambassador-pledges-to-uphold-good-friday-agreement-at-all-costs/38008404.html

Bell, C. (2003) "Dealing with the Past in Northern Ireland," *Fordham International Law Journal*, 26(44): 1096–1118.

Bennett, B. (2021) "How a Diplomatic Spat Shook up Biden's First Day in the UK", *TIME*, June 10. Available from: https://time.com/6072737/biden-united-kingdom-northern-ireland/

Biden, J. (2007) *Promises to Keep: On Life and Politics*. New York: Random House.

Blessing, P. (1980) "Irish," in *Harvard Encyclopedia of American Ethnic Groups*. Cambridge, MA: Harvard University Press, p 528.

Boffey, D. and Walker, P. (2021) "Joe Biden Supports EU Position on Northern Ireland, Says Von der Leyen," *The Guardian*, November 10. Available from: https://www.theguardian.com/politics/2021/nov/10/frost-repeats-threat-to-trigger-article-16-but-says-agreement-is-possible

Bolton, M. (2023) "Sinn Féin Dispute Report Finding United Ireland Could Cost €20B for 20 Years," *Connaught Telegraph*, April 4. Available from: https://www.con-telegraph.ie/2024/04/04/study-shows-united-ireland-could-cost-e20bn-for-20-years/

Bond, D. (2022) "Minister Risks Inflaming Tensions with US over Northern Ireland," *Evening Standard*, June 15.

Booth, W. (2019) "Pelosi Warns There Will Be No U.S.-U.K. Trade Deal if Brexit Harms the Irish Peace Accord," *Washington Post*, April 16. Available from: https://www.washingtonpost.com/world/pelosi-warns-there-will-be-no-us-uk-trade-deal-if-brexit-harms-the-irish-peace-accord/2019/04/16/51dff152-6049-11e9-bf24-db4b9fb62aa2_story.html

Borger, J. (2019) "We'll Block Trade Deal if Brexit Imperils Open Irish Border, Say US Politicians," *The Guardian*, July 31. Available from: https://www.theguardian.com/politics/2019/jul/31/brexit-mess-with-good-friday-and-well-block-uk-trade-deal-us-politicians-warn

Borger, J. (2021) "Why Joe Biden is so Invested in Defending Good Friday Agreement," *The Guardian*, June 10. Available from: https://www.theguardian.com/us-news/2021/jun/10/why-joe-biden-is-so-invested-in-defending-good-friday-agreement

Boulter, S. (2023) "Will Ireland's Neutrality Survive Putin's Aggression?" *CEPA*. Available from: https://cepa.org/article/will-irelands-neutrality-survive-putins-aggression/

Boutcher, J. (2024) *Operation Kenova Northern Ireland "Stakeknife" Legacy Investigation. Interim Report*, Operation Kenova, Bedfordshire Police. Available from: https://www.psni.police.uk/sites/default/files/2024-03/Operation%20Kenova%20Interim%20Report%202024.pdf

Brady, H., Verba, S., and Shlozman, K.L. (1995) "Beyond SES: A Resource Model of Political Participation," *American Political Science Review*, 89: 271–294.

Brogan, D.W. (1954) *Politics in America*. New York: Harper & Brothers.

Brundage, D. (2016) *Irish Nationalists in America: The Politics of Exile, 1798–1998*. Oxford: Oxford University Press.

Calamur, K. (2017) "Why Keep State Department Special Envoys?" *The Atlantic*, August 30. Available from: https://www.theatlantic.com/international/archive/2017/08/tillerson-special-envoys/538377/

Campbell, J. (2019) "Brexit: Nancy Pelosi Steps up Pressure on UK over Irish Border," *BBC News*, April 18. Available from: https://www.bbc.com/news/uk-northern-ireland-47979214

Carr, H. (2021) "US Representatives Issue Warning to the UK over Triggering Article 16," *JOE.ie*. Available from: https://www.joe.ie/news/us-representatives-warn-uk-article-16-735375

Carroll, R. (2022) "'One-Sided': Unionists React with Scorn as US Delegation Arrives in Ireland," *The Guardian*, May 23. Available from: https://www.theguardian.com/politics/2022/may/23/unionists-react-with-scorn-as-us-delegation-arrives-in-ireland-brexit

Carswell, S. (2019a) "'No Chance' of US Deal if Brexit Leads to Hard Border," *Irish Times*, March 22. Available from: https://www.irishtimes.com/news/ireland/irish-news/no-chance-of-us-deal-if-brexit-leads-to-hard-border-1.3835621

Carswell, S. (2019b) "US Politicians and Brexiteers Clash on 'Concocted Border Issue,'" *Irish Times*, April 17. Available from: https://www.irishtimes.com/news/ireland/irish-news/us-politicians-and-brexiteers-clash-on-concocted-border-issue-1.3862750

Carswell, S. (2020) "Loyalists on Brexit: 'A One-Way Route to an Economic United Ireland,'" *Irish Times*, January 30. Available from: https://www.irishtimes.com/news/politics/loyalists-on-brexit-a-one-way-route-to-an-economic-united-ireland-1.4155385

Carswell, S. (2022) "Dispute over NI Protocol Appears 'Manufactured' – Richard Neal," *Irish Times*, May 24. Available from: https://www.irishtimes.com/news/politics/dispute-over-ni-protocol-appears-manufactured-richard-neal-1.4886946

Carter, J. (1977) "Northern Ireland Statement on US Policy," The American Presidency Project, April 30. Available from: https://www.presidency.ucsb.edu/node/244190

Carty, T. (2001) "The Catholic Question: Religious Liberty and JFK's Pursuit of the 1960 Democratic Presidential Nomination," *The Historian*, 63(3): 577–599.

Casalicchio, E. (2021) "Fears of Brexit Hold-up over UK-US Steel Spat," *Politico*, December 1. Available from: https://www.politico.eu/article/fears-of-brexit-hold-up-over-uk-us-steel-spat/

Casalicchio, E. (2022) "US Rejects Invite for Face-to-Face Talks on UK Steel Dispute," *Politico*, January 13. Available from: https://www.politico.eu/article/us-wont-negotiate-on-steel-tariffs-in-london/

Casalicchio, E. and Cooper, C. (2019) "Boris Johnson Loses Majority as MPs Seek to Stop No-Deal Brexit," *Politico*, September 3. Available from: https://www.politico.eu/article/tories-lose-commons-majority-as-phillip-lee-defects/

Casalicchio, E., Lanktree, G., and Whale, S. (2022) "Joe Biden Could Ghost Boris Johnson over Northern Ireland Brexit Row," *Politico*, May 19. Available from: https://www.politico.eu/article/us-president-joe-biden-could-ghost-boris-johnson-in-brexit-row/

Census Bureau (2012) *Irish-American Heritage Month (March) and St. Patrick's Day (March 17): 2012*. CB12-FF.03.

Charlton, L. (1978) "Dublin's Prime Minister Denounces Biaggi on Ulster," *New York Times*, February 22, p A1.

Chatzky, A. and Siripurapu, A. (2020) "What Would a No-Deal Brexit Look Like?" *Council on Foreign Relations*, December 14. Available from: https://www.cfr.org/in-brief/what-would-no-deal-brexit-look

Childs, S. and Krook, M.L. (2009) "Analysing Women's Substantive Representation: From Critical Mass to Critical Actors," *Government and Opposition*, 44(2): 125–145. https://doi.org/10.1111/j.1477-7053.2009.01279.x

Committee on the Administration of Justice (2023) *The Road to the Northern Ireland Troubles (Reconciliation and Legacy) Act 2023. A Narrative Compendium of CAJ Submissions*. Available from: https://caj.org.uk/wp-content/uploads/2023/11/The-Road-to-the-Legacy-Bill-A-compendum-of-CAJ-submissions-FINAL.pdf

"Congressional Friends of Ireland: Celebrating 40 Years 1981–2021" (2021) Irish Department of Foreign Affairs. Available from: https://www.dfa.ie/media/missions/usa/newsandevents/Friends-of-Ireland.pdf

Connolly, C. (2007) "Seeking the Final Court of Justice," *San Diego International Law Journal*, 9: 81–133.

"Conservative Party Manifesto" (2015) Available from: https://www.theresavilliers.co.uk/sites/www.theresavilliers.co.uk/files/conservativemanifesto2015.pdf

Cooper, J. (2017) *The Politics of Diplomacy: U.S. Presidents and the Northern Ireland Conflict, 1967–1998*. Edinburgh: Edinburgh University Press.

Cordon, G. (2021) "Biden's 'Candid' Message to Johnson on Northern Ireland Brexit Row," *Belfast Telegraph*, June 13. Available from: https://www.belfasttelegraph.co.uk/news/northern-ireland/bidens-candid-message-to-johnson-on-northern-ireland-brexit-row/40534818.html

Corwin, E. (1957) *The President: Office and Powers 1787–1957*. New York: New York University Press.

Cosgrove, N. (2020) "Using COVID-19 to Cover Breaking Good Friday Commitments Reprehensible," *The Ancient Order of Hibernians*, March 24. Available from: https://aoh.com/2020/03/24/aoh-u-k-using-covid-19-to-cover-breaking-good-friday-commitments-reprehensible/

"Cost of Election" (no date) *Open Secrets*. Available from: https://www.opensecrets.org/elections-overview/cost-of-election?cycle=2020&display=T&infl=N

Cotton, T. (2019) "Press Release: Cotton, Colleagues Pen Letter Pledging to Back Britain after Brexit." Available from: https://www.cotton.senate.gov/news/press-releases/cotton-colleagues-pen-letter-pledging-to-back-britain-after-brexit

Cowell-Meyers, K. and Gallaher, C. (2021) "Parsing the Backstop: Northern Ireland and the Good Friday Agreement in the Brexit Debates," *British Politics*, 16: 219–238.

Crerar, P. (2022a) "No US Trade Deal on the Horizon, Admits Truss as She Flies in for Biden Meeting," *The Guardian*, September 20. Available from: https://www.theguardian.com/politics/2022/sep/20/no-us-trade-deal-on-the-horizon-admits-truss-as-she-flies-in-for-biden-meeting

Crerar, P. (2022b) "UK Aims to End Stormont Row before Planned Joe Biden Visit in 2023," *The Guardian*, September 21. Available from: https://www.theguardian.com/uk-news/2022/sep/21/six-month-deadline-to-solve-northern-ireland-protocol-row-say-government-sources

Crisp, J. (2020) "Government Delays Internal Market Bill Vote until End of Month," *The Telegraph*, November 10. Available from: https://www.telegraph.co.uk/politics/2020/11/10/government-delays-internal-market-bill-vote-end-month/

Crisp, J. (2023) "Joe Biden Offers Help to Ireland over Opposition to Legacy Bill," *The Telegraph*, September 22. Available from: https://www.telegraph.co.uk/world-news/2023/09/21/joe-biden-help-ireland-legacy-bill-amnesty-troubles-killers/

Crisp, J. and Yorke, H. (2021) "Exclusive: EU Threatens Sausage Trade War," *The Telegraph*, June 7. Available from: https://www.telegraph.co.uk/politics/2021/06/07/eu-threatens-sausage-trade-war/

Crothers, L. (2020) "Gerry Adams Asks Irish-Americans to Lobby for Unity Referendum," *Irish Times*, June 5.

Cunningham, P. (2021) "Biden's Irish Affections Beneficial for 'Old Country.'" *RTÉ*. Available from: https://www.rte.ie/news/analysis-and-comment/2021/0317/1204611-taoiseach-biden-meeting-analysis/

Cusick, J., Corderoy, J., and Geoghegan, P. (2019) "Revealed: The Files That Expose ERG as a Militant 'Party within a Party,'" *Open Democracy*. Available from: https://www.opendemocracy.net/en/freedom-of-information/revealed-the-files-that-expose-erg-as-a-militant-party-within-a-party/

Dallison, P. (2019) "Donald Trump: Theresa May 'Didn't Listen' to Me on Brexit," *Politico*, March 14. Available from: https://www.politico.eu/article/donald-trump-theresa-may-didnt-listen-to-me-on-brexit/

DeConde, A. (1992) *Ethnicity, Race and American Foreign Policy: A History*. Boston, MA: Northeastern University Press.

DeGregorio, C. (1997) *Networks of Champions: Leaders, Access and Advocacy in the US House of Representatives*. Ann Arbor, MI: University of Michigan Press.

Dewind, J. and Segura, R. (2014) *Diaspora Lobbies and the US Government: Convergence and Divergence in Making Foreign Policy*. New York: New York University Press.

# REFERENCES

"Did Money Win?" (no date) Available from: https://www.opensecrets.org/elections-overview/winning-vs-spending

"The Disappeared" (no date) Independent Commission for the Location of Victims' Remains. Available from: https://www.iclvr.ie/en/iclvr/pages/thedisappeared

Dolan, J. (2008) *The Irish Americans: A History*. New York: Bloomsbury Press.

Donlon, S. (2018) "Should Donald Trump Appoint Ambassador to Dublin and Envoy to Belfast? For and against," *Irish Times*, June 9. Available from: https://www.irishtimes.com/opinion/should-donald-trump-appoint-ambassador-to-dublin-and-envoy-to-belfast-for-and-against-1.3524087

Dooley, B. and Fernandez-Powell, M. (2024) "Ireland Takes British Amnesty Law to Court," *Human Rights First Blog*, January 24. Available from: https://humanrightsfirst.org/library/ireland-takes-british-amnesty-law-to-court/

Downing, J. (2022) "Haughey, Thatcher and the Falklands Stance That Led to Low-Point in Irish-British Relations," *The Independent*, June 13. Available from: https://www.independent.ie/opinion/haughey-thatcher-and-the-falklands-stance-that-led-to-low-point-in-irish-british-relations/41749634.html

Duffy, B. et al (2019) *Divided Britain? Polarisation and Fragmentation Trends in the UK*. London: The Policy Institute/King's College London.

Duffy, R. (2021) "British Officials Were 'Apoplectic' after Gerry Adams Was Granted a US Visa in 1994," *The Journal*, December 28. Available from: https://www.thejournal.ie/gerry-adams-us-visa-5632405-Dec2021/

Dugan, J. and Doyle, D. (2024) "How Irish Unification Is Boosted by Brexit and Demographics," *Bloomberg*, February 7. Available from: https://www.bloomberg.com/news/articles/2024-02-08/irish-unification-how-brexit-and-demographics-give-it-a-boost

Dumbrell, J. (1995) "The United States and the Northern Irish Conflict 1969–94: From Indifference to Intervention," *Irish Studies in International Affairs*, 6: 107–125.

Dunn, T. (2018) "Trump's Brexit Blast," *The Sun*, July 13. Available from: https://www.thesun.co.uk/news/6766531/trump-may-brexit-us-deal-off/

Elgot, J. (2017) "Ireland Threatens to Block Progress of Brexit Talks over Border Issue," *The Guardian*, November 17. Available from: https://www.theguardian.com/politics/2017/nov/17/irish-pm-brexit-backing-politicians-did-not-think-things-through

Elgot, J. (2020) "Johnson Risks Rift with Biden by Pressing Ahead with Brexit Bill," *The Guardian*, November 8. Available from: https://www.theguardian.com/politics/2020/nov/08/dominic-raab-joe-biden-no-deal-brexit

Elgot, J. (2022) "Irritation All Round at Handling of Move against Brexit Protocol," *The Guardian*, May 17. Available from: https://www.theguardian.com/politics/2022/may/17/brexit-northern-ireland-protocol-truss-johnson-analysis

Elgot, J. and Adu, A. (2022) "NI Deal Will Be Sorted by Good Friday Anniversary, Sunak Promises Biden," *The Guardian*, November 16. Available from: https://www.theguardian.com/uk-news/2022/nov/16/ni-deal-will-be-sorted-by-good-friday-anniversary-sunak-promises-biden

*Endgame in Ireland* (2021) Directed by Anderson, M. and M. Gold. BBC.

Engler, S., Mauelshagen, F., and Werner, J. (2013) "The Irish Famine of 1740–1741: Famine Vulnerability and "Climate Migration'," *Climate of the Past*, 9(3): 1161–1179.

Erwin, A. (2024) "Raymond McCord Loses Challenge over Ending Preparatory Work for Halted Inquest into his Son's Murder," *Belfast Telegraph*, April 19. Available from: https://www.belfasttelegraph.co.uk/news/courts/raymond-mccord-loses-challenge-over-ending-preparatory-work-for-halted-inquest-into-his-sons-murder/a381010342.html

Esman, M. (1994) *Ethnic Politics*. Ithaca, NY: Cornell University Press.

EU-US IPM (2022) "84th Transatlantic Legislators Dialogue – Joint."

Everett, M. (2023) "War in Ukraine Sees Ireland Reckon with Its Policy of Neutrality," *Al Jazeera*, September 1. Available from: https://www.aljazeera.com/features/2023/9/1/war-in-ukraine-sees-ireland-reckon-with-its-policy-of-neutrality

Fealty, M. (2024) "New Air of Seriousness about EU/UK Negotiations Promises to Defuse the NI Protocol for Unionists," *Slugger O'Toole*, April 8. Available from: https://sluggerotoole.com/2023/01/12/new-air-of-seriousness-about-eu-uk-negotiations-promises-to-defuse-the-ni-protocol-for-unionists/

Fedor, L. and Politi, J. (2023) "US Calls for Revived UK Trade Talks after Northern Ireland Deal," *Financial Times*, March 3. Available from: https://www.ft.com/content/362f4d28-91dd-4aca-81bb-582287026f5c

Fieldhouse, E. et al (2019) "Brexit and the Reshaping of British Electoral Politics," in *Electoral Shocks: The Volatile Voter in a Turbulent World*. Oxford: Oxford University Press, pp 163–187.

# REFERENCES

Finn, C. (2024) "Sinn Féin Has Placed Ads in Papers across the US – But There's a Softer Approach This Year," *The Journal*, March 13. Available from: https://www.thejournal.ie/sinn-fein-omit-irish-unity-lettering-in-us-newspaper-advert-6326299-Mar2024/

FitzGerald, G. (2021) "The Catholic Dimension of Irish Soft Power: Brexit and the Ancient Order of Hibernians," Berkley Center for Religion, Peace & World Affairs. Available from: https://berkleycenter.georgetown.edu/posts/the-catholic-dimension-of-irish-soft-power-brexit-and-the-ancient-order-of-hibernians

Fitzgerald, J. and Morgenroth, E. (2024) "Northern Ireland Subvention: Possible Unification Effects," *Institute of International and Economic Affairs*. Available from: https://www.iiea.com/publications/northern-ireland-subvention-possible-unification-effects

Fitzpatrick, M. (2019) *John Hume in America: From Derry to DC*. Notre Dame: University of Notre Dame Press.

*Foreign and Defense Policy Summary* (no date) Available from: https://www.opensecrets.org/industries/indus?cycle=2020&ind=Q04

Forgey, Q. (2019) "Trump Praises Boris Johnson as the 'Britain Trump,'" *Politico*, July 23. Available from: https://www.politico.com/story/2019/07/23/trump-boris-johnson-british-prime-minister-1426714

Franchot, J. (2022) *Roads to Rome: The Antebellum Protestant Encounter with Catholicism*. Berkeley, CA: University of California Press.

Fresh Air (2014) "The Case for Tammany Hall Being on the Right Side of History," March 5. Available from: https://www.npr.org/2014/03/05/286218423/the-case-for-tammany-hall-being-on-the-right-side-of-history

Friends of Sinn Féin USA (2023) [X] 15 March. Available from: https://x.com/FOSFUSA/status/1635996545882390534

Gallaher, C. (2007) *After the Peace: Loyalist Paramilitaries in Post-Accord Northern Ireland*. New York: Cornell University Press.

Gallardo, C. (2022a) "3 Things to Know about the UK Plan to Rip up Northern Ireland Brexit Trade Rules," *Politico*, May 17. Available from: https://www.politico.eu/article/3-things-know-uk-solo-plan-northern-ireland-trade-brexit-protocol/

Gallardo, C. (2022b) "New Northern Ireland Elections Loom as Coveney Says Protocol Row Won't Be Resolved before Deadline," *Politico*, October 7. Available from: https://www.politico.eu/article/uk-northern-ireland-protocol-bill-simon-coveney/

Gallardo, C. and Webber, E. (2023) "Britain and EU Close to New 'Mini-Deal' on Post-Brexit Trade in Northern Ireland," *Politico*, January 13. Available from: https://www.politico.eu/article/eropean-union-united-kingdom-northern-ireland-close-to-further-mini-deals-on-post-brexit-northern-ireland-trade/

Gallardo, C., Webber, E., and Kijewski, L. (2023) "Inside the Deal: How Boris Johnson's Departure Paved the Way for a Grand Brexit Bargain," *Politico*, February 28. Available from: https://www.politico.eu/article/uk-eu-deal-boris-johnson-departure-paved-the-way-brexit-bargain-northern-ireland-protocol-liz-truss-rishi-sunak-tory-conservatives/

Gardiner, N. (2021) "Joe Biden Should Keep His Sneering Anti-British, Anti-Brexit Views to Himself," *The Telegraph*, June 10. Available from: https://www.telegraph.co.uk/politics/2021/06/10/joe-biden-should-should-keep-sneering-anti-british-anti-brexit/

Garry, J. (2016) *The EU Referendum Vote in Northern Ireland: Implications for our Understanding of Citizens' Political Views and Behaviour*. Queen's University Belfast. Available from: https://www.qub.ac.uk/brexit/Brexitfilestore/Filetoupload,728121,en.pdf

Geoghegan, P. (2020) "A Corruption of Conservatism: How a Cartel of Tory MPs Broke British Politics," *Open Democracy Dark Money Investigations*. Available from: https://www.opendemocracy.net/en/dark-money-investigations/a-corruption-of-conservatism-how-a-cartel-of-tory-mps-broke-british-politics/

George, S. (1990) *An Awkward Partner: Britain in the European Community*. Oxford: Oxford University Press.

Gietel-Basten, S. (2016) "Why Brexit? The Toxic Mix of Immigration and Austerity," *Population and Development Review*, 42(4): 673–680.

Glancy, J. (2021) "US Trade Deal 'Blown by Our Man in Washington': A New Report Accuses Kim Darroch of Failing to Sell Brexit Britain. He blames the Chaos in London," *Sunday Times*, January 31, p 18.

Glazer, N. and Moynihan, D.P. (1963) *Beyond the Melting Pot: The Negroes, Puerto Ricans, Jews, Italians and Irish of New York City*. Cambridge, MA: Massachusetts Institute of Technology Press.

Glynn, N. (2022) "Joe Kennedy III Confirmed as US Special Envoy to Northern Ireland," *BBC*, December 19. Available from: https://www.bbc.com/news/uk-northern-ireland-64028400

Goodall, L. (2022) Available from: https://twitter.com/lewis_goodall/status/1526964423931351045?s=24&t=tENYlGy5yNUOFNl764hcxQ

Golway, T. (2014) *Machine Made: Tammany Hall and the Creation of Modern American Politics*. New York, NY: Liveright Press.

Gramer, R., de Luce, D., and Lynch, C. (2017) "How the Trump Administration Broke the State Department," *Foreign Policy*. Available from: https://foreignpolicy.com/2017/07/31/how-the-trump-administration-broke-the-state-department/

Grant, T. (2014) "St. Patrick's Day Graph: Irish in America Are Protestant, not Catholic," *Religion News Service*, March 17.

Greeley, A. (1973) *That Most Distressful Nation: The Taming of the American Irish*. Chicago: Quadrangle Books.

Greenslade, R. (2016) "Most of the National Press Lashes David Cameron's EU 'Settlement,'" *The Guardian*, February 3. Available from: https://www.theguardian.com/media/greenslade/2016/feb/03/most-of-the-national-press-lashes-david-camerons-eu-settlement

Greve, F. (1995) "Ethnic Lobby Powers up," *Armenian Reporter*, 28(50): 16.

Guelke, A. (1996) "The United States, Irish-Americans and the Peace Process," *International Affairs*, 72(3): 521–536.

Gutteridge, N. and Crisp, J. (2022) "We Won't Give in to US over Brexit Protocol, Says Minister," *Daily Telegraph*, May 21.

Halloran, C. (2019) "US Wants Brexit That Encourages Stability in Ireland – Pence," *RTÉ*, September 2. Available from: https://www.rte.ie/news/ireland/2019/0902/1073245-pence-visit/

Hamill, P. (1972) "A Guide to the Goyim," *New York Magazine*, March 13.

Hancock, L. (2012) "Transitional Justice and the Consultative Group: Facing the Past or Forcing the Future," *Ethnopolitics*, 11(2): 204–228.

Haney, P. and Vanderbush, W. (1999) "The Role of Ethnic Interest Groups in US Foreign Policy: The Case of the Cuban American National Foundation," *International Studies Quarterly*, 43(2): 341–361.

Haverty, D. (2024) "How Brexit Lit the Fuse in Northern Ireland," *Foreign Policy* April 13. Available from: https://foreignpolicy.com/2021/04/13/brexit-loyalist-unionist-violence-uvf-northern-ireland/

Haverty, D. and Reaney, B. (2018) "Why the Irish Border Matters," *New Atlanticist*, December 10. Available from: https://www.atlanticcouncil.org/blogs/new-atlanticist/why-the-irish-border-matters/

Hayward, K. and Murphy, M. (2012) "The (Soft) Power of Commitment: The EU and Conflict Resolution in Northern Ireland," *Ethnopolitics*, 11(4): 439–452.

Hayward, K. and Rosher, B. (2023) *Political Attitudes in Northern Ireland 25 Years after the Agreement*. ARC. Available from: https://www.ark.ac.uk/ARK/sites/default/files/2023-04/update151.pdf

"Hibernians Webinar – Legacy Justice Appeal" (2021) *Ancient Order of Hibernians*, January 23. Available from: https://aoh.com/event/hibernians-webinar-legacy-justice-appeal/

Hickey, S. (2022) "NI Minister Cannot Name a Single US Backer of Govt's Protocol Overhaul," *LBC*, June 13. Available from: https://www.lbc.co.uk/radio/presenters/andrew-marr/ni-minister-grilled-over-american-support-for-ni-protocol-overhaul/

HMIC (2013) *Inspection of the Police Service of Northern Ireland Historical Enquiries Team*. London. Available from: https://assets-hmicfrs.justiceinspectorates.gov.uk/uploads/inspection-of-the-police-service-of-northern-ireland-historical-enquiries-team-20130703.pdf

Hobolt, S. (2016) "The Brexit Vote: a Divided Nation, a Divided Continent," *Journal of European Public Policy*, 23(9): 1259–1277.

Hobolt, S. and Tilley, J. (2022) *Do "Remainers" and "Leavers" Still Exist?* London: UK in a Changing Europe. Available from: https://ukandeu.ac.uk/wp-content/uploads/2022/02/UKICE-British-Politics-after-Brexit.pdf

Holan, M. (2017) "Ireland's Famine Children 'Born at Sea,'" *Prologue Magazine*, 49(4). Available from: https://www.archives.gov/publications/prologue/2017/winter/irish-births#:~:text=The%20online%20database%20shows%208%2C075,among%202%2C883%20total%20reported%20fatalities

Honeycombe-Foster, M. (2022) "Everything You Wanted to Know about Rishi Sunak But Were Too Afraid to Ask," *Politico*, October 24. Available from: https://www.politico.eu/article/rishi-sunak-united-kingdom-liz-truss-britain-latest-prime-minister/

Hutton, B. (2024) "DUP Declares 'Guerrilla Warfare' on Northern Ireland Protocol," *Irish Times*, April 8. Available from: https://www.irishtimes.com/news/ireland/irish-news/dup-declares-guerrilla-warfare-on-northern-ireland-protocol-1.4497441

Hyland, P. (2022) "US Politicians Warn UK Government it is Undermining Good Friday Agreement," *Irish Independent*, June 22. Available from: https://www.independent.ie/irish-news/us-politicians-warn-uk-government-it-is-undermining-good-friday-agreement/41779974.html

Ignatiev, N. (1995) *How the Irish Became White*. Abingdon: Routledge.

International Body on Arms Decommissioning (1996) *Report of the International Body on Arms Decommissioning*, January 22. Available from: https://cain.ulster.ac.uk/events/peace/docs/gm24196.htm

*Irish Echo* (2019) "Ad Hoc Group Forms to Protect GFA," *Irish Echo*, February 19. Available from: https://www.irishecho.com/2019/2/ad-hoc-group-forms-to-protect-gfa

*Irish Echo* Staff (2020) "Despite Covid, Mulvaney Fully Engaged as Envoy," *Irish Echo*, September 14. Available from: https://www.irishecho.com/2020/9/despite-covid-mulvaney-fully-engaged-as-envoy

# REFERENCES

*Irish Echo* Staff (2022) "Keating Pens Envoy Letter to Biden," *Irish Echo*, August 4. Available from: https://www.irishecho.com/2022/8/keating-pens-envoy-letter-to-biden

*Irish Echo* Staff (2024) "Congress Members See Great Opportunities," *Irish Echo*, November 17. Available from: https://www.irishecho.com/2022/11/congress-members-see-great-opportunities

*Irish Legal News* (2021) "US Secretary of State under Pressure to Condemn UK Government's Troubles Plan," November 16. Available from: https://www.irishlegal.com/index.php/articles/us-secretary-of-state-under-pressure-to-condemn-uk-governments-troubles-plan

*Irish News* (2020) "Irish America 'Building a Green Wall' to Safeguard 1998 Peace Accord," October 1. Available from: https://www.irishnews.com/news/northernirelandnews/2020/10/01/news/irish-america-building-a-green-wall-to-protect-good-friday-agreement-2083577/

*Irish News* (2021) "US Senate Resolution Will Support Protocol and Good Friday Agreement," March 13. Available from: https://www.irishnews.com/news/northernirelandnews/2021/03/13/news/us-senate-resolution-will-support-protocol-and-good-friday-agreement-2253237/

*Irish Times* (2021) "Boris Johnson Says NI Protocol Needs to Be 'Fixed or Ditched,'" October 1. Available from: https://www.irishtimes.com/news/politics/boris-johnson-says-ni-protocol-needs-to-be-fixed-or-ditched-1.4689097

*IrishCentral.com* (2022) "AOH Urges Biden to Appoint US Special Envoy to Northern Ireland," May 4. Available from: https://www.irishcentral.com/news/politics/aoh-biden-special-envoy-northern-ireland

Johnson, R. (2007) "An Unlikely Champion: Congressman Mario Biaggi and the Beginnings of a Negotiated Settlement in Northern Ireland," University of New Orleans Theses and Dissertations. Available from: https://scholarworks.uno.edu/td/518

Judah, B. (2021) *A "Washington Strategy" for British Diplomacy*. Policy Exchange.

Kenealy, D. (2016) "How Did We Get Here? A Brief History of Britain's Membership of the EU," *European Futures Blog*, May 24. Available from: https://www.pure.ed.ac.uk/ws/portalfiles/portal/26891390/European_Futures_Article_No_106_Kenealy.pdf

Kennedy, L. (2017) "How Irish America Thinks, Votes and Acts: Is the US Irish Community Growing More Conservative as Their Prosperity Increases?" *Irish Times*, June 3. Available from: https://www.irishtimes.com/life-and-style/abroad/how-irish-america-thinks-votes-and-acts-1.3104336

Kennedy, L. (2019) "How Brexit Is Leading a Resurgent Irish American Influence in US Politics," *The Conversation*, August 7. Available from: https://theconversation.com/how-brexit-is-leading-a-resurgent-irish-american-influence-in-us-politics-12134

Kenny, K. (2000) *The American Irish: A History*. London: Longman.

Kenny, K. (2013) "Abraham Lincoln and the American Irish," *American Journal of Irish Studies*, 10: 39–64.

Kustra, T. and James, P. (2022) "The Importance of Immigrants on American Intervention in International Crises," paper presented at Midwest Political Science Association Annual Conference, 7–10 April, Chicago, IL.

Landler, M. (2022) "Washington Warns Britain to Temper Its Spat with EU over Northern Ireland," *New York Times*, May 20. Available from: https://www.nytimes.com/2022/05/20/world/europe/washington-eu-britain-northern-ireland.html

Landler, M. (2023) "In Northern Ireland, Glamorous U.S. Envoy Meets Less Than Glamorous Job," *New York Times*, April 18. Available from: https://www.nytimes.com/2023/04/18/world/europe/northern-ireland-joe-kennedy.html

Lanktree, G. (2023) "Biden Quietly Shelves Trade Pact with UK before 2024 Elections," *Politico*, December 18. Available from: https://www.politico.eu/article/us-president-joe-biden-shelves-trade-pact-with-uk-2024-election/

Lanktree, G. and Bade, G. (2023) "Revealed: Joe Biden and Rishi Sunak seek UK/US Trade Pact before 2024 Elections," *Politico*, October 3. Available from: https://www.politico.eu/article/revealed-joe-biden-rishi-sunak-seek-uk-us-trade-pact-before-2024-elections/

Lawder, D. and Shalal, A. (2020) "USTR Lighthizer Says Bilateral Trade Pacts Conflict with Multilateral Trading System," *Reuters*, July 9. Available from: https://www.reuters.com/article/idUSKBN24A2VF/

Lawless, J. (2024) "What's in the Deal That Has Broken Northern Ireland's Political Deadlock?" *AP News*, January 31. Available from: https://apnews.com/article/northern-ireland-dup-government-agreement-explainer-409efa7f72ca5e558e272028a911903d

Lawther, C. (2010) "'Securing' the Past: Policing and the Contest over Truth in Northern Ireland," *The British Journal of Criminology*, 50(3): 455–473

Leahy, P. (2021a) "Growing Fears That British Government Will Shortly Invoke Article 16 of Protocol," *Irish Times*, November 4. Available from: https://www.irishtimes.com/news/politics/growing-fears-that-british-government-will-shortly-invoke-article-16-of-protocol-1.4718672

Leahy, P. (2021b) "NI Protocol Tensions Threaten UK-Ireland, UK-EU and UK-US Relations," *Irish Times*, June 11. Available from: https://www.irishtimes.com/news/politics/ni-protocol-tensions-threaten-uk-ireland-uk-eu-and-uk-us-relations-1.4589953

Leahy, P. (2022) "Reflections on the Taoiseach's Covid-Hit Week in Washington," *Irish Times*, March 19. Available from: https://www.irishtimes.com/opinion/letters/pat-leahy-reflections-on-the-taoiseachs-covid-hit-week-in-washington-1.4830565

Leahy, P. (2024) "Sunak Victory Boosts Dublin Hopes of Deal on Northern Ireland Protocol," *Irish Times*, April 9. Available from: https://www.irishtimes.com/politics/2022/10/24/sunak-victory-boosts-dublin-hopes-of-deal-on-northern-ireland-protocol/

Leahy, P. and Wall, M. (2022a) "'God Love Him': Sympathy for the Taoiseach as Washington Trip Affected by Covid," *Irish Times*, March 18. Available from: https://www.irishtimes.com/news/politics/god-love-him-sympathy-for-the-taoiseach-as-washington-trip-affected-by-covid-1.4830415

Leahy, P. and Wall, M. (2022b) "Mr Martin Goes to Washington – Virtually: The Taoiseach Had Been Having the Week of His Life – Until Disaster Struck," *Irish Times*, March 19, p 6.

Leebody, C. (2021) "President Biden Should 'Reflect on Reality' of Protocol Says DUP's Poots," *Belfast Telegraph*, June 10. Available from: https://www.belfasttelegraph.co.uk/news/politics/president-biden-should-reflect-on-reality-of-protocol-says-dups-poots/40524255.html

Leebody, C. (2022) "DUP's Diane Dodds Writes to Powerful US Committee in Complaint over Chair Richard Neal's Protocol Comments," *Belfast Telegraph*, May 24. Available from: https://www.belfasttelegraph.co.uk/news/brexit/dups-diane-dodds-writes-to-powerful-us-committee-in-complaint-over-chair-richard-neals-protocol-comments/41685089.html

Lindsay, J. (1994) *Congress and the Politics of US Foreign Policy*. Baltimore, MD: Johns Hopkins University Press.

Lindsay, J. (2002) "Getting Uncle Sam's Ear: Will Ethnic Lobbies Cramp America's Foreign Policy Style," *Brookings Institution Commentary* (December 1). Available from: https://www.brookings.edu/articles/getting-uncle-sams-ear-will-ethnic-lobbies-cramp-americas-foreign-policy-style/

Lippman, D. (2020) "Mick Mulvaney to Finally Travel for Northern Ireland Envoy Gig," *Politico*, September 16. Available from: https://www.politico.com/news/2020/09/16/mick-mulvaney-irish-envoy-travel-416357

Lobo, A.P. and Salvo, J.J. (1998) "Resurgent Irish Immigration to the US in the 1980s and early 1990s: A Socio-demographic Profile," *International Migration*, 36(2): 257–280.

Loomis, B. (1983) "A New Era: Groups and the Grass Roots," in A. Cigler and B. Loomis (eds) *Interest Group Politics*, 2nd edn. Washington, DC: CQ Press, pp 169–190.

Loomis, B. and Cigler, A. (1995) "Introduction," in A. Cigler and B. Loomis (eds) *Interest Group Politics*. 3rd edn. Washington, DC: CQ Press, pp 1–31.

"Lord Frost Speech at British-Irish Association: 4 September 2021" (2021) *Gov.uk*. Available from: https://www.gov.uk/government/speeches/lord-frost-speech-at-british-irish-association-4-september-2021

Lynch, G. (2023) "Once again, America chooses Ireland over the UK," *UnHerd*, 25 January. Available from: https://unherd.com/newsroom/once-again-america-chooses-ireland-over-the-uk/?us=1

O'Loughlin, G. (2023) "Ad Hoc Committee to Protect the Good Friday Agreement Writes to PM Sunak," *Friends of Sinn Fein*. Available from: https://friendsofsinnfein.com/ad-hoc-committee-to-protect-the-good-friday-agreement-writes-to-pm-sunak/

Luce, E. (2019) "Dublin's Irish-American Trump Card," *Financial Times*, March 15. Available from: https://www.ft.com/content/c0aa6358-4698-11e9-a965-23d669740bfb

Lundy, P. and McGovern, M. (2007) "Attitudes towards a Truth Commission for Northern Ireland in Relation to Party Political Affiliation," *Irish Political Studies*, 22(3): 321–338.

Lynch, S. (2019a) "Brexit: US Congress Members Urge May to Ensure Hard Irish Border Avoided," *Irish Times*, March 11. Available from: https://www.irishtimes.com/news/world/us/brexit-us-congress-members-urge-may-to-ensure-hard-irish-border-avoided-1.3822274

Lynch, S. (2019b) "May Tells Irish-Americans She'll Uphold Good Friday Agreement," *Irish Times*, March 1. Available from: https://www.irishtimes.com/news/politics/may-tells-irish-americans-she-ll-uphold-good-friday-agreement-1.3811493

Lynch, S. (2019c) "Trump Not 'Picking Sides' in Brexit Negotiations, Says Chief of Staff," *Irish Times*, September 19, p 9. Available from: https://www.irishtimes.com/news/politics/trump-not-picking-sides-in-brexit-negotiations-says-chief-of-staff-1.4024187

Lynch, S. (2020) "Trump to Break with Tradition for St. Patrick's Day Celebrations," *Irish Times*, March 9. Available from: https://www.irishtimes.com/news/world/us/trump-to-break-with-tradition-for-st-patrick-s-day-celebrations-1.4196868

Lynch, S. (2021a) "Coveney Supports Appointment of Northern Ireland Envoy by US Government," *Irish Times*, May 18. Available from: https://www.irishtimes.com/news/ireland/irish-news/coveney-supports-appointment-of-northern-ireland-envoy-by-us-government-1.4568735

Lynch, S. (2021b) "How Irish America Will Be at the Heart of the Biden Administration," *Irish Times*, January 20. Available from: https://www.irishtimes.com/news/world/us/how-irish-america-will-be-at-the-heart-of-the-biden-administration-1.4462569

Lynch, S. and McGee, H. (2019) "Pence Voices Support for Johnson in Brexit Talks after Varadkar Meeting," *Irish Times*, September 3. Available from: https://www.irishtimes.com/news/politics/pence-voices-support-for-johnson-in-brexit-talks-after-varadkar-meeting-1.4006887

Lynch, T. (2004) *Turf War: The Clinton Administration and Northern Ireland*. London: Routledge.

Mackey, R. (2019) "Nancy Pelosi Takes Control of U.S. Foreign Policy on Brexit with Stark Warning to U.K.," *The Intercept*, April 17. Available from: https://theintercept.com/2019/04/17/nancy-pelosi-brexit-ireland/

Mackinnon, A. and Quinn, C. (2020) "Biden's Irish Roots Promise a New Kind of Special Relationship," *Foreign Policy*, November 19. Available from: https://foreignpolicy.com/2020/11/19/joe-biden-irish-ireland-special-relationship/

MacLeod, A. (2016) *International Politics and the Northern Ireland Conflict: The USA, Diplomacy and the Troubles*. London: I.B. Tauris.

Madhani, A. and Superville, D. (2022) "US-UK Relations Enter New Chapter as New PM, King Settle in," *AP News*. Available from: https://apnews.com/article/russia-ukraine-queen-elizabeth-ii-biden-boris-johnson-united-kingdom-7b9a61b6358d2291c457c33a091fcfcd

Maguire, P. and Wright, O. (2021) "G7 Summit 2021: Joe Biden Accuses Boris Johnson of 'Inflaming' Irish Tensions," *The Times*, June 10. Available from: https://www.thetimes.co.uk/article/g7-summit-2021-joe-biden-accuses-boris-johnson-of-inflaming-irish-tensions-r88lcv6cg

Major, J. and Reynolds, A. (1993) "Joint Declaration on Peace, Also Known as the Downing Street Declaration." Available from: https://cain.ulster.ac.uk/events/peace/docs/dsd151293.htm

Mallie, E. and McKittrick, D. (1996) *The Fight for Peace: The Secret Story behind the Irish Peace Process*. London: Heinemann.

Manley, J. (2020) "Irish America 'Building a Green Wall' to Safeguard 1998 Peace Accord," *Irish News*, October 1.

Manley, J. (2022) "Analysis: US Pressure Unlikely to Derail Protocol legislation But Then It's Nothing More Than a Paper Exercise," *Irish News*, May 27. Available from: https://www.irishnews.com/news/northernirelandnews/2022/05/27/news/analysis-us-pressure-unlikely-to-derail-protocol-legislation-but-then-it-s-nothing-more-than-a-paper-exercise-2724554/

Martin, R. (2016) "Ted Kennedy and the Troubles, Part 1," *First Year 2017: Where the Next President Begins*, May 17. Available from: http://firstyear2017.org/blog/ted-kennedy-and-the-troubles-working-with-president-carter-on-northern-irel.html

May, T. (2019) "British PM May's Brexit Statement to Conservative Lawmakers," *Reuters*, March 27. Available from: https://www.reuters.com/article/idUSL8N21E6G2/

Mayhew, D. (2004) *Congress: The Electoral Connection*, 2nd edn. New Haven: Yale University Press.

McAdam, D., Tarrow, S., and Tilly, C. (2001) *Dynamics of Contention*. Cambridge: Cambridge University Press.

McAlpine, A. (1997) *One a Jolly Bagman: Memoirs*. London: Weidenfeld & Nicolson.

McBride, S. (2021) "US President Joe Biden Says He Backs the Irish Sea Border, Further Isolating Unionists Attempting to Have It Removed," *Belfast News Letter*. Available from: https://www.newsletter.co.uk/news/politics/us-president-joe-biden-says-he-backs-the-irish-sea-border-further-isolating-unionists-attempting-to-have-it-removed-3169803

McCaffrey, L. (1975) *The Irish Diaspora in America*. Washington, DC: Catholic University Press.

McCarthy, G. (2018) "A View from the Hill," in *Congress and Diaspora Politics: The Influence of Ethnic and Foreign Lobbying*. Albany, NY: State University of New York Press, pp 223–244.

McCormack, J. (2019) "Brexit: How the Irish Border Issue Was Viewed during Campaigning," *BBC News*, October 12. Available from: https://www.bbc.com/news/uk-northern-ireland-politics-49988057

McCormack, J. (2022) "New US Special Envoy to NI Expected 'Very Soon,'" *BBC News*, December 11. Available from: https://www.bbc.com/news/uk-northern-ireland-63918945

McDonagh, B. (2022) "Bobby McDonagh: Rishi Sunak Knows Brexit Britain Can't Play Silly Buggers Anymore," *Irish Times*, December 30. Available from: https://www.irishtimes.com/politics/2022/12/30/bobby-mcdonagh-rishi-sunak-knows-brexit-britain-cant-play-silly-buggers-any-more/

McEvoy, K. (2001) *Paramilitary Imprisonment in Northern Ireland: Resistance, Management, and Release*. Oxford: Oxford University Press.

McEvoy, K. (2006) *Making Peace with the Past: Options for Truth Recovery in and about Northern Ireland*. Belfast: Healing through Remembering. Available from: https://healingthroughremembering.org/wp-content/uploads/2015/11/Making-Peace-with-the-Past_2006.pdf

McGee, H. (2008) "SF Figures Show US Is Key Source of Funds," *Irish Times*, August 15.

McGovern, M. (2015) "State Violence and the Colonial Roots of Collusion in Northern Ireland," *Race & Class*, 57(2): 3–23.

McGrath, D. (2022) "Nancy Pelosi Threatens to Block Trade Deal over Northern Ireland Protocol Plans," *The Independent*, May 20. Available from: https://www.independent.co.uk/news/uk/northern-ireland-protocol-nancy-pelosi-northern-ireland-government-liz-truss-b2083312.html

McGurk, T. (2019) "Can Irish America Protect the Backstop?" *Business Post*, February 10.

McKeone, M. (2019) "How Green Is Capitol Hill?" *Business Post*, October 13.

McKercher, B.J.C. (2017) *Britain, America and. the Special Relationship since 1941*. New York: Routledge.

McLeish, H. (2020) "Boris Johnson's Brexit Plans Underestimate America's Commitment to Northern Ireland's Peace Process," *The New Scotsman*, September 21.

McLoughlin, P. and Meagher, A. (2019) "The 1977 'Carter Initiative' on Northern Ireland," *Diplomatic History*, 43(4): 671–698.

McMahon-IM, V. (2014) "Police Waiting for Us to Die off, Claim Bloody Sunday Relatives," *Irish Mirror*, January 30.

McManus, F.S. (1997) *The Macbride Principles*. Irish National Caucus.

Meagher, T. (2005) *The Columbia Guide to Irish American History*. New York: Columbia University Press.

Mearsheimer, J. and Walt, S. (2007) *The Israel Lobby and U.S. Foreign Policy*. New York: Farrar, Straus & Giroux.

Meyer, D. and Minkoff, D. (2004) "Conceptualizing Political Opportunity," *Social Forces*, 82(4): 1457–1492.

Milligan, E. (2022a) "UK and EU Are Close to Breakthrough in Long-Running Brexit Spat," *Bloomberg.com*, November 8. Available from: https://www.bloomberg.com/news/articles/2022-11-08/uk-and-eu-are-close-to-breakthrough-in-long-running-brexit-spat

Milligan, E. (2022b) "UK Expects to Secure Six Trade Deals with US States This Year," *Bloomberg.com*, May 18. Available from: https://www.bloomberg.com/news/articles/2022-05-18/uk-expects-to-secure-six-trade-deals-with-us-states-this-year

Milner, H. and Tingley, D. (2015) *Sailing the Water's Edge: The Domestic Politics of American Foreign Policy*. Princeton: Princeton University Press.

Moore, A. (2021) "US Political Leaders Visit Dublin to Re-affirm Support for Good Friday Agreement," *Irish Examiner*, October 11. Available from: https://www.irishexaminer.com/news/arid-40718376.html

Moore, D., Vazquez, G., and Dolan, R. (2021) *Happy St. Patrick's Day to the One Out of 10 Americans Who Claim Irish Ancestry*. Washington, DC: Census Bureau.

Moats Miller, R. (1990) *Bishop G. Bromley Oxnam: Paladin of Liberal Protestantism*. Nashville, TN: Abingdon Press.

Morales, A. (2022) "UK Seeks to Deepen US Trade Links Even as FTA Talks on Hold," *Bloomberg.com*, March 16. Available from: https://www.bloomberg.com/news/articles/2022-03-16/u-k-seeks-to-deepen-u-s-trade-links-even-as-fta-talks-on-hold

Morgan, G. (2016) "Brexit and the Elites: The Elite Versus the People or the Fracturing of the British Business Elites," *Socio-Economic Review*, 14(4): 825–829.

Morgenthau, H. (1951) *In Defense of the National Interest*. New York: Knopf.

Morris, C. (2020) "Brexit: Why Is the Internal Market Bill Controversial?," *BBC News*, December 8. Available from: https://www.bbc.com/news/54088596

Mortimore, R. (2016) "Polling History: 40 Years of British Views on 'In or Out' of Europe," *The Conversation*, June 21. Available from: https://theconversation.com/polling-history-40-years-of-british-views-on-in-or-out-of-europe-61250

Moss, J. and Clarke, N. (2021) "A Folk Theory of the EEC: Popular Euroscepticism in the Early 1980s," *Contemporary British History*, 35(4): 545–568.

Murphy, C. (2019) "Extra Innings: The Dangers of Brexit for the Special Relationship." London School of Economics, March 20. Available from: https://www.lse.ac.uk/lse-player?id=4668

Murphy, C. (2021) Letter to Prime Minister Johnson. Available from: https://www.murphy.senate.gov/imo/media/doc/northern_ireland_letter.pdf

National Parks Service (2021) "Commemorating Camelot: Three Women Who Shaped JFK's Legacy," *John Fitzgerald Kennedy National Historic Site*, February 10. Available from: https://www.nps.gov/articles/000/commemorating-camelot-three-women-who-shaped-jfk-s-legacy.htm

"New British Government Should Keep Its Manifesto Promise and Immediately Repeal Northern Ireland Legacy Act" (2024) *Human Rights First Blog*, July 5. Available from: https://humanrightsfirst.org/library/new-british-government-should-keep-its-manifesto-promise-and-immediately-repeal-northern-ireland-legacy-act/

Newhouse, J. (1992) "Socialism or Death," *The New Yorker*, April 19, pp 52–83.

Newhouse, J. (2009) "Diplomacy, Inc. – The Influence of Lobbies on US Foreign Policy," *Foreign Affairs*, 88(3): 73–92.

Newport, F. (2020) *Religious Group Voting and the 2020 Election*. Gallup. Available from: https://news.gallup.com/opinion/polling-matters/324410/religious-group-voting-2020-election.aspx

"Northern Ireland Human Rights Commission Responds to Legacy Judgment" (2024) Northern Ireland Human Rights Commission. Available from: https://nihrc.org/news/detail/northern-ireland-human-rights-commission-responds-to-legacy-judgment

O'Brien, S. (2020) "Donald Trump Appointed Envoy Mick Mulvaney to Win Irish Votes, Claims SDLP Leader," *The Times*, March 8. Available from: https://www.thetimes.co.uk/article/donald-trump-appointed-envoy-mick-mulvaney-to-win-irish-votes-claims-sdlp-leader-8wwn9j5n5

O'Carroll, L. (2022a) "Tory MP Steve Baker Apologises to Ireland and EU for Behaviour during Brexit," *The Guardian*, October 2. Available from: https://www.theguardian.com/politics/2022/oct/02/tory-mp-steve-baker-apologies-to-ireland-and-eu-for-behaviour-during-brexit

O'Carroll, L. (2022b) "US 'Will Not Entertain' UK Trade Deal That Risks Good Friday Agreement," *The Guardian*, March 24. Available from: https://www.theguardian.com/uk-news/2022/mar/24/us-will-not-entertain-uk-trade-deal-that-risks-good-friday-agreement

O'Carroll, L. (2023) "UK to Further Delay Calling Northern Ireland Election as Brexit Talks Continue," *The Guardian*, January 13. Available from: https://www.theguardian.com/uk-news/2023/jan/13/uk-to-further-delay-calling-northern-ireland-election-as-brexit-talks-continue

O'Carroll, L. and Borger, J. (2022) "Brexit: Unilateral Action on NI Protocol 'Not Conducive' to Trade Deal, Warns US," *The Guardian*, June 22. Available from: https://www.theguardian.com/uk-news/2022/jun/22/brexit-unilateral-action-northern-ireland-protocol-us-uk-trade-deal

O'Carroll, L. and Rankin, J. (2023) "NI Protocol: UK and EU Agree Deal on Trade Data Sharing," *The Guardian*, January 9. Available from: https://www.theguardian.com/politics/2023/jan/09/ni-protocol-uk-and-eu-agree-deal-on-trade-data-sharing

O'Carroll, L. and Walker, P. (2021) "Senior Loyalist Says NI Post-Brexit Tensions 'Most Dangerous for Years,#" *The Guardian*, May 19. Available from: https://www.theguardian.com/uk-news/2021/may/19/senior-loyalist-says-ni-post-brexit-tensions-most-dangerous-for-years

O'Carroll, L., Mason, R. and Rankin, J. (2019) "Boris Johnson and Leo Varadkar Say They 'See Pathway' to Brexit Deal," *The Guardian*, October 10. Available from: https://www.theguardian.com/politics/2019/oct/10/boris-johnson-and-leo-varadkar-say-they-see-pathway-to-brexit-deal

O'Clery, C. (1996) *The Greening of the White House: The Inside Story of How America Tried to Bring Peace to Ireland*. Dublin: Gill and MacMillan.

O'Clery, C. (1997) *Daring Diplomacy: Clinton's Secret Search for Peace in Ireland*. Boulder, CO: Roberts Rinehart.

O'Clery, C. (2015) "Reagan in the White House Leaned on Thatcher to Reach Historic Agreement: The US President Encouraged Thatcher to Be More Flexible and Work towards Compromise," *Irish Times*, November 6. Available from: https://www.irishtimes.com/news/politics/reagan-in-the-white-house-leaned-on-thatcher-to-reach-historic-agreement-1.2429179

O'Donovan, B. (2019a) "Former US Special Envoy to Northern Ireland Outlines Brexit Concerns," *RTÉ*, October 15. Available from: https://www.rte.ie/news/brexit/2019/1015/1083626-us-brexit-concerns/

O'Donovan, B. (2019b) "Washington Monument Reopens with Irish Plaque on Show," *RTÉ*, September 19. Available from: https://www.rte.ie/news/us/2019/0919/1077008-washington-monument/

O'Donovan, B. (2021) "Biden Urged to 'Stand up' for Good Friday Agreement," *RTÉ*, June 7. Available from: https://www.rte.ie/news/2021/0607/1226482-joe-biden-ni-protocol/

O'Dowd, N. (1985) "Behind the McBride Principles," *Irish America*. Available from: https://www.irishamerica.com/2022/10/the-macbride-principles/

O'Dowd, N. (2018) "E3 Bill Dies Thanks to Senator Tom Cotton and Incredibly, an Irish Journalist Neil Munro," *Irish Central*, December 21. Available from: https://www.irishcentral.com/news/politics/e3-bill-dies-thanks-to-senator-tom-cotton-and-incredibly-an-irish-journalist-neil-munro

O'Dowd, N. (2022) "Northern Envoy Appointment Offers Kennedy a Political Lifeline," *Irish Times*, December 19. Available from: https://www.irishtimes.com/opinion/2022/12/19/northern-envoy-appointment-offers-kennedy-a-political-lifeline/

O'Gráda, C. (2015) *Famine in Ireland, 1300–1900*. Dublin: University College Dublin.

O'Grady, J. (1996) "An Irish Policy Born in the U.S.A.: Clinton's Break with the Past," *Foreign Affairs*, 75(3): 2–7.

O'Grady, J. (1998) "The Mitchell Appointment to the Belfast Talks: How Did an Ex-United States Senator Win That Task?," *Canadian Journal of Irish Studies*, 24(2): 77–88.

O'Hanlon, R. (2018) "Hibernians Press Pompeo on North Envoy," *Irish Echo*, June 11. Available from: https://www.irishecho.com/2018/6/hibernians-press-pompeo-on-north-envoy

O'Hanlon, R. (2020) "Despite Covid, Mulvaney Fully Engaged as Envoy," *Irish Echo*, September 14. Available from: https://www.irishecho.com/2020/9/despite-covid-mulvaney-fully-engaged-as-envoy

O'Hanlon, R. (2022) "Ad Hoc Committee Urges Blinken Intervention," *Irish Echo*, June 22. Available from: https://www.irishecho.com/2022/6/ad-hoc-committee-urges-blinken-intervention

O'Leary, B. 2022. *Making Sense of a United Ireland: Should It Happen? How Might It Happen?* Dublin: Sandycove.

O'Leary, B. (1999) "The Nature of the British-Irish Agreement," *New Left Review*, 233(1): 66–96.

O'Leary, B. and McGarry, J. (1993) *The Politics of Antagonism: Understanding Northern Ireland*. London: Athlone Press.

O'Loan, N. (2007) *Statement by the Police Ombudsman for Northern Ireland on Her Investigation into the Circumstances Surrounding the Death of Raymond McCord Junior and Related Matters*. Police Ombudsman for Northern Ireland. Available from: https://www.policeombudsman.org/getmedia/54f70b0c-1899-4c7f-a1bf-287204061228/BALLAST-PUBLIC-STATEMENT-22-01-07-FINAL-VERSION.aspx?ext=.pdf

O'Loughlin, G. (2023) "Irish Unity and the Role of Irish America with Gerry Adams, Joe Crowley and Christine Kineally," *Friends of Sinn Féin*. Available from: https://friendsofsinnfein.com/irish-unity-and-the-role-of-irish-america-with-gerry-adams-joe-crowley-and-christine-kineally/

O'Loughlin, G. (2023) "Ad Hoc Committee to Protect the Good Friday Agreement Writes to PM Sunak," *Friends of Sinn Féin*. Available from: https://friendsofsinnfein.com/ad-hoc-committee-to-protect-the-good-friday-agreement-writes-to-pm-sunak/

O'Malley, P. (2023) "Irish Whiteness and the Nineteenth-Century Construction of Race," *Victorian Literature and Culture*, 51(2): 167–198.

O'Reilly, J. (2016) "The Fault Lines Unveiled by Brexit," *Socio-Economic Review*, 14(4): 808–814.

O'Shea, K. (2021a) "'Cold Frost' if Good Friday Agreement Jeopardized, US Experts Say," *Irish Central*, November 11. Available from: https://www.irishcentral.com/news/politics/cold-frost-us-uk-relations-good-friday-agreement

O'Shea, K. (2021b) "Warning of 'Repercussions,' US Experts Urge UK to Withdraw Amnesty Proposals," *Irish Central*, September 8. Available from: https://www.irishcentral.com/news/ad-hoc-committee-urges-johnson-withdraw-amnesty

O'Shea, K. (2022) "Congressional Group Reiterates US Commitment to Northern Ireland," *Irish Central*, August 5. Available from: https://www.irishcentral.com/news/northern-ireland-congressional-commitment

Olson, M. (1965) *The Logic of Collective Action*. Cambridge, MA: Harvard University Press.

Organski, A.F.K. (1990) *The $36 Billion Bargain: Strategy and Politics in US Assistance to Israel*. New York: Columbia University Press.

*PA Reporter* (2022) "Sir Jeffrey Donaldson: US Delegation Is Most Undiplomatic Visit I've Ever Seen." Available from: https://www.newsletter.co.uk/news/politics/sir-jeffrey-donaldson-us-delegation-is-most-undiplomatic-visit-ive-ever-seen-3710045

"PAC Dollars to Incumbents, Challengers, and Open Seat Candidates" (no date) Available from: https://www.opensecrets.org/elections-overview/pacs-stick-with-incumbents?cycle=2022

"PAC Profile: Irish American Democrats" (no date) Available from: https://www.opensecrets.org/spending-section.

"Pat Finucane and the Inquiries Act – Amnesty International Calls for Boycott" (2005) Pat Finucane Centre. Available from: https://www.patfinucanecentre.org/collusion-pat-finucane/pat-finucane-and-inquiries-act-amnesty-international-calls-boycott

Paul, D. and Paul, R. (2009) *Ethnic Lobbies & US Foreign Policy*. Boulder, CO: Lynne Rienner.

Paul, R. (2002) "Serbian-American Mobilization and Lobbying: The Relevance of Jasenovac and Kosoov to Contemporary Grassroots Efforts in the United States," in T. Ambrosio (ed) *Ethnic Identity Groups and U.S. Foreign Policy*, Westport, CT: Praeger, pp 93–113.

Payne, S. (2020) "Lords Vote on Brexit Bill Poses Early Test for Johnson-Biden Relations," *Financial Times*, November 8. Available from: https://www.ft.com/content/874ef7b6-91f9-4f5e-b2ae-5a3def68e250

Pelosi, N. (2019) "In Conversation with U.S. House Speaker Nancy Pelosi." US Centre at the London School of Economics, April 15. Available from: https://www.lse.ac.uk/lse-player?id=4675

Perry, C. (2019) *The Tribe: The Inside Story of Irish Power and Influence in US Politics*. Dublin: Gill.

Phoenix, É. (2018) "How Britain Tried to Stop Gerry Adams Getting US Visa," *Irish Times*, December 31. Available from: https://www.irishtimes.com/news/ireland/irish-news/how-britain-tried-to-stop-gerry-adams-getting-us-visa-1.3739551

Pogatchnik, S. (2022) "Sunak Seeks Negotiated Solution to Brexit Trade Row in First Talks with Ireland," *Politico*, November 10. Available from: https://www.politico.eu/article/rishi-sunak-brexit-trade-tensions-ireland-talks-protocol/

Pogatchnik, S. (2023) "A United Ireland Looks More Likely Thanks to Brexit, New Study Finds," *Politico*, April 23. Available from: https://www.politico.eu/article/united-ireland-look-more-likely-brexit-study-uk-belfast/

Powell, J. (2019) Available from: https://twitter.com/jnpowell1/status/1184776605308276736

Powell, J. (2023) "Comments Delivered as Part of a Council on Foreign Relations Forum 'Lessons from History Series: The Good Friday Agreement Twenty-Five Years Later,'" March 23. Available from: https://www.cfr.org/event/lessons-history-series-good-friday-agreement-twenty-five-years-later.

Prasad, S.K. and Savatic, F. (2023) "Diasporic Foreign Policy Interest Groups in the United States: Democracy, Conflict, and Political Entrepreneurship," *Perspectives on Politics*, 21(3): 831–848.

Preston, A. (2022) "Richard Neal Responds to Criticism over Use of 'Planter' Term as Arlene Foster Highlights US Congressman's Previous Tributes to IRA Members," *Belfast Telegraph*, May 25. Available from: https://www.belfasttelegraph.co.uk/news/brexit/richard-neal-responds-to-criticism-over-use-of-planter-term-as-arlene-foster-highlights-us-congressmans-previous-tributes-to-ira-members/41688478.html

"Pro-Israel Summary" (no date) Available from: https://www.opensecrets.org/industries/indus?cycle=2022&ind=Q05

Prosser, C. (2016) "Calling European Union Treaty Referendums: Electoral and Institutional Politics," *Political Studies*, 64(1): 182–199.

"Protecting the Good Friday Agreement from Brexit" (2019) Washington, DC. Available from: https://www.congress.gov/event/116th-congress/house-event/110131?s=2&r=10

"Public Briefing on Truth and Accountability for Victims of the Troubles in Northern Ireland" (2022) Available from: https://democrats-foreignaffairs.house.gov/2022/7/public-briefing-on-truth-and-accountability-for-victims-in-northern-ireland_2

Quinn, C. (2019) "Why Did Nancy Pelosi Visit Ireland? Congressional Delegation Trip Comes as Irish-US Relationship Is in Flux," *Irish Times*, April 25. Available from: https://www.irishtimes.com/opinion/why-did-nancy-pelosi-visit-ireland-1.3870328

Rahman, M. (2020) "On Brexit, Johnson Is Caught between Biden and His Own MPs," *Politico*, November 12. Available from: https://www.politico.eu/article/on-brexit-boris-johnson-is-now-caught-between-joe-biden-and-his-own-mps/

Rankin, J. and Elgot, J. (2019) "EU Rejects Boris Johnson Request to Remove Backstop," *The Guardian*, August 20. Available from: https://www.theguardian.com/politics/2019/aug/20/donald-tusk-rejects-boris-johnsons-bid-to-remove-the-backstop-brexit

Rea, A. (2019) "It's Not Donald Trump the UK Should Be Wooing to Get a Trade Deal: It's Nancy Pelosi," *New Statesman*, September 6. Available from: https://www.newstatesman.com/politics/the-staggers/2019/09/it-s-not-donald-trump-uk-should-be-wooing-get-trade-deal-it-s-nancy-pelosi

Refugee Action (2016) "Britain Welcomes More Than 4,000 Syrian Refugees over the Past Year." Available from: https://www.refugee-action.org.uk/britain-welcomes-4000-syrian-refugees-past-year/

Riordon, W. (1963) *Plunkitt of Tammany Hall: A Series of Very Plain Talks on Very Practical Politics*. New York: Signet Classics.

RTÉ News (2022) "Preserving Peace 'Number One' Issue for Us in Ireland," May 24. Available from: https://www.rte.ie/news/ireland/2022/0524/1300909-richard-neal/

Rubenzer, T. (2008) "Ethnic Minority Interest Group Attributes and US Foreign Policy Influence: A Qualitative Comparative Analysis," *Foreign Policy Analysis*, 4(2): 169–185.

Rubenzer, T. and Redd, S. (2010) "Ethnic Minority Groups and US Foreign Policy: Examining Congressional Decision Making and Economic Sanctions," *International Studies Quarterly*, 54(3): 755–777.

Sabbagh, D. and Barr, C. (2018) "Jacob Rees-Mogg and the Shadowy Group of Tories Shaping Brexit," *The Guardian*, February 6. Available from: https://www.theguardian.com/politics/2018/feb/06/jacob-rees-mogg-and-the-shadowy-group-of-tories-shaping-brexit

Sanders, A. (2019) *The Long Peace Process: The United States of America and Northern Ireland, 1960–2008*. Liverpool: Liverpool University Press.

Savage, M. (2022) "Liz Truss Rejects Plea from Biden Ally Not to Rewrite the Northern Ireland Protocol," *The Observer*, May 22. Available from: https://www.theguardian.com/politics/2022/may/22/liz-truss-rejects-plea-from-biden-ally-not-to-rewrite-the-northern-ireland-protocol

Schlozman, K.L. and Tierney, J. (1986) *Organized Interests and American Democracy*. New York: Harper & Row.

Schmidt, A. (1980) *Fraternal Organizations*. Westport, CT: Greenwood Press.

Schumer, C. (2019) "Letter to the Honorable Michael Pompeo." Available from: https://www.democrats.senate.gov/newsroom/press-releases/in-new-letter-to-secretary-pompeo-schumer-says-he-will-vigorously-and-vociferously-oppose-any-potential-us-uk-trade-deal-that-undermines-the-good-friday-agreement-or-a-return-to-a-hard-border-

Schütze, R. (2022) "Britain in the European Union: A Very Short History," *Global Policy*, 13(2): 39–46.

Scott, F. and Osman, A. (2002) "Identity, African-Americans, and US Foreign Policy: Differing Reactions to South African Apartheid and the Rwandan Genocide," in T. Ambrosio (ed) *Ethnic Identity Groups and US Foreign Policy*. Westport, CT: Greenwood Publishing Group, pp 71–92.

Secretary of State for Northern Ireland (2021) *Northern Ireland Protocol: The Way Forward*. CP 502. Her Majesty's Government. Available from: https://assets.publishing.service.gov.uk/media/6109b4be8fa8f5042d17a2d9/CCS207_CCS0721914902-005_Northern_Ireland_Protocol_Web_Accessible__1_.pdf

Sheahan, F. (2021) "'Copy the Irish' UK Diplomats Told after Ireland's Wins in US," *Irish Independent*, February 1. Available from: https://www.independent.ie/irish-news/politics/copy-the-irish-uk-diplomats-told-after-irelands-wins-in-us/40036471.html

Shipman, T. (2023) "Is Rishi Sunak Finally Getting Brexit Done?" *The Times*, January 14. Available from: https://www.thetimes.co.uk/article/is-rishi-sunak-finally-getting-brexit-done-0kwdj85b8

Shipman, T. and Wheeler, C. (2023) "Angry Boris Johnson Kept in the Dark as Tories Turn Fire on Each Other," *The Times*, February 25. Available from: https://www.thetimes.co.uk/article/angry-boris-johnson-kept-in-the-dark-as-tories-turn-fire-on-each-other-p9zk9pbrl

Simons, N. and Waugh, P. (2019) "Nancy Pelosi Clashed with Tory Brexiteers over Northern Ireland Border," *Huffington Post*, April 17. Available from: https://www.huffingtonpost.co.uk/entry/nancy-pelosi-clashed-with-tory-brexiteers-over-northern-ireland-border_uk_5cb6f0dbe4b0ffefe3b96fe0

Smith, A. (2019) "This is What the US Wants from the UK before It Will Sign a Trade Deal," *NBC News*, June 3. Available from: https://www.nbcnews.com/news/world/what-u-s-wants-u-k-it-will-sign-trade-n1013081

Smith, A. (2020) "Biden Warns UK That Irish Peace Deal Cannot Become a 'Casualty of Brexit,'" *NBC News*, September 17. Available from: https://www.nbcnews.com/news/world/biden-warns-u-k-northern-ireland-peace-deal-cannot-become-n1240302

Smith, T. (2000) *Foreign Attachments: The Power of Ethnic Groups in the Making of American Foreign Policy.* Cambridge, MA: Harvard University Press.

Smyth, C., Waterfield, B., and Charter, D. (2022) "Boris Johnson Defies Warnings over Northern Ireland Protocol," *The Times*, May 16. Available from: https://www.thetimes.co.uk/article/boris-johnson-defies-warnings-over-northern-ireland-protocol-mvtskzfvs

Smyth, T. (2020) "Irish American Organizations and the Northern Ireland Conflict in the 1980s: Heightened Political Agency and Ethnic Vitality," *Journal of American Ethnic History*, 39(2): 36–61.

Sparrow, A. (2019) "What Does the Johnson-Varadkar Brexit Statement Mean?" *The Guardian*, October 10. Available from: https://www.theguardian.com/politics/2019/oct/10/what-does-the-johnson-varadkar-brexit-statement-mean

Stacey, K. (2022) "UK Minister Warns US politicians to Mind Their Language over Northern Ireland," *Financial Times*, June 15. Available from: https://www.ft.com/content/7b737d11-d2c7-4487-bf1a-1663106811d0

Stacey, K. et al (2023) "Rishi Sunak Plans US Trip with Northern Ireland High on Agenda," *The Guardian*, February 1. Available from: https://www.theguardian.com/politics/2023/feb/01/rishi-sunak-plans-us-trip-with-northern-ireland-high-on-agenda

Staunton, D. (2021) "What Lay behind Frost and Lewis's Inflammatory Article on the Protocol?" *Irish Times*, July 10. Available from: https://www.irishtimes.com/opinion/what-lay-behind-frost-and-lewis-s-inflammatory-article-on-the-protocol-1.4616169

Steerpike (2018) "Boris Johnson's speech to DUP Conference: 'We Are on the Verge of a Historical Mistake,'" *The Spectator*, November 24. Available from: https://www.spectator.co.uk/article/boris-johnson-s-speech-to-dup-conference-we-are-on-the-verge-of-making-a-historic-mistake/

Stewart, H. (2021a) "Britain's Hopes of Early Post-Brexit Trade Deal with US Appear Dashed," *The Guardian*, September 21. Available from: https://www.theguardian.com/politics/2021/sep/21/britains-hopes-of-early-post-brexit-trade-deal-with-us-appear-dashed

Stewart, H. (2021b) "From Climate to Covid Rules: How Johnson and Biden Match Up," *The Guardian*, September 21. Available from: https://www.theguardian.com/politics/2021/sep/21/from-climate-to-covid-rules-how-johnson-and-biden-match-up

Stewart, H. and Sabbagh, D. (2021) "Boris Johnson Flies to New York to Tighten Transatlantic Ties after Strained Summer," *The Guardian*, September 17. Available from: https://www.theguardian.com/politics/2021/sep/17/boris-johnson-flies-to-new-york-to-tighten-transatlantic-ties-us-joe-biden

Sullivan, A. (2019) "Could Irish-America Stop UK-US Deal?" *Deutsche Welle*, August 27. Available from: https://www.dw.com/en/the-real-special-relationship-could-irish-america-thwart-a-us-uk-trade-deal/a-50181175

Sullivan, K. and Adam, K. (2019) "Boris Johnson Suffers Two Major Losses in Parliament, Leaving His Governing Authority and the Terms of Brexit in Doubt," *Washington Post*, September 4. Available from: https://www.washingtonpost.com/world/europe/uk-parliament-brexit-vote/2019/09/04/cc934b1c-cb6d-11e9-9615-8f1a32962e04_story.html

Sullivan, R.D. (2018) "Infographic: The Irish Diaspora in the United States," *Jesuit Review*, February 22. Available from: https://www.americamagazine.org/politics-society/2018/02/22/infographic-irish-diaspora-united-states

Suzberger, C.L. (1971) "Karl Marx and the Irish," *New York Times*, December 1. Available from: https://www.nytimes.com/1971/12/01/archives/karl-marx-and-the-irish.html

Sutton, M. (no date) *An Index of Deaths from the Conflict in Ireland: Summary of Organization Responsible for Death*. CAIN Archives. Available from: https://cain.ulster.ac.uk/sutton/tables/Organisation_Summary.html

Targeted News Service (2022) "Senator Menendez Issues Statement on St. Patrick's Day," 18 March.

Taylor, P. (1997) *Behind the Mask: The IRA and Sinn Féin*. New York: TV Books.

Taylor, P. (1999) *Loyalists: War and Peace in Northern Ireland*. New York: TV Books.

Tharoor, I. (2016) "New Pro-Brexit Ad Gets Linked to Nazi-Era Propaganda," *Washington Post*, June 16. Available from: https://www.washingtonpost.com/news/worldviews/wp/2016/06/16/new-pro-brexit-ad-gets-linked-to-nazi-era-propaganda/

The Economist (2019) "The Irish Conquest of America," March 16. Available from: https://www.economist.com/united-states/2019/03/16/the-irish-conquest-of-america

The Economist (2020) "Biden Puts Pressure on Johnson to Do a Deal with the EU," November 12. Available from: https://www.economist.com/britain/2020/11/12/biden-puts-pressure-on-johnson-to-do-a-deal-with-the-eu

The Journal (1983) "St. Patrick's Parade 'Held with Dignity,'" 17 March, p 3.

The Migration Observatory (2025) "UK Public Opinion Toward Immigration: Overall Attitudes and Level of Concern," *The Migration Observatory Briefings*, January 24. Available from: https://migrationobservatory.ox.ac.uk/resources/briefings/uk-public-opinion-toward-immigration-overall-attitudes-and-level-of-concern/

*The United States and Ireland – A Partnership in Combating Global Hunger and Supporting Shared International Development Priorities* (2023) United States Agency for International Development. Available from: https://web.archive.org/web/20230516131758/https://www.usaid.gov/news-information/fact-sheets/apr-13-2023-united-states-and-ireland-partnership-combating-global-hunger-and-supporting-shared-international-development-priorities

The White House (2021) "Readout of Vice President Kamala Harris Meeting with First Minister Arlene Foster and Deputy First Minister Michelle O'Neill of Northern Ireland." Available from: https://www.whitehouse.gov/briefing-room/statements-releases/2021/03/17/readout-of-vice-president-kamala-harris-meeting-with-first-minister-arlene-foster-and-deputy-first-minister-michelle-oneill-of-northern-ireland/

The White House (2022) "Readout of President Joe Biden's Call with Prime Minister Liz Truss of the United Kingdom." Available from: https://www.whitehouse.gov/briefing-room/statements-releases/2022/09/06/readout-of-president-joe-bidens-call-with-prime-minister-liz-truss-of-the-united-kingdom/

The White House (2023) "Statement from President Joe Biden on the Windsor Framework." Available from: https://web.archive.org/web/20230607022349/https://www.whitehouse.gov/briefing-room/statements-releases/2022/09/06/readout-of-president-joe-bidens-call-with-prime-minister-liz-truss-of-the-united-kingdom/

Thody, P. (1997) *An Historical Introduction to the European Union*. Abingdon: Routledge.

Thompson, J. (2001) *American Policy and Northern Ireland: A Saga of Peacebuilding*. Westport, CT: Praeger.

Thurber, J., Campbell, C., and Dulio, D. (2018) "Congress and Diaspora Politics: The Influence of Ethnic and Foreign Lobbying," in J. Thurber, C. Campbell and D. Dulio (eds) *Congress and Diaspora Politics: The Influence of Ethnic and Foreign Lobbying*. Albany, NY: State University of New York Press, pp 1–18.

Trounstine, J. (2008) *Political Monopolies in American Cities: The Rise and Fall of Bosses and Reformers*. Chicago: University of Chicago Press.

Trubowitz, P. (1998) *Defining the National Interest: Conflict and Change in American Foreign Policy*. Chicago: University of Chicago Press.

Truman, D. (1951) *The Governmental Process: Political Interests and Public Opinion*. New York: Alfred A. Knopf.

"UK 'First in Line' for US Trade Deal, Says John Bolton" (2019) *BBC News*, August 13. Available from: https://www.bbc.com/news/uk-49325620

# REFERENCES

"UK Government Appoints Special Envoy to the US on Northern Ireland" (2021) *Gov.uk*. Available from: https://www.gov.uk/government/news/uk-government-appoints-special-envoy-to-the-us-on-northern-ireland

US Census Bureau (2023) "Irish American Heritage Month and St. Patrick's Day: March 2023." Available from: https://www.census.gov/newsroom/facts-for-features/2023/irish-american-heritage.html

US House (2019) House Res. 88. 116th Congress (2019-2020). Available from: https://trackbill.com/bill/us-congress-house-resolution-88-expressing-the-opposition-of-the-house-of-representatives-to-a-hard-border-between-northern-ireland-and-the-republic-of-ireland/1660244/

US House (2021) House Res. 888, 117th Congress (2021–2022). Available from: https://legiscan.com/US/text/HR888/id/2497041

US House (2022) *Congressional Record: Expressing Hope for the Victims of Bloody Sunday*. Available from: https://www.congress.gov/congressional-record/volume-168/issue-48/house-section/article/H3798-2

US House (2023) House Res. 33, 118th Congress (2023–2024). Available from: https://www.congress.gov/bill/118th-congress/house-resolution/33

US Mission to the United Kingdom (2022) Department of State Counselor Derek Chollet visit to Belfast, Northern Ireland, U.S. Embassy & Consulates in the United Kingdom.

US Senate (2021) Sen. Res. 117. 117th Congress (2021–2022). Available from: https://www.congress.gov.bill/117th-congress/senate-resolution/117/text

Uslaner, E. (2002) "Cracks in the Armor? Interest Groups and Foreign Policy," in A. Cigler and B. Loomis (eds) *Interest Group Politics*. Washington, DC: CQ Press, pp 355–377.

USTR Press Office (2020) "Statement of USTR Robert Lighthizer on the Launch of U.S.-UK Trade Negotiations, United States Trade Representative." Available from: https://ustr.gov/about-us/policy-offices/press-office/press-releases/2020/may/statement-ustr-robert-lighthizer-launch-us-uk-trade-negotiations

Vargo, T. (2019) *Shenanigans: The US-Ireland Relationship in Uncertain Times*. New York: Girl Friday Productions.

Villiers, D. (2021) "How the US Impacts Brexit's Northern Ireland Protocol," *The Hill*, December 8. Available from: https://thehill.com/opinion/international/584866-how-the-us-impacts-brexits-northern-ireland-protocol/

Vinjamuri, L. (2022) "The Myth of Global Britain: Brexit Left London Even More Dependent on Washington," *Foreign Affairs*, February 15. Available from: https://www.foreignaffairs.com/articles/united-states/2022-02-15/myth-global-britain?check_logged_in=1)

Viser, M. (2021) "Irish Humor, Irish Temper: How Biden's Identity Shapes His Political Image," *Washington Post*, March 18. Available from: https://www.washingtonpost.com/politics/biden-irish-st-patricks/2021/03/17/6b59390c-8740-11eb-8a8b-5cf82c3dffe4_story.html

Von Bismarck, H. (2022) "Whisper It, But the UK and the EU Are Starting to Mend Their Broken Relationship," *The Guardian*, November 18. Available from: https://www.theguardian.com/world/commentisfree/2022/nov/18/uk-eu-mend-broken-relationship-brexit-neighbours

Walker, P. (2020) "Brexit: UK Risks Being 'International Pariah' under Biden, Says Labour," *The Guardian*, November 9. Available from: https://www.theguardian.com/politics/2020/nov/09/uk-risks-becoming-international-pariah-by-rewriting-brexit-bill

Wall, M. (2022a) "Ancient Order of Hibernians Votes to Continue as Male-Only Organisation," *Irish Times*, June 18. Available from: https://www.irishtimes.com/world/americas/2022/07/18/ancient-order-of-hibernians-votes-to-continue-as-male-only-organisation/

Wall, M. (2022b) "Coveney Optimistic Deal on Northern Ireland Can Be Achieved," *Irish Times*, November 16. Available from: https://www.irishtimes.com/politics/2022/11/16/coveney-optimistic-deal-on-northern-ireland-can-be-achieved/

Wall, M. (2022c) "Washington Must Tread Carefully on Britain's NI Protocol Plans at G7 Summit," *Irish Times*, June 23. Available from: https://www.irishtimes.com/ireland/2022/06/23/washington-must-tread-carefully-on-britains-ni-protocol-plans-as-leaders-set-to-meet-at-g7-summit/

Wall, M. (2022d) "When Irish Ties Are Waning: Our Diplomatic Struggle in the United States," *Irish Times*, March 12. Available from: https://www.irishtimes.com/news/ireland/irish-news/when-irish-ties-are-waning-our-diplomatic-struggle-in-the-united-states-1.4824397

Wall, M. (2022e) "White House Probably Does Not Need Another Headache, Dealing with the NI Protocol Row," *Irish Times*, June 17. Available from: https://www.irishtimes.com/world/us/2022/06/17/white-house-probably-does-not-need-another-headache-dealing-with-the-ni-protocol-row/

Wall, M. (2023) "Friends of Sinn Féin in US Raise over $2m in Last Five Years," *Irish Times*, June 26. Available from: https://www.irishtimes.com/politics/2023/06/26/friends-of-sinn-fein-in-us-raise-over-2m-in-last-five-years/

Walsh, J. (2024) "A United Ireland is Growing Ever More Likely – Thanks to the Failures of Brexit Britain," *The Guardian*, February 26. Available from: https://www.theguardian.com/world/commentisfree/2024/feb/26/ireland-unity-brexit-britain

Warhurst, C. (2016) "Accidental Tourists: Brexit and Its Toxic Employment Underpinnings," *Socio-Economic Review*, 14(4): 819–825.

Watkin, E. (2002) *Enter the Irish-American*. Lincoln, NE: iUniverse.

Webber, E. (2022) "Tony Blair 'Helping' in UK's Northern Ireland Protocol Row with EU," *Politico*, September 21. Available from: https://www.politico.eu/article/tony-blair-helping-in-uks-northern-ireland-protocol-row-with-eu/

Weinraub, B. (1981) "24 Politicians Urge US Role in Ending Ulster Strife," *New York Times*, March 17.

Wheeler, C., Shipman, T., and Wheeler, C. (2022) "Brexit Bill on Ice as Hopes Rise of EU Deal," *The Times*, December 11. Available from: https://www.thetimes.co.uk/article/brexit-bill-on-ice-as-hopes-rise-of-eu-deal-9wl67c99r

Whelan, I. (2005) "Religious Rivalry and the Making of Irish-American Identity," in *Making the Irish American: History and Heritage of the Irish in the United States*. New York: Glucksman Ireland House and New York University, pp 271–285.

Whelan, S. (2022) "US Cross-Party Committee Strongly Criticises UK on Protocol Plans," *RTÉ*. June 17. Available from: https://www.rte.ie/news/2022/0617/1305362-adhoc-committee-good-friday-agreement-northern-ireland-protocol/

Wickham, A. (2023) "Rishi Sunak Is Privately Drafting Plans to Rebuild Britain's Ties with the EU," *Bloomberg.com*, February 11. Available from: https://www.bloomberg.com/news/articles/2023-02-11/rishi-sunak-wants-stronger-ties-with-eu-to-limit-brexit-dangers

Wickham, A. and Donaldson, K. (2022) "Biden Eyes Envoy to Give US a Bigger Role in Northern Ireland," *Bloomberg.com*, December 6. Available from: https://www.bloomberg.com/news/articles/2022-12-06/biden-eyes-envoy-to-give-us-a-bigger-role-in-northern-ireland

Wilcock, D. (2021) "Biden Security Chief Warns Boris Johnson over Northern Ireland Plans," *Mail Online*, October 8. Available from: https://www.dailymail.co.uk/news/article-10072067/Joe-Bidens-aide-Jake-Sullivan-warns-Boris-Johnson-scrapping-Northern-Ireland-protocol.html

William, A. and Mace, H. (2019) "Members of US Congress Warn UK over Irish Border," *Financial Times*, February 7. Available from: https://www.ft.com/content/79cdf2a8-2b02-11e9-a5ab-ff8ef2b976c7

Williams, A. and Bound, A. (2021) "US Delays Deal to Lift Trump-Era UK Steel Tariffs over N Ireland Fear," *Financial Times*, December 2. Available from: https://www.ft.com/content/c99a20ff-4fa0-41ea-ba4b-b9f2706393cb

Wilson, A. (1995) *Irish America and the Ulster Conflict, 1968–1995*. Belfast: Blackstaff Press.

Wilson, E. (2023) "Beyond the Blarney, What Does Biden's Irish American Identity Actually Mean?" *The Hill*, September 7. Available from: https://thehill.com/opinion/white-house/4192202-beyond-the-blarney-what-does-bidens-irish-american-identity-actually-mean/

Winters, R. (2018) "New Figures Reveal Scale of Unsolved Killings from the Troubles," *The Detail*, April 9. Available from: https://www.thedetail.tv/articles/new-figures-reveal-scale-of-unsolved-killings-from-the-troubles

Wintour, P. and Boffey, D. (2020) "Angry Tory MPs Reject Joe Biden's Comments on UK-EU Brexit Talks," *The Guardian*, September 17. Available from: https://www.theguardian.com/politics/2020/sep/17/angry-tory-mps-reject-joe-biden-comments-uk-eu-brexit-talks

Wintour, P. and O'Carroll, L. (2022) "Us Urges No More 'Flare ups' from UK over Northern Ireland," *The Guardian*, October 6. Available from: https://www.theguardian.com/world/2022/oct/06/us-urges-no-more-flare-ups-from-uk-over-northern-ireland

Witte, G. and Adam, K. (2019) "A Chaotic Final Night for Parliament Leaves Johnson with Bleak Choices on the Path to Brexit," *Washington Post*, September 10. Available from: https://www.washingtonpost.com/world/europe/a-chaotic-final-night-for-parliament-leaves-johnson-with-bleak-choices-on-the-path-to-brexit/2019/09/10/443a835a-d33a-11e9-8924-1db7dac797fb_story.html

Wokeck, M. (1989) "German and Irish Immigration to Colonial Philadelphia," *Proceedings of the American Philosophical Society*, 133(2): 128–143.

Working Group on Unification Referendums (2021) *Final Report*. London: Constitution Unit, University College London. Available from: https://www.ucl.ac.uk/constitution-unit/sites/constitution-unit/files/working_group_final_report.pdf

Wright, J. (1996) *Interest Groups in Congress*. Needham Heights, MA: Allyn & Bacon.

Wright, O. (2020) "Why Does the Internal Market Bill Matter to Joe Biden?" *The Times*, November 9. Available from: https://www.thetimes.co.uk/article/why-does-the-internal-market-bill-matter-to-joe-biden-jrdtg6vnv

Wright, O. and Charter, D. (2021) "Joe Biden Raises Pressure on Boris Johnson to Solve Northern Ireland Impasse," *The Times*, June 7. Available from: https://www.thetimes.co.uk/article/joe-biden-raises-pressure-on-boris-johnson-to-solve-northern-ireland-impasse-x2wgx87ph

Young, D. (2019) "Nancy Pelosi Urged to Only Back US-UK Trade Efforts That Protect Peace Deal," *Belfast Telegraph*, September 3. Available from: https://www.belfasttelegraph.co.uk/news/republic-of-ireland/nancy-pelosi-urged-to-only-back-us-uk-trade-efforts-that-protect-peace-deal/38463828.html

Zeffman, H. (2021) "Damaging Northern Ireland Peace Process Will Hinder US Deal, Says Nancy Pelosi," *The Times*, September 17. Available from: https://www.thetimes.co.uk/article/damaging-northern-ireland-peace-process-will-hinder-us-deal-says-nancy-pelosi-6h35c0r9c

Zeffman, H., Charter, D., and Wright, O. (2021) "Joe Biden Is Wrong about Northern Ireland, Says George Eustice," *The Times*, September 22. Available from: https://www.thetimes.co.uk/article/biden-sinks-hopes-of-quick-trade-deal-with-us-6h7v0d529

# Index

References in **bold** type refer to tables. References to footnotes show both the page number and the note number (95n1).

## A

Adams, Gerry 41, 204, 210
  US visa 2, 43–44, 45, 202, 226
Ad Hoc Committee on Irish Affairs (ACCIA) 39–40
Ad Hoc Committee to Protect the Good Friday Agreement (Ad Hoc Committee) 8, 13, 48, 58, 66, 94, 96
  activism on legacy 184, 185–186
  bipartisan support 67–68
  border poll 215
  high-level meetings 98, 148, 185
  HR 888 117th Congress (2021–2022) 151
  influence 95, 165–168, 231
  and Joe Biden 142
  letters to Theresa May 97–8, 221–222
  letter to Leo Varadkar 97–98
  name 226
  Northern Ireland Protocol 146, 153
  political re-engagement 98–99, 107
  pressure on the UK 234
Ahern, Bertie 172–173
Ahrari, M. 52
Alfaro, Mariana 133n1
Ambrosio, Thomas 58, 61
American Brexit Committee (ABC) 8, 13, 95–96
American Catholics 81
American Ireland Funds 151
American Irish State Legislators Caucus (AISLC) 8, 48, 148, 212, 235
American Israel Political Action Committee (AIPAC) 56, 57, 60, 61
American Jews 54
American role 9, 117, 167, 229
amnesties 179, 183
Ancient Order of Hibernians (AOH) 8, 13, 25, 94, 96, 184
  Belfast/Good Friday Agreement 148
  cultural issues and immigration 93
  HR 888 117th Congress (2021–2022) 151
  Irish American organization 219
  Legacy Justice Webinar (2021) 185
  letter to Bill Keating 141
  letter to Mike Pompeo 121
  letter to Tom Cotton 108
  membership 2, 83
  political positions 210–212
  "radical flank effect" 212
  visas 84–85
Anglo-Americans 28, 52
Anglo-Irish Agreement (1985) 36–37, 42, 45
Anglo-Irish Treaty (1921) 4, 199n1
Anglo-Saxon Protestant domination 19, 34
antebellum America 28
Anti-Catholicism in Northern Ireland 4
Anti-Catholicism bordering US 28n5, 29, 45
Arab American lobby 61, 62
Armenian Americans 54, 62
Arthur, P. 35, 36–37
Article 16 *see* Northern Ireland Protocol
assimilation (of ethnic groups into the US) 52, 53, 54–55

# INDEX

The Atlantic Declaration (2023) 127n3
Attlee, Clement 71
Australia 106, 123, 147

## B

Backstop 98, 100–101, 105, 112–113, 119
  *see also* Northern Ireland Protocol; Withdrawal Agreement
Baker, Steve 158
Ballymurphy inquest 181
Barr, C. 102n5
Battle of the Boyne 22
BBC 113, 133, 144, 161
  *Question Time* 111–112, 114
Beattie, Doug 155
Beirne, Hilary 206
Belfast/Good Friday Agreement (1998) 1–2, 3, 45
  25th anniversary 159–160
  approaches to truth and justice 172, 173–174
  and the Backstop 98
  bipartisan support 67–68, 221
  and Brexit 8, 70, 79–80, 107
  consociational peace agreement 171
  framework for peace 5, 183
  importance to American interests 222–223
  Loyalists withdrawing support 140
  referenda on a united Ireland 193, 197–202
  and Rishi Sunak 159
  UK and Ireland EU membership 78
  US as "guarantor" 97, 107, 221
  use of term by authors 18
  US-UK trade deal 96, 99, 104–105, 107, 115, 127, 129, 130, 151
*Belfast Telegraph* 14, 108
Bercow, John 101
Biaggi, Mario 39–40
Biden Administration 8, 132–135
  *démarche* (2021) 143
  Irish American lobbying 132, 187
  pressuring the UK 223–224
  Protocol Bill 153
  Russian invasion of Ukraine 11, 149, 158
  Special Envoy for Economic Development 160–162

St. Patrick's Day celebrations 137–139, 151
  united Ireland 213
  Windsor Framework 163, 164
Biden, Joe 132–168
  Belfast/Good Friday Agreement 127, 130, 158
  G7 summit 2021 141–143
  Irish America cabinet 134–135
  Irish American identity 8, 64, 132–134
  Legacy Act 188
  Northern Ireland expertise 65–66
  the Protocol 139–140, 159
  special envoy for Northern Ireland 141, 141n5
  UK-EU trade row 142–143
Biden, Neilia 133n1
bipartisanship 36, 67–68, 93, 94, 189
  *see also* US Congress
Birmingham Six 133
Black Americans 28–29, 28–29n5
Blair, Tony 77
Blinken, Antony 127–128, 153, 186, 187, 188, 223
Bloody Sunday Inquiry (Saville Inquiry) 175, 180
*Bloomberg* 161
Bobroske, Alexander 154
Bolton, John 102, 106, 107
border between Northern Ireland and Ireland 6–7, 80
  border infrastructure 79
  CODEL visiting 104
  cross-border trade 6–7, 10, 79
  and the EU 6, 79
  hard border 8, 15, 69, 86–89, 106–109, 170, 189–190
  in the Irish Sea 6, 87, 163, 205, 208
  legacy issues 221
  *see also* Ad Hoc Committee to Protect the Good Friday Agreement (Ad Hoc Committee); Brexit; European Union (EU); Ireland; Trump, Donald; Unionist; US-UK Trade Deal
  open border 10, 88, 163, 168, 232
Borger, J. 133, 154
Boston, MA 26, 31, 32
Boutcher, Jon 179, 191
Boyle, Brendan 68, 97, 104, 121, 123, 164
Bradley, Denis 175

277

Bradley, Karen 99
Brady, H. 55
Brehon Law Society 96
Brexit 5–8, 62, 70–91, 206
  Belfast/Good Friday Agreement 8, 79–80, 107
  cross-border trade 6–7, 206
  cultural factors 75–76
  debates over Northern Ireland 77
  economic factors 74–75
  English interests 77
  and EU 165–166
  Irish American lobbying 3, 12, 221
  Irish American responses 9, 86–91
  Leavers and Remainers 74
  political miscalculations 76–77
  UK-Ireland relationship 9
  UK-US special relationship 9–10, 68, 100, 143
  UK withdrawal negotiations 48–49
  and a united Ireland 193–194, 198
  US strategic considerations 9
  US-UK trade deal 106
  *see also* European Union (EU); United Kingdom (UK); Withdrawal Agreement
Brexiteers 100, 104, 112–113, 117, 130–131, 165–166, 224
British American lobby 62
British-Irish Association 144–145
British-Irish Council (BIC) 159
British-Irish Intergovernmental Conference 141, 158
Brogan, D.W 33
Brown, Jerry 43
Bryson, Jamie 204
Burns, Conor 155–156, 166–167, 186
Bush, George H.W. 42–43, 133
Butler, Robin 9n5

## C

Caine, Jonathan, Baron Caine 186
Camelot 34–35, 34n8
Cameron, David 73, 75, 76–77
campaign contributions 56
  Irish America 2–3, 57, 94
Campbell, John 103
Canosa, Jorge Mas 57
Carey, Christopher 196
Carey, Hugh 37
Carswell, Simon 100, 103, 104, 155
Carter, Jimmy 39

Carty, T. 34
Casalicchio, E. 147, 149, 150, 154, 156
Catholic Association 30
Catholic Church 30–32
Catholic Nationalists 194
Catholics
  anti-British sentiment 25
  civil rights marches 1960s 5
  émigrés in 1700s 23–24
  fealty to Rome 34
  as "green" 26
  Northern Ireland 4
  Penal Laws 22
  plantation period 23
  second wave of migrants 21, 24, 25, 194–195
  unique history 78
  voting politically 81
Center for Responsive Politics 56
Charter, D. 142, 155, 156
"Chequers Plan" (2018) 90–91
Chicago 32
Chollet, Derek 149, 153, 158, 160, 163–164, 223
Churchill, Winston 35
Cigler, A. 55
civil society organizations 93–94
Clan na Gael 27
Clark, William 41
Clinton, Bill 1–2, 43–45, 115, 202
coalition building by ethnic lobbies 58
Cold War 36
collective action 12, 51–52, 221
Collins, Susan 138, 164
colonialism 4, 22–23
  Penal Laws 22
  Famine 25–27
Committee on the Administration of Justice 179
common historical traumas 52
Common Travel Area (CTA) 6n3
Congressional delegations (CODELs) 101–104, 115–116, 154–155, 188, 223
  *see also* US Congress
Congressional Friends of Ireland Caucus 2, 8, 64, 138, 210
  bipartisan group 67, 93
  formation 40, 93
  Irish unity 212
  letter to Boris Johnson 107
  membership 83

pressure on the UK  111, 148, 153, 164
Protocol Bill  153
Connorton, John  181
Conservative Party  69
  1922 Committee  105
  and the DUP  113
  and the EU  73, 76–77
  legacy issues  170, 190
  Manifesto 2019  178
  reunification  198–199
consociationalism  171
constitutional Nationalist approaches  209, 212
Consultative Group on the Past  175–176
Coons, Chris  164
Cooper, J.  42
Corbyn, Jeremy  101
Corderoy, J.  102n5
Cordon, G.  143
the Cotton letter  106, 107–108, 115
Cotton, Tom  106
Council of Europe  182n4
Coveney, Simon  95, 99, 109, 138, 158, 162
Crawford, Ed  108
Crisp, J.  129–130
Crowley, Joseph (Joe)  81–82, 84, 87, 193
Cuban American National Foundation (CANF)  57
Cuban Americans  54, 59
Cullen, Paul  31
Cummings, Michael  181, 198–199, 207
Cunningham, Paul  134
Cusick, J.  102n5

**D**

Daly, Mark  123, 212, 216
Davis, Susan  82, 200, 201–202
Dearie, John  43
decommissioning weapons  44–45
DeConde, A.  52n2
de Gaulle, Charles  72
de Klerk, F.W.  173
de Luce, D.  89
Democratic Party  31–32
Democratic Unionist Party (DUP)  7, 77
  and Boris Johnson  112–113
  challenging the Protocol  140–141
  denunciations of CODELs  155
  elections 2019  119
  intransigence of hardliners  205
  Windsor Framework  163
demographic changes  81–83
dense networks  15, 220
*deorai* ("involuntary exile")  23
Dewind, J.  60, 61
The Disappeared  174–175
dishonest graft  33
dissident Republicans  88
  *see also* Republicans (Northern Ireland)
Dodds, Diane  155
Dodds, Nigel  113
Dolan, Jay  23–24, 30–31
Donaldson, Jeffrey  204
Donaldson, K.  161
Donilon, Mike  134
Donlon, Sean  41–42, 121
Downing Street Declaration (1993)  43–44
Durbin, Dick  151
Dutch Protestants  19, 22

**E**

Eames, Robin  175
Easter Rising (1916)  27, 123, 124
Eastwood, Colum  122
ECHR and ECtHR  177, 180, 182n4
*Economist, The*  53, 63–64, 130
Elgot, J.  155, 156
Elliott, Susan  203, 208
Engel, Elliot  127
Esman, M.  49–50, 52, 57
ethnic bond  51, 52n2
ethnic cohesion  52
ethnic groups  54–63
  influencing US foreign policy  48
  mobilization  50
  policy circles  58–59
  salience  53
ethnic "homelands"  6, 11n6
ethnic lobbies  49–63
  defining US strategic interests  49
  effectiveness  53–59
  Irish America  11–12, 218–219
  organizational strength  57
  PACs  56
  public ignorance of international affairs  61
  supporting the status quo  63
  and US foreign policy  60–63

ethnic-oriented PAC money 56
European Coal and Steel Community (ECSC) 72
European Convention for the Protection of Human Rights (ECHR) 177, 180, 182n4
European Court of Human Rights (ECtHR) 169–170, 177, 180, 182, 182n4
European Economic Community (EEC) 71
European Free Trade Area 72
European Research Group (ERG) 102, 102n5, 103, 116
European Social Summit (Gothenberg, 2017) 88
European Union (EU)
  Backstop 105
  Charter of Fundamental Rights 72–73
  conflict resolution funding 79
  "entente-cordiale" (2023) 162
  Irish border 69, 79
  PEACE Programmes 79
  single market 6
  and Liz Truss 158
  and the UK 71–73
  UK-EU negotiations 48–49, 160, 162–163
  UK-EU trade deal 120, 129, 137, 142–143
  united Ireland 194
  *see also* Brexit; Withdrawal Agreement
Eurosceptics 76–77, 102
EU-US Inter-Parliamentary Meeting (EU-US IPM) 154

**F**

Farrell, Henry 113–114
Fealty, Mick 162
Federal Election Commission (FEC) 3
Fedor, L. 164
*Financial Times* 130, 146–147, 190
Finucane, Pat 175
Fitzgerald, Garret 41
FitzGerald, Ger 212
Fitzpatrick, Brian 188
"formers" 13, 116
Foster, Arlene 205
Four Horsemen 37, 40–41, 212
freedom of movement 6n3

Friendly Sons of St. Patrick 24
Friends of Ireland Caucus 41, 141, 219
Friends of Sinn Féin 186, 193, 209–210
Frost, David, Baron Frost 143, 144–145
fundraising 56–57
  *see also* political action committees (PACs)

**G**

Gallardo, C. 152, 165
Galvin, Martin 87, 181, 190–191, 213
Gardiner, N. 143
Gaulle, Charles de 72
Gaza 60, 61
Geoghegan, P. 102n5
Georgia 23
Glancy, J. 136
Glazer, Nathan 34, 50
Goldin, Harrison 42
Golway, Terry 33
Good Friday Agreement (GFA) *see* Belfast/Good Friday Agreement (1998)
Gove, Michael 76, 135
Gramer, R. 89
Grant, Tobin 21
Grassley, Chuck 106
Great Awakening 24
Great Britain *see* United Kingdom (UK)
Great Famine (1840s) 24, 24–27, 32
Great Frost (1741) 22–23
"Great Transformation" (Polanyi) 74
Greek Americans 62
Green Wall 1, 95, 116, 227
Greer, Bonnie 111, 114
Greve, F. 62
*Guardian, The* 129, 130, 140, 154, 155, 156, 164, 222

**H**

Haass, Richard 124
Haddock, Mark 176–177
Halloran, C. 109
Hamill, P. 35
Hammond, Philip 101
Hart, Gary 94, 108
Hayward, Katy 191, 208–209, 230–232

# INDEX

Heath, Edward (Ted) 71
Heaton-Harris, Chris 137, 158, 163
*Hill, The* 147
Historical Enquiries Team
  (HET, PSNI) 177
Historical Investigations Unit
  (HIU) 177–178
Hoover, Herbert 34
House of Commons Defence
  Committee 178, 185
Houston, Norman 86, 205
Huey, Erik 65, 197–198, 220
Hughes-Jennett, Lyndon 136
human rights 39–40, 58, 93, 177–180, 186, 190
Hume, John 39, 41, 140, 213
hunger strikes (1981) 36, 40–41, 173

## I

Ignatiev, Noel 28, 28–29n5, 28n4
illegal immigrants to the US 27n3
Independent Commission for the
  Location of Victims' Remains
  (ICLVR) 174–175, 178
Independent Commission on
  Information Retrieval
  (ICIR) 178
Independent Reporting Commission
  (IRC) 201, 201n2
*Intercept, The* 104
internal border 113
International Fund for Ireland
  (IFI) 44
interview source materials 12–14, 224–228, **236–239**
"involuntary exile" (*deorai*) 23
Ireland
  action against UK in
    ECtHR 169–170
  Anglican dominance 22
  border with Northern Ireland 6, 79, 116–117
  Brexit 9, 15, 62, 69, 88, 90, 115–116, 122, 224
  culturally incompatible with
    American 29
  Department of Foreign Affairs 133
  emigration 22–26
  Great Famine (1840s) 24–27, 32
  Great Frost (1741) 22–23
  Irish "brand" or ethos 16
  lobbying Congress 62

neutrality 35, 149n7
partition 4
Penal Laws 22
  Sacramental Test Act 1704 22
as a "secondary" player 150
soft power 67
*see also* Irish immigration; St.
  Patrick's Day celebrations
Ireland Funds 56–57, 59, 94
"Ireland House" 235
Irish America 21–27
  approaches to unification 209–215
  Brexit referendum 3, 80
  Brexit strategy 96–97
  and Catholic Church 30–31
  class and geographic differences 25
  communal organization 29
  decline in engagement 85–86
  demographic changes 81–83
  dense networks 114–115, 220
  discrimination 28–29n5
  economic ladder 32
  effectiveness 15, 45, 167–168
  ethnic awakening 3
  ethnic lobby 11–12, 47–69, 218–219
  as "green" 194–195, 197, 209
  halls/rooms of power 65–66, 220
  Irish peace process 1, 8–9, 40–45
  key actors 36–38, 115–116
  media assessments 233
  members of Congress 8, 65, 115–116, 187–188
  message discipline 227
  organizational changes 83
  paternalism 207
  political culture 53, 63–64
  political ladder 28–35, 45–46, 63–68, 220
  religion 81
  remobilizing 63, 92–93
  resisting the British 29
  self-assessment 226–228
  shallow ethnic identity 50
  societal goodwill 16, 67, 221
  as "stuck in the past" 83
  Unionists and Loyalists 202–207
  as unique 15
Irish American activism 8–9, 14, 170, 188–189, 192
  *see also* soft power
Irish American Democrats 56, 83
Irish American influence 223–226

and the UK 3, 15, 104, 116, 129–131, 156, 166–167, 224–225, 229–233
 on US policies 3, 15, 35, 68–69, 92, 110, 114–118, 124, 131, 222, 230–231
Irish American lobbying 8–12, 21–22, 38, 41–44, 56–57, 62, 92, 95–99, 106–108, 110–111, 113–114, 141–142, 146, 148, 150–151, 153, 166–167, 184–187, 224–225
Irish American PACs 3, 56, 83, 218
Irish American remobilization 9–10, 12, 62, 63, 92–93
Irish American Unity Conference (IAUC) 83, 186
Irish ancestries
 Joe Biden 132–133
 political coalition 38
 US Censuses 18, 19, 21, 50
Irish Catholics 21, 30–31, 204
*Irish Echo* 14, 98, 122, 151
Irish Free State *see* Ireland
Irish immigration 19–20
 1700s (first wave) 21, 24, 26, 194
 1800s (second wave) 21, 24–28, 194–195
 Battle of the Boyne 22
 Catholics 23–24
 class and geographic differences 25
 decline in numbers 81
 Great Famine (1840s) 25–27
 religious differences 25
 supporting Irish independence 195
 War of 1812 24
 *see also* Ireland
Irish machine politics *see* machine politics
Irish National Caucus (INC) 83
Irish Nationalism 26–27, 209
*Irish News* 139, 156
Irish Northern Aid Committee (NORAID) 13, 36, 37–38
Irish Republican Army (IRA) 2, 40
 approaches to unification 209
 ceasefire 44
 hunger strike 36, 40–41, 173
 *see also* Sinn Féin
Irish reunification *see* reunification
*Irish Times* 139, 143, 151, 154–155
Irish unity *see* reunification

Irish War of Independence (1919—1921) 4, 199n1
Israel 60, 61

## J

Jeanne-Pierre, Karine 154
Jewish American lobby 60, 62
Jewish Americans 58, 59
Johnson, Boris 89
 and the Biden Administration 130, 147–148
 fanciful promises 206
 internal crisis 110
 Internal Markets Bill 10
 intransigence 165
 Irish American lobbying 224–225
 no-deal Brexit 8, 116
 Northern Ireland Protocol 112–113, 116, 145, 156–157
 as Prime Minister 105–107
 resignation 157
 Windsor Framework 167
 Withdrawal Agreement (2020) 92, 114, 119–121
 working with Americans 167
Johnson, R. 40
Judah, Ben 135–137
Juncker, Jean-Claude 112
justice mechanisms 171–172

## K

Keating, Bill 113, 127, 141–142
 CODELs 187–188
 HR 888 117th Congress (2021–2022) 151
 "mood music" 162
 Protocol Bill 153
 trade deal 190
 US-UK relationship 164
Kelley, Mike 93
Kelly, Stephen 230
Kennedy, Joe III 97, 99–100, 160–162, 160n10, 163
Kennedy, John Fitzgerald 34–35
Kennedy Onassis, Jacqueline 34n8
Kennedy Smith, Jean 65
Kennedy, Ted 37, 65, 82, 93, 133n1
Kenova report (2024) 191–192
Kentucky 26
Kijewski, L. 165
King, Peter 99, 110–111, 127
Kissel, Peter 182, 183, 195, 207

# INDEX

Klain, Ron 158
Know-Nothing Movement 29

## L

Labour Party 71, 73, 111, 130
Landler, M. 149, 150, 155
Lanktree, G. 149, 150, 154, 156
'late ethnicity' 50
Leahy, Pat 66, 138, 142, 143, 221
"Leave.EU" 75
Leavers (Brexit identity) 74
legacy issues
  activism 183–188, 189–192, 226, 234
  Belfast/Good Friday Agreement 183
  early efforts to address 174–180
  and trade 170, 184, 189–190
Legacy Justice Webinar (AOH, 2021) 185
legacy legislation 169, 171–174, 178–183, 188–192
  troubles-related crimes 169, 177, 179
Lempert, Yael 143
Lewis, Brandon 126, 128, 137, 178, 184–185, 186
Leyen, Ursula von der 146, 159
Lidington, David 101
Lighthizer, Robert Emmet 126–127
Lindsay, J. 63
Lippman, Daniel 128
Lisbon Treaty (2007) 72–73
Lloyd, Tony 111
lobbying 8, 9–10
  *see also* Irish American lobbying
Loomis, B. 55
Lowe, Sam 147
Loyalist Communities Council 140
Loyalist paramilitaries 5, 5n2, 173
Loyalists 78, 140–141, 172–173, 201–209
  *see also* Protestants; Unionists
Luce, Ed 66
Lundy, P. 172
Lynch, C. 89
Lynch, Suzanne 109, 134–135

## M

MacBride Principles 42
machine politics 15, 20, 33, 58, 65, 211
Mackey, R. 104

Madhani, A. 158
Major, John 43–44, 77
Mandela, Nelson 173
Manley, John 157
March Madness 138–140
  *see also* St. Patrick's Day celebrations
Martin, Carmel 134
Martin, Micheál 134, 163
mayors 33
May, Theresa 77, 90–91, 97, 99, 101–102, 105, 222, 224–225
McAlpine, Robert, Baron McAlpine of West Green 42
McBride, Sam 139–140
McCaffrey, L. 27, 30
McCarthy, Gina 134
McCarthy, John 134, 221
McCord, Raymond Jr. 176–177, 179
McCord, Raymond Sr. 176–177
McCormick, Jane 161
McDonagh, B. 167
McDonald, Mary Lou 188
McDonough, Denis 134
McEvoy, K. 173
McFall, John, Baron McFall of Alcluith 188
McGarry, J. 25
McGee, H. 109
McGovern, M. 172, 173
McGrath, D. 152–153
McGuinness, Martin 94, 204–205
McGurk, Tom 98–99, 219–220
McKeone, Marian 112, 115
McKerr cases (ECtHR) 177, 180
McLeish, Henry 67
Meagher, T. 27
Menendez, Robert 138, 151–152, 153, 164
migration waves 22–24
Mitchell, George 1, 44–45, 216
Mordaunt, Penny 147
Morrison, Bruce 43–44, 94, 97–98, 116, 185, 199–200, 213, 226
Moynihan, Daniel Patrick 34, 37, 50, 82, 93
Mulhall, Daniel (Dan) 64, 67, 90, 95, 101, 103, 116, 122–125, 129, 161, 228–229
Mulvaney, Mick 68
  Backstop 90
  Belfast/Good Friday Agreement 109–110
  Internal Market Bill 153

283

legacy issues 182, 184–185
reunification 200–201
as special envoy 121–125, 128, 131, 204
Trump Administration 220
Murphy, Chris 100–101, 102, 146

**N**

Narain, Paul 209
Nason, Geraldine Byrne 95
National Committee on American Foreign Policy 44
National Health Service 215
Nationalists 5n2, 7, 78, 139n2, 140, 175–176
  *see also* Republicans (Northern Ireland)
National Park Service 34n8
nativism 29
naturalization of immigrants to US 32–33
Neal, Richard (Richie)
  Appropriations Committee 69
  CODELs 101, 154–155
  Congressional Friends of Ireland Caucus 93, 99–100, 111
  House Ways and Means Committee 103, 115–116, 189
  Internal Market Bill 127
  role in 2020/2021 227–228
Negroponte, Diana Villiers 147
Newhouse, John 57
New Ireland Forum 41
New York 31, 32, 43
New York Draft Riot (1863) 28–29
*New York Times* 122, 149, 150, 233
no-deal Brexit 104, 106–107
no-popery campaigns 29
North Atlantic Treaty Organization (NATO) 11, 35
Northern Ireland
  Brexit debates 77–80
  Catholics 4
  consociational peace agreement 171
    *see also* Belfast/Good Friday Agreeement
  creation 199n1
  government wanting it to work 191
  Great Britain unconcerned with 78n1
  Inspector General of Constabulary 177

Police Ombudsman (PONI) 176
Police Service (PSNI) 172, 177
Protestants 4
Reports on Human Rights Abuses 40
Royal Ulster Constabulary 5, 40, 173
street violence 140–141
UK subsidy 214
Northern Ireland Assembly 5, 7, 41, 79, 163
Northern Ireland Bureau (NIB) 13, 136–137
Northern Ireland Civil Service (NICS) 13
Northern Ireland Executive 5, 177
Northern Ireland High Court 180
*Northern Ireland Life and Times* (NILT) survey (2022) 194
Northern Ireland Office (NIO) 13, 78, 178–179
Northern Ireland Protocol 7, 129, 137–162
  Article 16 137, 138, 144, 146–147, 152, 189
  Biden White House 139–140
  deadline 145–146
  replacing the Backstop 112–113
  UK renegotiating 144–145
  *see also* Backstop; Withdrawal Agreement
Northern Ireland Protocol Bill 149, 152–157, 159–160, 163
"Northern Ireland Protocol: The Way Forward" (UK command paper) 144–145
Northern Ireland Troubles (Legacy and Reconciliation) Bill *see* United Kingdom (UK) legislation, Legacy Act 2022
North-South Ministerial Council 141

**O**

Obama, Barack 68, 222
O'Carroll, L. 140, 154, 158
O'Clery, C. 42
O'Connell, Daniel J. "Danny" (AOH President) 84–85, 205, 206, 212
O'Connell, Daniel ("The Great Liberator") 29–30, 220
O'Donovan, B. 108, 142
O'Dowd, Niall 133n1, 203, 206, 207–208, 210, 220

O'Dwyer, Brian 53, 80, 84, 87, 124, 196–197
O'Gráda, C. 22
O'Grady, J. 43
O'Hanlon, Ray 124
O'Leary, Brendan 6, 25, 79
O'Leary, Stella 67
O'Loan, Nuala 176–177, 179
O'Loughlin, G. 210
Olson, Mancur 51
O'Malley Dillon, Jennifer 134
O'Malley, Kevin 45–46
O'Malley, P. 28–29n5
O'Neill, Michelle 192
O'Neill, Tip 36, 37, 42, 93
O'Reilly, J. 68–69, 74
Organski, A.F.K. 60
Osborne, George 77

**P**

Paisley, Ian 5
Paisleyites 5
paramilitary prisoners 36, 40–41, 173
partition 4
paternalism 207
patronage 32–33
Paul, D. 3, 53, 54, 55, 56, 57
Paul, R. 3, 52, 53, 54, 55, 56, 57–58
peace process 1, 8–9, 38, 40–45, 68, 80, 85, 93, 94
PEACE Programmes (EU) 79
Pelosi, Nancy 69
  CODELs 101, 102–103, 115–116
  Internal Market Bill 127
  Legacy Bill 189
  Northern Ireland Protocol 145, 152–153
  US-UK trade deal 107, 111, 151
Pence, Mike 59, 109–110
Perry, Caitríona 47–48, 51, 67, 221
Plunkitt, George Washington 33
Pogatchnik, S. 159
Polanyi, Karl 74
Police Ombudsman of Northern Ireland (PONI) 176
Police Service of Northern Ireland (PSNI) 172, 177
Policy Exchange 135–137, 166, 224
political action committees (PACs) 2–3, 56, 83
political engagement 2, 54–55, 219–220

*Politico* 130, 147, 149, 150, 156, 165, 233
Politi, J. 164
Pompeo, Mike 107–108, 121, 122, 128
Powell, Charles, Baron Powell of Bayswater 135
Powell, Jonathan 113, 174
Power, Samantha 134
"practicing Catholic" notion 31
Prasad, S.K. 55, 58
Presbyterians 4, 22–23, 22n2
prisoner releases 172
Protestant Ascendancy 22
Protestants 26
  first wave of migrants 21, 24, 26, 194
  as Irish Americans 81
  Northern Ireland 4
  unique history 78
Protocol, renegotiating 154
Protocol on Ireland/Northern Ireland *see* Northern Ireland Protocol
Provisional IRA 5
Psaki, Jen 139

**Q**

*Question Time* (BBC) 111–112, 114
Quinn, Ciarán 64, 87, 100
Quinn, Colm 65, 81
Quinn, Paul 47, 65

**R**

Raab, Dominic 107–108, 127, 129, 130
Rahman, M. 130
Rea, Ailbhe 117
Reagan, Ronald 36, 41–42, 202
Redd, S. 55
Rees-Mogg, Jacob 103
referenda
  Brexit 6, 7, 70, 75, 219, 222
  Irish unity 193–194, 210, 213–215
Reiss, Mitchell 85, 183, 201, 203, 204, 206, 213, 226
religious differences 25, 204
Remainers (Brexit identity) 74
Repeal Movement 30
Republican paramilitaries 5n2, 36, 40–41, 173
Republicans (Northern Ireland) 5n2, 36, 78, 88, 172, 202, 204–205, 209
*see also* Nationalists

Republicans (US) 36, 81–82, 115, 215–216
reunification 85, 193–217
  Brexit and the EU 194, 198
  constitutional and legal changes 214
  Friends of Sinn Féin 209–210
  health and education 215
  incremental and consensual approaches 212
  national symbols 215
  proceed with caution camp 212–215
  push camp 209–212
Reynolds, Albert 43–44
Ringland, Trevor 136, 166–167
Riordon, William 33
Robinson, Peter 94
Royal Ulster Constabulary (RUC) 5, 40, 173
*RTE News* 154
Rubenzer, T. 55
Russian invasion of Ukraine (2022) 10–11, 149–152, 165
Ryan, Evan 134

**S**

Sabbagh, D. 102n5
Savatic, F. 55, 58
Saville Inquiry (Bloody Sunday Inquiry) 175, 180
Schengen Agreement 72
Schultz, George 42
Schuman Declaration (1950) 72
Schuman, Robert 72
Schumer, Chuck 107–108, 153
Schütze, R. 72
"Scots Irish" or "Scotch-Irish" 19n1, 21, 26
Second World War 35, 71
Securing the Union deal (2024) 7
security forces collusion with paramilitaries 173, 190–191
Šefčovič, Marcoš 138
Segura, R. 60, 61
Shamrock Friendly Association 24
*Shenanigans* (Vargo) 47
Shipman, T. 233
Shlozman, K.L. 55
Simons, Ned 103
Single Market and the Customs Union 113
Sinn Féin 2, 192
  absence from Westminster 77–78

Belfast/Good Friday Agreement 44, 87
  courting American involvement 210
  engaging in elections 40–41
  Republican approaches 209
  reunification 211–212
  violence and the peace process 87–88
  *see also* Irish Republican Army (IRA)
Sloat, Amanda 66, 113–114, 134, 158, 163
*Slugger O'Toole* (website) 162
Small, Joseph 9n5
Smith, A. 126, 127
Smith, Al 33–34
Smith, Jean Kennedy 65
Smith, Julian 107
Smith, Tony 3
  accessing the President 60
  ethnic communities as political force 57
  impact of Irish America 54–55
  Irish American activism 26, 50, 63
  powerful ethnic groups 58
  voting strength 56
Smyth, C. 155, 156
Smyth, Ted 35, 195, 199–201, 212–213
Social Democratic Labour Party (SDLP) 209, 212
Society of St. Tammany (Tammany Hall) 32–33, 32–33n7
soft power 67, 114, 220–221
  *see also* Irish American activism; St. Patrick's Day celebrations
South Africa 173
South Carolina 23
Soviet Union 36
Special Branch 176–177
special relationship *see* US-UK special relationship
*Spectator, The* 112
"spheres of influence" 79–80
Stakeknife (agent) 191–192
Starmer, Keir 192
Staunton, Denis 144
steel and aluminum tariffs 146–147, 150
*Steerpike* (gossip column *The Spectator*) 112
Stephenson, Barbara 53, 79–80, 198, 226–227

Stormont House Agreement
    (SHA, 2014) 177–178, 183
St. Patrick's Day celebrations 15, 124
  Biden Administration 2021 134, 138
  Biden Administration 2022 150, 151
  diplomacy and lobbying 45–46,
    66–67, 220–221
  Gerry Adams in the US 44
  March Madness 138–140
  see also Ireland; soft power
strategic convergence 60–61
Sullivan, A. 107
Sullivan, Jake 66, 94, 98, 134,
    142–143, 145–146, 158, 163–164
Sullivan, Kevin 86–87, 94, 199, 204,
    207, 210, 216–217, 227
Sullivan Principles 42
"Summary for Lobbying" (ABC) 95
*Sun, The* 77, 90–91
Sunak, Rishi 159–160, 162, 165–166,
    167, 186, 224–225
*Sunday Times* 136
Suozzi, Tom 111, 187
SuperPACs 56
Superville, D. 158
Sutton Index of Deaths 187n6
Syrian Civil War refugees 75–76

**T**

Tai, Katherine 143, 153, 223
Tammany Hall (Society of St.
    Tammany) 32–33, 32–33n7
Taylor, P. 172
Teggart, Grainne 187
*Telegraph, The* 129–130, 143
Thatcher, Margaret 40–42, 72–73,
    133, 173, 202
Thune, John 164
*Times, The* 130, 142, 143, 155, 156,
    161, 162
Tóibín, Peadar 1
Toomey, Pat 146, 151
trade deals *see* UK-EU trade deal;
    US-UK trade deal
Tranghese, William (Bill) 67, 104,
    180, 189, 195–196, 227–228
Transatlantic Parliamentary Dialogue
    (EU-US IPM) 154
transatlantic relations *see* US-UK
    special relationship
Trevelyan, Anne-Marie 147, 153–154
Trimble, David 140

the Troubles 3–4, 5, 35–36, 83–85,
    170, 172
Trubowitz, Peter 61
Trump Administration 8, 59
  advocates for Irish America 108
  and Brexiteers 130–131
  CODELs 102, 104
  Internal Market Bill 128
  and Mick Mulvaney 122, 220
  US-UK trade deal 126
Trump, Donald 89–91, 101
  and Brexit 68, 97
  concerns about the border 108–109
  impeachment proceedings 123
  praising Boris Johnson 105–106
  undermining democratic
    norms 102n5
Truss, Liz 8, 145, 152, 157–159, 165,
    224–225
truth and reconciliation
    commissions 172–174
Turkey 75
Turkish Americans 58, 62
Tusk, Donald 88–89

**U**

Ulster 4
  see also Northern Ireland
Ulster Defence Association 140n4
Ulster Presbyterians 26
Ulster Volunteer Force (UVF) 140n4,
    176–177
*UnHerd* 233
unification *see* reunification
Unionists
  betrayal by Conservatives 206
  Consultative Group on the
    Past 176
  contempt for 207
  and Irish America 86, 202–208, 232
  isolated from Westminster 206
  Northern Ireland Protocol 119,
    139, 139n2
  opposing reunification 78,
    201–202, 213
  Protocol Bill 152
  sea border 7, 208
  use of force 5n2
  *see also* Loyalists; Protestants
united European 11
United Kingdom Independence Party
    (UKIP) 73, 76

United Kingdom (UK) 4–8
  anti-immigrant sentiment 75
  bridge between Europe and US 71
  control of Ireland 4
  credibility problem 154–155
  diplomacy 135–137, 155
  domestic contexts 190
  elections 2019 114, 119–120
  EU opt-outs 72–73
  G7 summit 2021 142
  House of Commons Defence Committee 178, 185
  Irish American remobilization 62
  joining the EEC/EU 71–72
  military colluding with paramilitaries 173, 190–191
  negotiations with the EU 48–49, 160, 162–163
  Parachute Regiment 181
  parliamentary inquiries 175
  political chaos 2019 110
  relations with Ireland 9
  relations with the EU 142
  role of Irish America 99
  Secretary of State for Northern Ireland (SOSNI) 126, 137, 158
  Special Envoy to the US on Northern Ireland 136–137
  Supreme Court 110
  unconcerned with Northern Ireland 78, 78n1
  US's role 9, 73
  White Paper 2020 125–126
  withdrawal negotiations 48
  *see also* Brexit; US-UK special relationship; US-UK trade deal
United Kingdom (UK) legislation
  Act of Union 1800 25, 30, 214
  Catholic Relief Act 1829 30, 30n6
  European Union (Withdrawal) (No. 2) Act 2019 (Benn Act) 110
  Inquiries Act 2005 175
  Internal Market Act 2020 10, 125–131
  Legacy Act 2023 69, 169, 178–183, 192
  Northern Ireland Protocol Bill 149, 152–157, 159–160, 163
  Police (Northern Ireland) Acts 1998 and 2000 176
  Tribunals of Inquiry (Evidence Act) 1921 175
UK-EU trade deal 120, 129, 137, 142–143

United States (US)
  19th century politics 29
  ethnic identity and immigrant experience 50
  Immigration and Nationality Act 1965 (Hart-Celler Act) 27
  influencing UK policy on Brexit 224
  internationalized Brexit 231–232
  lobbying on trade deals 60
  midterm elections (2018) 68–69
  national origins quota system 27
  and the peace process 8–11
  role in border poll 215–217
  US Censuses 19n1, 50, 81, 219
  US Commerce Department 146
  US Congress
    bipartisanship 36, 67–68, 93, 94
    committees 56, 187–188
    Congressional districts 54
    ethnic lobbies 59–60
    Irish Americans 8, 34, 45
    pressure on Biden and UK 187–188
    ratification of trade deals 10
    *see also* Congressional delegations (CODELs)
  US Congress, House Resolutions (HR)
    HR 88 116th Congress (2019–2021) 97
    HR 585 116th Congress (2019–2021) 111
    HR 888 117th Congress (2021–2022) 151, 223
    HR 33 118th Congress (2023–2024) 164
    HR 3653 118th Congress (2023–2024) 164, 164n11
  US foreign policy 11–12, 60–63
    and AIPAC 60
    Belfast/Good Friday Agreement 61, 67
    and Brexit 61
    ethnic groups influencing 12, 48, 60, 222
    Irish America influencing 35–36
    strategic interests 8–11, 12, 60–61
  US House Foreign Affairs Subcommittee on Europe 141
  "Protecting the Good Friday Agreement from Brexit." 113
  US House Ways and Means Committee 154–155

US Senate, Senate Resolutions (SR)
  SR 117 117th Congress
    (2021–2022) 138–139
  SR 157 118th Congress
    (2023–2024) 164, 164n12
US Senate UK Trade Caucus 115
US Special Advisor for Economic
  Initiatives 44, 160n10
US Special Envoy for Economic
  Development 160–162, 160n10
US State Department 188
  Report on Human Rights Abuses 40
US Trade Representative (USTR) 153
US-UK special relationship 8–9, 35,
  100, 145
  and Brexit 68, 100, 143–144
  *démarche* (2021) 143
  Irish American activism 8–9
  media fiction 96
  shared views 62
  UK breaching international law 10
  Ukraine war 150–151
  UK taking for granted 36, 166
US-UK Supplemental Extradition
  Treaty (1986) 133
US-UK trade deal 99–104
  "Atlantic Declaration" 127n3
  Boris Johnson meeting Joe Biden 145
  and Donald Trump 126
  and a hard border 106–107
  Internal Market Bill 129
  Irish America leverage 10, 222
  and John Bolton 106
  and legacy issues 170, 184, 189–190
  linking to Belfast/Good Friday
    agreement 96, 99, 104–105, 107,
    115, 127, 129, 130, 151
  Northern Ireland Protocol 145,
    146–147, 153–154, 158
  and US Congress 115
  US withholding 117
US visas
  granting to Gerry Adams 2, 44,
    202, 226
  for Irish citizens 84–85, 106, 123
  overstaying 27n3

**V**

Vance, Cy 39
Varadkar, Leo 88, 97, 109, 112, 116, 188
Vargo, Trina 47–48, 51, 82, 121
Verba, S. 55

Villiers, Theresa 78
Vinjamuri, Leslie 147–148
violence 87–88, 108, 140–141, 213
Viser, Matt 133n1
Vote Leave campaign 75

**W**

Walker, P. 140
Wall, Martin 138, 150, 221
Walsh, Jim 1
  Gerry Adams' visa 81
  Ad Hoc Committee 94, 95, 97–98,
    116, 185, 226
  relationships with Unionists 85–86, 205
  reunification 198
Walsh, Marty 134
War of 1812 24, 31
Washington Ireland Program
  (WIP) 94, 134
*A "Washington Strategy" for British
  Diplomacy* (Ben Judah, Policy
  Exchange) 135–137, 166, 224
Waterfield, B. 155, 156
Waugh, Paul 103
Wave Trauma Center 187
Webber, E. 165
Whale, S. 149, 150, 154, 156
Wheeler, C. 233
Whig Party 32
whiteness 28, 28n4
Wickham, A. 161
Wilcock, D. 145–146
William of Orange 22
Wilson, A. 42
Wilson, Eliot 133
Windsor Framework (2023) 7, 95,
  163–164, 165, 184
Withdrawal Agreement 7, 95, 184
  2019 agreement (Theresa
    May) 88, 91
  2020 agreement (Boris Johnson) 92,
    114, 119–121
  and the Internal Markets Bill 10
  *see also* Backstop; Brexit; European
    Union (EU); Northern
    Ireland Protocol
Workman, Garrett 154
Wright, O. 130, 142

**Y**

Young, D. 111
Young Friends of Ireland 148, 235

www.ingramcontent.com/pod-product-compliance
Lightning Source LLC
Chambersburg PA
CBHW051529020426
42333CB00016B/1851